THE LAST POSSE

Also by Gale E. Christianson

This Wild Abyss:
The Story of the Men Who Made Modern Astronomy

In the Presence of the Creator:
Isaac Newton and His Times

Fox at the Wood's Edge:
A Biography of Loren Eiseley

Writing Lives Is the Devil!
Essays of a Biographer at Work

Edwin Hubble:
Mariner of the Nebulae

Isaac Newton and the Scientific Revolution

Greenhouse:
The 200-Year Story of Global Warming

THE LAST POSSE

*A Jailbreak, a Manhunt, and the End
of Hang-'Em-High Justice*

Gale E. Christianson

The Lyons Press
Guilford, Connecticut
An imprint of The Globe Pequot Press

The Lyons Press is an imprint of the Globe Pequot Press.

Printed in the United States of America

10 9 8 7 6 5 4 3 2 1

Design by Compset, Inc.

Library of Congress Cataloging-in-Publication Data

Christianson, Gale E.
    The last posse: a jailbreak, a manhunt, and the end of hang 'em high justice/ Gale E. Christianson.
        p. cm.
    Includes bibliographical references and index.
    1. Morley, Charles A., d. 1959. 2. Gray, Shorty, d. 1912. 3. Dowd, John, d. 1912. 4. Nebraska State Penitentiary. 5. Escapes—Nebraska—Lioncoln. 6. Prisoners—Nebraska—Lincoln—Biography. I. Title.
HV8658.M67 C57 2001
365'.641—dc21
                                                                    2001029900

ISBN 1-58574-384-4

To Rhonda

When the conductor was gone the big man turned to me with a glimmer of amusement in his eyes. "Stranger," he appealed before I could return to my book, "tell me a story." In all the years since I have never been addressed by that westernism "stranger" on a New York train. And never again upon the Pennsylvania Railroad has anyone asked me, like a pleading child, for a story.

Loren Eiseley, *All the Strange Hours*

CONTENTS

❧ PROLOGUE ❧

Morley's spare, ascetic face was like that of a monk who had long since grown accustomed to his cell. The transformation had taken decades to complete, all traces of the once surly and defiant young man now gone. Gone was the shock of unruly black hair, the week's accumulation of dark stubble, the wild eyes that had betrayed a morphine addict. A reporter sent by the *Lincoln Star* to interview him, in December of 1940, found Morley seated at a small desk. The convict reminded the newsman of a balding professor rather than the defiant outlaw who had once stood behind the barricaded door of a farmhouse, a .38 revolver in his hand, and dared any lawman to set foot on the porch.

Charles A. Morley, alias Edward Craig, was a lifer. Sentenced in 1912 for gunning down prison warden James Delahunty, before escaping into a March blizzard with fellow convicts Shorty Gray and John Dowd, Morley had spent more time in the Nebraska State Penitentiary than any other criminal in the history of the institution. After thirty years behind bars he had finally been granted a hearing by the Board of Pardons and Paroles, which usually let a convicted murderer off in less than half the time that Morley had already served. Win or lose, January 8, 1941, promised to be an exciting day.

Until then, there was little to do but what he had always done: think back on those lost thirty years, during which the arching sun had notched 120 seasons, 360 months, 1,560 weeks, 10,950 days. Prison had taken Morley out of the natural cycle of things, creating an unchanging regimen of its own, dependent on nothing beyond the gray ramparts and the barbed wire fence stretching into the distance until they became one with the horizon.

There were times when it seemed that his past had happened to someone else: the deafening exchange of gunfire, the mad dash into the blinding snowstorm, the blood of the mortally wounded warden and his dying assistants coagulating on the prison floor. Then the taking of hostages, the kidnapping, and the anxious days spent in hiding, followed by a headlong chase across the snow-covered Gretna Hills, with six posses, the state militia, scores of lathered horses, and dozens of wagons, buggies, and sleds in hot pursuit.

It was not the *Titanic* disaster of 1912 that many landlocked citizens of the Midwest and the Great Plains counted as their most vivid childhood memory. Nor was it Pancho Villa's brazen raid into New Mexico in 1916 and the killing of several U.S. citizens. Instead, it was the violent escape from a Nebraska penitentiary that they remembered, an escape planned and carried out by a trio of notorious robbers and safe-blowers.

Rifles were removed from closets, loaded, and placed within easy reach by anxious fathers who slept in their clothes on the living room sofa with one eye open. Doors and windows were bolted and locked for the first and only time, giving every citizen a part, however small, in the unfolding drama. For one brief moment the "desperadoes," as they were labeled by the press, made the front pages from New York to California, resurrecting the Old West of the imagination. As the years passed and the dark deeds receded into history, they took on the coloring of myths passed down through the generations like family heirlooms.

With his sixty-fourth birthday approaching, Morley told his interviewer that all he wanted was to return to his native Missouri, where he claimed to have been born in the Clay County home of the outlaw brothers Frank and Jesse James. A sister and a few old family friends promised to make a place for him. Only thirty more days and nights to go before his fate would be decided; yet to Morley it must have seemed like another lifetime as the migratory ghosts of his days on the run returned to trouble his sleep once again.

"STAND UP FOR JESUS"

The 240-acre Nebraska State Penitentiary was known locally as Lancaster, after the nearby post office on the Burlington line. Hopes that a town would eventually materialize went unfulfilled, and, by 1910, little beyond the prison grounds and railroad tracks remained, except for a forlorn signpost, a post office without a postmaster, and a small store that sold root beer and not much else.

Constructed of magnesium limestone from quarries located nine miles away, Lancaster's most distinguishing feature was its three-and-one-half-story administration building, flanked by matching Victorian turrets that were visible for miles around. Extending from two sides of this rectangular monstrosity were the east and west cell houses, which, like the building to which they were connected, faced a public road and were topped by battlements inspired by a Europe that had long since faded into myth. A high wall—gray, gloomy, and infested with snakes and vermin—extended from the ends of both cell houses to the south, on top of which stood six towers, each occupied by a guard with a loaded rifle. A historian of the period tersely observed: "The external appearance of this building is very imposing, at once suggesting to the observer the use for which it was intended."

Visitors to the prison took the streetcar marked PENITENTIARY, which left downtown Lincoln every forty minutes from 10th and O Streets. After a three-mile ride that extended well beyond the city's southern limits, they were dropped off near a set of heavy iron doors guarding the prison's main entrance. On entering, they were directed to a reception room on the right. A yellowing card on the door read: COME WITHOUT KNOCKING; GO THE SAME WAY, a relic of a former keeper who hated to be disturbed. Here those wishing to tour the prison were asked to wait for usher E. G. Heilman, who would be along soon to collect them and their ten-cent admission fee.

Sundays were for church. And every Sunday, Deputy Warden Edward D. Davis marked the occasion by wearing a flower in his lapel. But this Sunday, February 11, 1912, the deputy wore no flower.

Shortly before the service began, an elderly Negro trusty named Frank spoke with Deputy Clerk Walter Wilson about it. "Did you notice," Frank asked, "that the deputy warden does not wear a flower this morning? It looks strange, for it is the first Sunday morning that I have ever seen him without a flower of some sort."

Wilson thought the same and made a hurried detour to the prison greenhouse, residence of an ever-blooming lantana vine that was as large as a tree, and of "Old Bill," a goldfish that was believed to be the biggest in Nebraska. He returned with a white tuberose, which he took up to the deputy warden's apartment, on the third floor.

Davis was in a jovial mood. When Wilson asked why he was sporting no flower, Davis replied, "Well, you see the ladies are forgetting me."

"Take a look at him and see whether we are forgetting him or not," Mrs. Davis laughingly countered. "Look at his new suit and the new tie I got him."

Wilson inserted the tuberose in the deputy warden's button-hole. "Please thank Frank for the flower," Davis said.

On descending the stairs they encountered Warden James Delahunty, who was carrying his usual copy of the Sunday paper. Wilson smiled to himself. It was customary for the warden to sit in Davis's office during services, as a precautionary measure, out of sight but within earshot of everything that transpired. Privately, Delahunty could not abide the chaplain's hellfire and brimstone oratory, and he had once remarked: "We have had plenty of hell and damnation right here." Thus, the paper was a welcome distraction.

Standing over his flock while the final hymn was sung, Prison Chaplain Porter C. Johnson resembled a patriarch of yore. The Civil War veteran had served under George McClellan in the Peninsular Campaign and had been wounded near Richmond. At seventy-five, the chaplain still sported a formidable white beard that broadened below his chin into a cascading Niagara, though his powerful singing voice was no longer as commanding as it had once been. The loss was more than compensated for by the zeal of Miss Ruth Storm, the volunteer pianist, and the large congregation of prisoners, Sunday school teachers, and various guests from in and around Lincoln:

> **Stand up, stand up for Jesus!**
> **Ye soldiers of the cross;**
> **Lift high his royal banner,**
> **It must not suffer loss.**
> **From victory unto victory**
> **His army he shall lead**
> **Till every foe is vanquished**
> **And Christ is Lord indeed.**

As the last notes faded away the men remained standing for the benediction. Deputy Warden Davis took out his keys and began walking down the aisle, as he did every Sunday at the close of services, heading for the chapel's south door through which the prisoners had to pass into the yard, and from there into the cell houses. After dinner they would receive copies of the *Lincoln Daily Star* and other periodicals to read during their weekly afternoon of rest.

The attack was so swift and unexpected that few among the worshipers were able to testify as to exactly what had happened. Indeed, most of the four hundred or so prisoners had no idea that anything was wrong. Although he was standing on the rostrum not ten feet away from the first row of convicts, Chaplain Johnson saw what he thought was only a minor disturbance and addressed those nearest him in reassuring tones: "It's all right, boys. Be Quiet."

As Davis walked past the long rows of gray-clad inmates, Albert Prince, otherwise known as convict number 5374, was waiting for the deputy warden next to the outer aisle. Without warning, he pulled a homemade knife from beneath his jacket, stepped in front of Davis, and plunged the blade deep into his stomach. A man of "splendid physical power and courage," the former sheriff of Clay County, and onetime warden of the penitentiary, was now sixty-five years of age and in no condition to put up a fight. He extended an arm in self-defense and began backing up the aisle, still facing his attacker. Prince stabbed the deputy warden again and again, with the short underhand thrusts of a man familiar with the blade. Yet strangely, as if in deference to the solemnity of the occasion, Davis neither cried out in pain nor uttered a word.

He made it as far as his office before collapsing into a chair. Prince, still in close pursuit, was seized from behind and disarmed by Guard Charles Wagner before he could do further harm. Wagner handed the knife to Warden Delahunty, who had come out of

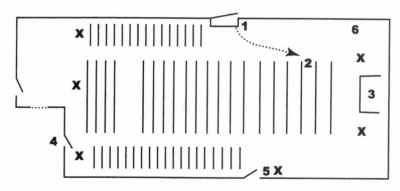

DIAGRAM OF PRISON CHAPEL SCENE OF ATTACK

1. **Deputy Warden Davis's path from the door to the Turnkey's Room (Cage). He was about to pass in front of the rostrum (3) and proceed to the south door (5).**
2. **Point where Prince was standing when he sprang at Davis.**
3. **Rostrum where Chaplain P. C. Johnson was standing.**
4. **Door to deputy warden's office to which Davis retreated during the attack.**
5. **South door at which Davis usually stood as the convicts filed into the yard and back to the cell houses.**
6. **Position of Guard Charles Wagner at the time of the attack.**
X **Positions of armed guards at the time of the attack.**

Davis's office. Passing his stricken deputy, Delahunty heard Davis say to him: "I am going to leave you, Jim."

While an unsuspecting Johnson pronounced the benediction as the convicts were marched back to their cells, Davis, who remained conscious, was walked to the prison hospital by trusty Frank Dinsmore and placed on the operating table. In the confusion that followed, Prince was told to go to the "hole," but no guard was delegated to accompany him. The solitary confinement cells happened to be located at one end of the hospital, leading to a second confrontation that threatened to become as deadly as the first.

Having done as he was told, Prince reached the hospital shortly after Dinsmore and Davis, the deputy's new gray suit and blue tie unrecognizable beneath a spreading river of crimson. Prince shouted at Dinsmore, "I want to finish him," then lunged at the helpless deputy. But the slightly built Prince was no match for Dinsmore, who, at six feet three and 180 pounds, was one of the tallest and most powerful men in the penitentiary. He literally held off the manic convict with one arm while administering to Davis with the other. The scuffling ended only after a guard following the trail of blood arrived and marched Prince off to solitary. Prince continued spewing obscenities while pleading with Dinsmore, known as the "convict physician," to dispatch the old man as a personal favor. "You finish him, Doc!"

Davis lingered through the afternoon and into the night. Weakened by shock and heavy bleeding, he spoke little, except to say that he knew of no reason why Prince should want to kill him. Dr. R. H. Spradling, the prison physician, was summoned from his home, and he immediately called in a Dr. Wilmeth for consultation. Their examination revealed that Prince's knife had found its mark half a dozen times. One blow struck a rib and narrowly missed the heart; three others pierced the abdomen; a fifth left a gash on the victim's cheek; and another had lacerated the hand Davis raised in self-defense. The doctors stanched the bleeding as best they could by stitching up the wounds and applying heavy bandages. Davis was then removed to his living quarters, where several visitors came to pay their respects in hushed tones.

Word of the attack spread quickly through the cell houses, and guards were told to be on the alert for any signs of a general uprising. Some of the younger prisoners could be heard shouting and cursing: "Let him die." "Bury him." The most raucous were escorted over to solitary, where they joined Prince's benighted chorus. According to the next day's newspaper accounts, some prisoners had been seen "weeping bitterly" in their cells. A distraught Warden Delahunty, fighting back tears of his own, called Davis "the most lenient official that the state prison has ever had. I have seen him allow a convict to go to work after a reprimand that, if I had been doing it, would have meant solitary confinement." The mystified warden believed that Prince's attack was aimed at the administration of the prison in general, rather than solely at the deputy warden.

Davis continued to weaken as the night wore on. Having determined that the internal bleeding had not been controlled, the doctors decided to operate as a last resort. The anesthetic was administered and the surgery was performed at eleven p.m. Forty-five minutes later, Davis passed away. He had never regained consciousness.

The funeral was held the following Wednesday, February 14, 1912, in the Lincoln home of George E. Hager, Lancaster County deputy attorney. Mrs. Hager was both the niece and the adopted daughter of the Davises. Her husband had already been given the task of prosecuting Albert Prince for murder and making sure that he would die on the gallows.

The crime that landed Prince in the Nebraska State Penitentiary had been committed in Omaha, in the late afternoon of November 1, 1909, shortly after police detective Michael J. Sullivan walked into Antokal's Saloon. After making his way to the cigar counter, where he began clipping a prize contest coupon from a copy of the *Omaha World Herald,* the detective was jostled from behind. He turned around to face a man he described as a slightly built "mulatto," with yellow, bloodshot eyes.

"What's the matter with you? Are you sick?" Sullivan asked him.

"Oh, I don't know as I'm sick," he replied surlily.

"Who are you?" Sullivan wanted to know.

"None of your damn business," the stranger shot back.

With that, he grabbed the lapel of Sullivan's coat, exposing his police badge. On seeing the star, the man drew a revolver from beneath his coat and fired it point-blank at the detective.

The bullet struck Sullivan in the right side of the chest, spinning him around but not felling him. Sullivan punched his assailant in the face, knocking him to the floor. Realizing that it would take too long to draw his own gun, the detective leapt on the man in an attempt to wrest the pistol from his grasp. Four more shots were fired during the struggle, three of which hit the officer.

Meanwhile, J. M. Antokal, the saloon keeper, had vaulted over the bar and attempted to grab the weapon. Antokal's finger caught in the trigger guard and was broken when Sullivan wrenched away the pistol and pointed it at his attacker. Prince was subdued by some customers and held in a corner while the police were called. A bleeding Sullivan made it to a chair but refused medical attention until his captive was hustled away in the police automobile.

While three surgeons operated on Sullivan at St. Joseph's Hospital, the gunman was placed in a cell. He pretended to be ill, moaning and groaning as if in agony. When no one responded, he suddenly leapt to his feet and began swearing at the top of his lungs. Then he quieted down and asked for a cigarette.

During his interrogation, the prisoner told the detectives that his last name was "Prim" and that he had arrived in Omaha the previous Saturday. An express claim found in his pocket enabled the officers to collect two suitcases at the depot that had been billed through St. Louis to an Albert Prince. Once his true identity was revealed Prince stated that his home was Cincinnati, but that he had left there six years ago. He described his mother as a "full blood Negro" and his father, whom he never knew, as a white man from Dublin, Ireland.

After leaving home, Prince said, he had traveled all over the United States, Mexico, and parts of South America, and he backed his claim with a fluent display of Spanish. Before coming to Omaha he had worked in an Arkansas town, where he purchased

Albert Prince, 1909

the pistol he was carrying "to protect himself." Prince admitted to Chief of Police Donahue that he had once shot a man in an Alabama coal mine because the "no-good" had tried to stab him with a knife. The incident had taken place several years ago and the man had recovered from his wounds—or so Prince claimed.

The gun with which Prince shot Sullivan was a .38-caliber Smith & Wesson. A subsequent body search yielded a full cartridge belt, a straight razor, and a large clasp knife. Detectives suspected that he was on dope, a charge that Prince denied at first, but to which he later confessed after an examination of his bags turned up an opium pipe, opium, and the utensils of an addict.

When asked why he had come to Omaha in the first place, Prince replied: "I had heard so much talk about it being a wide-open town, and I knew where there is so much gambling going on, there is something doing." He also claimed to have no recollection of the shooting, as he had been drunk for a week. What Prince did not say, and what the Omaha police soon learned, was that he was wanted in Kansas City for a number of daring stickups still classified by the law as "highway robbery." Suspicious of who Sullivan was in the bar, he panicked and went for his gun.

The case of *State of Nebraska v. Albert Prince* never made it to trial in Douglas County District Court. On the advice of his court-appointed attorney, Prince pled guilty to assault with intent to kill. Detective Sullivan had pulled through, luckily enough, so the charge was not murder. The surgeons removed a bullet from each of his shoulders and another from the bicep of his right arm. The first shot, which most likely would have been fatal, had struck a suspender buckle and been deflected.

On December 4, 1909, the defendant was brought to the courtroom to be read his sentence: "That . . . Albert Prince be taken by the sheriff of Douglas County, Nebraska, . . . to the penitentiary of the state of Nebraska, located at Lincoln, Lancaster County, Nebraska, and that he be there confined at hard labor for a term of twelve and a half years from this date, no part of which term shall by reason of this sentence be spent in solitary confinement."

By law, Sheriff E. F. Bailey had thirty days to deliver his prisoner to the penitentiary, but it took him only two. Prince, together with another miscreant named William Lewis, was committed by Warden T. W. Smith on December 6, 1909. With time off for good behavior he could become a free man in eight years, maybe less.

Sheriff Bailey and a manacled Prince proceeded to Warden Smith's office, located directly across the hall from the reception room. Smith filled out a receipt for the prisoner that was little different from the ones used by shopkeepers when they took delivery of groceries or a keg of beer. His business completed, the sheriff caught the next train back to Omaha.

After talking with the prisoner for a few minutes—what the warden called "sizing up the new man"—Smith took Prince next door to the chief clerk's office for booking. There he was given his convict number, 5374. The first felon to be admitted to Lancaster, back on February 1, 1871, was assigned the number 1, and the numbering had continued in consecutive order ever since. If a man was released and later returned after committing a second, third, or even fourth offense, he received a new number each time. Yet, unlike the inmates in many other penitentiaries, those in Lancaster were always addressed by their last names.

Prince's money and valuables were cataloged and placed in the clerk's vault. His cigarette papers and tobacco were tossed in the wastebasket (cigarettes were strictly forbidden owing to the danger of fire). If he behaved himself, he would be allowed to smoke an occasional cigar and chew all the tobacco he could afford.

From the clerk's office he was delivered to the aging turnkey, Claus Pahl, who carried out his duties from inside a large metal cage illuminated by a single bulb that dangled precariously from the ceiling at the end of a wire. Once a prisoner was admitted to this enclosure, and heard the sound of the key in the lock, the realization that he was truly behind bars suddenly hit home. Some men broke down and began to weep. Deputy Clerk Wilson, who had witnessed many such lapses of composure, reflected: "I believe that in more than half the cases, were [the prisoner] pardoned right then and there, he would never again trespass against the laws of the land."

The next stop was the Bertillon room, so named for the French criminologist Alphonse Bertillon, who was the first to apply the scientific method to criminal identification. The deputy warden recorded every mark and scar on Prince's body, then measured his height, the length and width of his head, the length of his nose, his left finger, his left forearm, and his left foot.

Prince, who said he was twenty-four, was five feet eight and three-fourths inches tall and weighed 139 pounds. Under complexion the deputy warden wrote "black." The new prisoner's most distinguishing features were multiple tattoos of red, green, and blue that wound around his torso and limbs like rivers encircling a miniature continent. On one arm was an American flag, an anchor, and a snake in olive, yellow, and green. On the other was a butterfly, an eagle, and a woman's head with the word LOVE printed beneath it. So numerous were these markings that the deputy warden ran out of space and simply wrote at the bottom: "Arms and legs tattooed."

Prince gave his religious preference as Baptist, and it was noted that he could read and write. His occupations were waiter and barber, although he had also mined coal and worked as a seaman. Under habits he was classified as "Intemperate," meaning he drank liquor, used tobacco, and had a taste for opium. He claimed to have a wife named Mary, for whom he provided only the general address of Cincinnati, Ohio. After this information was recorded, Prince was photographed from both front and side; his youthful looks were muted by a deep scowl and heavy black beard. Then his head and face were shaved and, like all new convicts, he was photographed a second time. He also signed a document giving the warden the authority to open and read his mail.

Now officially a convict, Prince was fitted for his uniform. The hated black-and-white, horizontal stripes had been replaced in the mid-1890s by Warden A. D. Beemer, at the urging of his then-

Nebraska State Penitentiary, Lincoln, Nebr.

The Nebraska State Penitentiary or "Lancaster," c. 1910 (Used by permission of The Nebraska State Historical Society)

assistant James Delahunty. The new clothes were made on-site of a dark gray material similar to the uniforms worn by mailmen, though of an inferior quality. After the process of checking in, the prisoner was finally turned over to the keeper responsible for assigning him to a cell.

The two wings in which the convicts were housed contained a total of 294 cells. Measuring five feet long by seven feet wide, each was equipped with a washstand, a primitive toilet, and narrow, double-deck bunks containing tick mattresses filled with straw. When a convict went to bed, mere inches separated his head and feet from the walls. Since the inmate population fluctuated between 400 and 450 men, many were required to double up, the newcomer taking the top bunk, from which he could reach out and touch the low ceiling while lying down. And though an effort was made to keep nonviolent first offenders in the east building, which had only sixty cells, the policy was impossible to maintain given the constraints on space. Cells too small for one man, let alone two, became perpetual torture chambers, made even more unbearable by the stifling summer heat and winter cold that permeated the limestone walls. Lancaster was a place where only fleas, bedbugs, and cockroaches thrived, little worse and little better than most other state prisons of the time.

Because of his potential for violence, Prince was placed in the west wing, where he spent his first month adapting to the mechanical routine. The morning bell rang at six o'clock. After dressing hurriedly, the inmates walked single-file to the dining room. They sat down on command, all facing in the same direction, and ate their bread and hash in silence. Talking could get one written up, and the result could be the loss of several days' good time or possibly a night or two in the dreaded hole. Once finished, the men filed back to their cells for a brief rest before the seven o'clock bell summoned them to work in one of the shops, where shirts, brooms, and rattan furniture were made under contract with private companies.

Work continued until noon, when the big whistle sounded the dinner break. The men returned to the dining room for their second, and largest, meal of the day; it was long on starch and boiled vegetables, but short on the fried meat that so many of them craved, well over half of Lancaster's inmates having been reared on farms. The dishes were passed by waiters drawn from the prison population; if a man wanted another slice of bread, he held up his right hand; if it was water or coffee he wanted, he held up his cup. Beyond this, seconds were prohibited.

The men were returned to their cells for half an hour's rest. The whistle blew again at one o'clock, and everyone went back to work until five in the afternoon. Then came the last trip to the dining room, after which the inmates spent the evening in their cells reading magazines and books borrowed from the prison library. The intemperate chewed tobacco and smoked cigars purchased from the stand at one end of the chapel. Those who had money in their prison bank accounts savored fruit and other delicacies ordered with the permission of the administration. The final bell of the day rang at exactly nine p.m. Moments later, the guards cut the electricity to the cells, plunging their numbed inhabitants into darkness.

To the surprise of Warden Smith and his deputies, Prince became something of a model prisoner. His one official reprimand was recorded in Lancaster's "Day Journal" some eight weeks into his sentence. On February 2, 1910, he and eight others were cited for stealing clothing from one of the prison's three labor contractors, the Platte Shirt Company. The penalty was severe: "Forfeit—30 days each—good behavior."

Rather than assign Prince to one of the shops on a permanent basis, the warden decided to take advantage of his barbering skills and make him a trusty. He went from shop to shop, shaving his fellow inmates, and cutting their hair, for a small monthly fee. In the evenings, while everyone else was locked up, he was allowed to move about the corridors of the west cell house unattended. The only complaints about his conduct were lodged by white inmates who couldn't afford a small tip. It was said that Prince would literally "tear" the whiskers from their faces by failing to sharpen his razor, then wipe them off with a towel previously used on a "darkey."

Lancaster's population included eighty or so Negro inmates, and Prince, by virtue of his position and race, got to know each of them. Among his favorites was thirty-nine-year-old Thomas Johnson, who was serving his second term in the penitentiary. Johnson was first committed in April of 1908, after an Omaha jury convicted him of robbing a saloon. He completed his sentence on the Fourth of July the following year and promptly returned to Omaha, where he took a job as a waiter at the Henshaw Hotel.

About nine o'clock on the night of October 14, 1909, Henry R. "Lucky" Frankland, a member of a bridge construction gang, was found lying under a viaduct in the rail yard of Omaha's Union Station. Frankland was bleeding profusely from a three-and-a-half-inch knife wound to the side of the throat, his jugular vein severed. Another seven-inch gash extended from his left cheek to the back of his neck; a third, six inches long, ran from the victim's neck to his scalp. A stretcher was called for, and Frankland was carried to the station's hospital room, where he died within minutes.

Frankland had been paid earlier that day and was planning to return to Chicago to see his wife and children. He had decided to celebrate by having a drink or two, but by late afternoon he was "well oiled," according to those who had seen him in Hunsinger's saloon, the very establishment Johnson had been sent up to Lancaster for robbing. Frankland eventually left for another tavern, where he was joined by a Negro described as thirty-five to forty years of age, about five feet seven inches tall, and weighing 155 pounds. The two men were last seen by Frank Galivan, the elevator boy at Union Station, walking arm-in-arm in the direction of the yards just a half hour before a dying Frankland was discovered by a night porter. His gold watch and chain were missing, and his pockets had been turned inside out. In his haste, Frankland's assailant had overlooked two ten dollar bills.

The watch and chain soon turned up in the pawnshop of Hascal Segal. The pawnbroker identified Johnson, who had already been detained by the Omaha police on suspicion of robbery and murder, as the man who had pawned the objects. His testimony was supported by Bernice Wilhoit, a prostitute, with whom Johnson had spent the night of the killing, in the Humbolt Hotel, on Dodge Street. According to Wilhoit, Johnson was wearing Frankland's watch and chain, and he had plenty of money on him. Johnson

**Thomas Johnson, 1910 (Used by permission of
The Nebraska State Historical Society)**

told police the money came from cashing his pension check for service in the Spanish-American War. Equally damaging was the fact that Johnson had been observed by two sisters scrubbing bloodstains from his clothing—these he said were weeks old and had come from a stint as a cook in Grand Island. The case against him was clinched when J. T. Donahue, a city detective, identified a knife he had found in the suspect's pocket at the time of his arrest, its blade smeared with blood. The alleged murder weapon, along with $2.50, had been stolen from the home of Dollie Walker during a visit Johnson had paid her three nights prior to the murder.

Johnson admitted to everything but the killing itself—this in the face of a witness list for the prosecution that ran to forty-five names. A newspaper account stated that he refused an offer to plead guilty in return for a life sentence, but that seems unlikely given the weight of evidence against him. On December 11, 1909, the jury found the Georgia-born defendant guilty of murder, but sentencing was postponed pending an appeal, which ultimately failed. On February 9, 1910, Johnson was sentenced to hang the following June. He was transferred to Lancaster the next day by Sheriff Bailey where he became 5407, his second, and last, convict number.

Johnson's execution day came and went pending another appeal, although no one, including the prisoner and his lawyer, held out much hope. If anyone was living on borrowed time, it was Thomas Johnson. Finally, after reviewing the evidence and the various rulings of the trial judge, the state supreme court reaffirmed the conviction. Prison authorities were ordered to proceed with the execution on Friday, May 19, 1911, between the hours of eleven a.m. and three p.m.

In early February, a cell keeper named Thomas Doody approached Warden Smith and told him a conspiracy was in the works. An informer claimed that Prince and Johnson were plotting an escape, and that other inmates were likely involved. Prince intended to kill the night cell keeper and any other prison official who crossed his path, open Johnson's cell, and together they would scale the walls to freedom.

Johnson was taken to the hole to await execution, while Prince was relieved of his barbering duties and assigned to work in the corn-broom shop. He denied knowing anything about an escape plan and requested a meeting with Smith. When he asked the warden why his work assignment had been changed, all Smith would say is that Prince had been the head barber for a year, that it was an easy job, and that the decision had been made to give it to a lifer for a while.

Two weeks later, a guard named Coakley came to Prince's cell and told him to fetch his coat and cap. He was wanted in the warden's office right away. Prince arrived to find two guards searching another prisoner for weapons and drugs, after which they escorted him to the hole. They then searched Prince and found nothing. As he was being placed in the hole by Coakley, he again asked what was happening, but the guard's mumbled reply was unintelligible because of Prince's poor hearing. Johnson, who was in the adjoining cell, thought he heard Coakley say something about a knife.

Doody, assisted by Kennison, the new prison barber, had made a search of the wooden towel and supply stand to which the barber chair was attached. Inside a locked drawer were a double-edged knife and a two-foot length of gas pipe. When Prince was confronted with the weapons he pled ignorance, claiming that he had once asked a guard why the drawer was locked and was told to pay it no mind.

The hole consisted of six cells, each lit by an opening in the ceiling about the size of a man's hand. Devoid of all furnishings, the stone floor served as both chair and bed, but this was not what concerned most convicts. What they truly feared was the practice of "stringing up" those in solitary confinement. This was done by backing the prisoner up to the cell bars, pulling his arms through, and shackling his wrists. Next a rope was passed through the shackles and looped around a bar overhead. As the rope was tightened, the arms were raised to a point even with, or sometimes above, the prisoner's head, until he was standing on tiptoes. There was no toilet—only a pail and a floor drain—and the prisoner either had to wait for his food to be delivered to relieve himself, or soil his pants, which happened repeatedly if one remained in the hole for any length of time.

About noon, a guard delivered two slices of stale bread and a cup of water, which the unsteady convict spilled more often than not for lack of feeling in his arms and hands. After eating, he was strung up again and remained that way until supper, when he received the same ration as before. Using his coat for a mattress and shoes for a pillow, he slept fitfully, if at all, in the company of rats, mice, and various species of roaches. Only on Sundays was the prisoner spared the ordeal of being trussed up like a turkey.

According to Prince, Warden Smith visited him on a Sunday morning, several days after he was placed in the hole. "Get up, I want to see you," the warden snapped at the reclining prisoner.

"He asked me how I was feeling," Prince recounted. "I told him that anyone confined there for four days without food would not feel very well. He told me that if that was the way I felt that he guessed I could stay there. Later Coakley came around and strung me up. All this time I had nothing to eat."

Johnson offered Prince some food, if only he could get to it through a small door held in place by a two-by-four and some pieces of iron. Prince kicked the door open without much difficulty, knocking out the metal braces and loosening the timber, then instantly regretted what he had done. There were many stories of men being beaten in solitary for lesser transgressions, so he made up his mind to keep the lumber and iron as protection.

Later that same day, a group of Negro citizens from Lincoln were admitted to Johnson's cell to pray and read the Bible with the condemned man. When they saw the damage Prince had done they reported him to the warden's office the next morning.

Guard Coakley was sent to Prince's cell to confirm the report. "I told him to come in and see," Prince recounted. "Then Coakley wanted to string me up. I refused. I knew if I was strung up, I would be helpless if they beat me." Coakley left and returned a few minutes later with Warden Smith. When Prince again refused to hand over the wood and iron, Smith said, "I was only making things harder on myself."

The two disappeared down the corridor, leaving Prince to ponder what would happen next. The answer came when Coakley reappeared with another guard, dragging the canvas fire hose. "Coakley pointed it in my face and ordered me to give him the stick and iron." Prince refused and moved behind the door where the full force of the water could not reach him.

In retaliation, Coakley ordered the other guard to get the "prodding pole" and use it to force Prince into the open. "After the guard had prodded me in the ribs until I couldn't stand it any longer, I went over to the other side of my cell and stood bending down with my back to the door. If I had stood up, it would have knocked me over."

Prince fought back by filling the waste bucket with water and throwing it at Coakley, who was soon soaked from head to foot. The battle of wills continued for a good half hour, with Prince refusing to go down so that he could be disarmed. Finally, when he could withstand the dousing no longer, he hollered for the guards to stop and handed over the pieces of wood and iron.

Coakley immediately strung Prince up. Totally spent and shivering uncontrollably from the cold draft, the convict feared he might catch pneumonia and asked the warden for some dry clothes, which were not sent until evening. When they arrived, Prince was stunned. Instead of the regulation prison gray the warden had sent a striped uniform not seen in Lancaster for years. After he had changed, Prince was walked over to the blacksmith shop, where a rarely used ball and chain were attached to one ankle. The next morning, as the other convicts were filing to work, Prince could be seen in the yard breaking stone with a sledgehammer. He couldn't remember just how long it was before they removed the ball and put him back to work in the corn-broom shop, but it was at least twenty-five days.

———————◇——◦●◦——◇———————

A somewhat quaint headline greeted the readers of the April 10, 1911, issue of the *Lincoln Daily Star:* DELAHUNTY DRIFTS INTO THE CITY. James Delahunty had arrived in Lincoln the previous day for an appointment with Nebraska Governor Chester Hardy Aldrich and Warden T. W. Smith.

A native of Peoria, Illinois, Jim Delahunty was nearing fifty-five and had spent most of the past fifteen years in one form of government service or another. Balding and dignified, he possessed a melancholy countenance and the slightly averted gaze of a man too well acquainted with the darker side of human nature. After serving a two-year term as deputy clerk of Clay County, Delahunty had been appointed steward at the state penitentiary. He later served as deputy warden under A. D. Beemer and under Beemer's successor, Edward D. Davis. So respected was he by the inmates that they circulated a petition asking Warden Smith to keep Delahunty on when he took over, something Smith had chosen not to do.

The reason for the meeting was a poorly kept secret. Wardens, like many other state officials, came and went in the aftermath of elections, and Smith, a Democrat, was on his way out. Indeed, he would have left sooner had not the Republican governor waited for the legislature to adjourn, so that he could appoint Delahunty warden without running afoul of the politically hostile Senate. Two days later, Smith departed and Delahunty moved into the warden's apartment on the second floor of the administration building. Having no wife, he appointed his widowed mother to

**Warden James Delahunty (Used by permission of
The Nebraska State Historical Society)**

the position of penitentiary matron, another perquisite of the
spoils system.

Delahunty was also in a position to repay an old friend and political benefactor. With the consent of Governor Aldrich, he selected Ed Davis, his onetime superior and fellow native of Clay
County, to be his deputy warden. Having served as warden himself
from 1901 to 1903, Davis knew the ropes and in Delahunty's judgment would make an excellent right-hand man.

One of Davis's first orders was to send for Prince. He was
brought before the deputy warden in stripes, lugging the ball and
chain.

"Don't you think that you have worn this thing long enough,
my boy?" Davis asked.

"Yes," a subdued and distant Prince replied.

"Well," said Davis, "I'll take it off right now, and here is a pass to the clothing department. You go over and pull off those stripes and get a new suit. Get to look like a man and act like one."

The application of the water cure followed by Prince's exclusion from the daily routine wrought a marked change in his personality. He became sullen and withdrawn and wanted to get even with someone, anyone, for his misfortune. Beneath his laconic exterior was a simmering hatred fed by Thomas Johnson's imminent appointment with the gallows.

------- ◦ ◦◉◦ ◦ -------

The nondescript building known as the "hanghouse" was located in the southwest corner of the penitentiary complex. When seen by visitors from a distance, it resembled a large woodshed and was normally used to store box lumber belonging to the broom shop. This had to be removed before George Stryker, the aptly named state executioner, could oversee the assembly of the gallows. Once this was done, the rope and trapdoor were tested, as was the circuitry that made the whole thing work. On Stryker's signal, he and three other men would each press a button, one of which would spring the trap, dropping the body into the void, and allowing each of the four men a degree of anonymity, and a clear conscience.

Johnson's hanging was scheduled for two o'clock in the afternoon. The prisoner spent the morning of May nineteenth with Ollie Jackson, described by the papers as a "colored minister." They prayed together, and Johnson wrote his final letters to friends and relatives. He refused to be interviewed by reporters. When asked for a final statement regarding his guilt, he tersely replied: "Don't say anything for me."

At one-thirty Johnson presented the clergyman with his glasses and a song he had recently composed. The prison gates were opened shortly before two, and the 150 men who had requested permission to witness the execution filed in. Minutes later, Johnson began the march from his cell to the gallows, his arms in the grasp of guards. He walked calmly, requiring no support. Others, including Jackson, fell in behind, with Warden Delahunty and his assistants bringing up the rear.

The spectators were in place by the time the cavalcade of death entered the hanghouse and stopped in front of the gallows. The stories and nervous jokes about past hangings abruptly ceased as necks craned to get a better view of the condemned. Johnson, wearing a cap, looked up at the gallows, then turned to survey the silent crowd. A familiar face greeted him and he nodded and smiled in recognition.

Supported by guards, he climbed the wooden stairs, followed by Jackson. Johnson turned and offered his hand to the minister. Then he spoke his last words in what the reporter from the *Lincoln Daily Star* characterized as "the melodious tones of the Southern Darkey, without trace of quaver or fear: 'Goodbye brother, I'll meet you in heaven.'"

Johnson was moved to the right side of the trapdoor while guards unwound the rope. Another guard removed his own hat out of respect, and Johnson did likewise, smiling and folding his hands. He was motioned to the trap, and he stepped onto the rectangular outline of wooden planks, then stood placidly as his wrists and ankles were bound and the black execution cap, looking like a relic from the Tower of London, was pulled over his face. The rope was adjusted so that the knot fit snugly under the left ear. Almost before the spectators knew what was happening, the wedge that prevented the door from tripping accidentally was kicked away, and the trap was sprung. The crowd surged forward to get a better look and had to be repelled by the guards. The body quivered slightly for a time before going limp. Eighteen minutes later, the six attending physicians required by law pronounced the prisoner dead. They noted that Johnson's neck had not snapped as it was supposed to, and that death had resulted from slow strangulation.

When Prince got the news of Johnson's extended ordeal, it pushed him closer to the edge. Still protesting angrily that he was "jobbed" by the administration, that the knife and gas pipe had been planted in the barber chair, he tried to start a mutiny in the corn-broom shop by encouraging fellow inmates to take sledge-hammers to the machinery. "And while you are doing that, I will go up on the guard stand and I will not only kill the bastard but will cut his head plumb off."

When no one rallied to this wild appeal, Prince decided to act alone. While working in the corn-broom shop he had discovered a knife hidden in one of the machines. He honed both edges of the blade to razor sharpness and fashioned a new handle of wood, then attached it to the blade with broom wire. Concealing the dirk in his clothing, he carried it back to his cell, where he hid it from the guards. The following Sunday, former warden T. W. Smith visited Lancaster and attended church services. Prince was present in the chapel and very much regretted the fact that he had not brought the knife along. "I would have put Smith on the bum," he later declared of the man who had ordered his torture.

But this encounter gave Prince an idea. He noticed how Deputy Warden Davis always walked down the outer aisle just before the benediction was pronounced. If only he could maneuver himself into the right seat he would be in the perfect spot from which to strike. By the time the guards responded it would be all over for him. The next Sunday Prince hid the knife under his gray coat and got into position for the attack. In the silence following the last hymn, he could hear the deputy warden's approaching footsteps echoing off the steel-lined walls. As the old man drew closer, he glimpsed him out of the corner of his eye. All of a sudden, Prince whirled and was on his victim in an instant.

When the dying man reached the operating room minutes later, he recognized his assailant in the gloom.

"What got into you this morning?" Davis asked Prince as he swayed, mortally wounded.

"You have been digging at me for long enough," Prince shot back.

"Why, I haven't spoken to you for over a month," countered the dying man.

BREAKOUT

Streetcars running between downtown Lincoln and the penitentiary were thronged by curiosity seekers within hours of the stabbing. Others came by horse and buggy or by automobile. When the news of Davis's late-night death hit the papers the next morning, their numbers swelled. Everyone wanted to get a look at the murderer, with more women arriving at the gates than men. All were politely but firmly turned away by Warden Delahunty and his staff. Prince remained in solitary confinement, where his attorney and spiritual adviser would be the only ones permitted to visit him.

Some of the rules governing prisoners locked in the hole were suspended in recognition of Prince's instant notoriety, and the feeling that he would surely hang. An electrical wire was strung to his cell so that he could see to read and write. A wooden shoe box became a combination table and desk, and a bed would soon follow. His first letters were written to his mother, in Cincinnati, and to his stepbrother, in New York, asking him to come to Lincoln as soon as possible. Prince was the recipient of many cards and religious tracts, and even received a box of candy, whose contents had a peculiar odor. Taking no chances, the warden ordered it thrown into a nearby lake. A card arrived later, on which the anonymous sender had sketched a skull and crossbones and had written: "Give

Satan my best regards, and I will send you down a chunk of ice." The card, like the candy, was never delivered, for it violated a long-established policy of not forwarding any mail to an inmate that might give him serious cause for worry.

At ten o'clock on the Tuesday morning following the slaying, a six-member coroner's jury assembled at the penitentiary in what one reporter described as "an atmosphere charged with the fiercest human passion." The witness list included the names of five guards, three doctors, one convict, and Prince himself. The jury listened intently while Dr. F. L. Wilmeth, who conducted the postmortem examination on Davis, testified that he died of wounds inflicted by a homemade knife with a six-inch blade, the same one that had been taken away from the accused prisoner in the chapel. Its point bent, the weapon in question was exhibited to the jury, dark clots of blood still clinging to the hilt. The guards, led by cell keeper Thomas Doody, then told of the foiled escape plan devised by Prince and the deceased convict Thomas Johnson.

All present agreed that the most impressive witness was the physically commanding Frank Dinsmore. The trusty had become a hero in the eyes of many for taking Prince by the collar and preventing him from assaulting Davis in the hospital. Possessed of curly dark hair and piercing blue eyes, the tall, muscular convict had been a grain buyer in Dawson County until the day he laced his wife's food with a fatal dose of arsenic. Lancaster's only inmate with a college education, Dinsmore was immaculate in his prison garb and spoke what was described as the "purest English." At the prompting of Coroner Jack Matthews, he recounted the details of the stabbing down to the words exchanged by Prince and Davis in the hospital. When pressed for more information about his role in protecting the deputy warden, Dinsmore modestly replied: "I had a little tussle with Prince, that was all."

Frank Dinsmore, the "convict physician" (Used by permission of The Nebraska State Historical Society)

When it came time for Prince to testify, Delahunty asked that the jury be allowed to visit him in solitary. Despite the fact that he had no court-appointed lawyer as yet, rumors were already circulating that Prince was planning an insanity defense, and Delahunty had issued orders that no guard should enter the inmate's cell unless another armed man was present. The coroner agreed to the warden's request, and the jury soon found itself staring at the convict through steel bars. "Calm, cold and self-possessed" was how Prince was described by a reporter from the *Lincoln Evening News*. He stood at his cell door, searching the faces of the clustered jurors, while Matthews informed him that he was not compelled to testify, or even make a statement, if he did not wish to. If he did choose to speak, whatever he might say could be used against him at a future trial.

"Do you wish to make a statement?" Matthews asked.

Prince said nothing but shook his head to indicate that he did not.

"Did you kill Deputy Davis?"

"I would rather not talk about it until my trial, if that is just the same to you," Prince replied.

The prisoner pointed to the warden and asked whether some heat could be directed to his chilly cell, and Delahunty promised to see what he could do. Then Prince turned away and disappeared into a darkened corner. As the jury slowly filed out of solitary, some of its members shuddered as they passed into the free and warmer air beyond.

The jury reached its verdict within minutes: "Edward Davis's death was caused by knife wounds inflicted on the body by one Albert Prince, colored, on February 11, 1912, at the close of chapel services at the penitentiary at Lancaster, Nebraska. We, the jury, recommend that Prince be given a speedy trial, signed C. H. Rudge, O. W. Webster, William Robertson, Jr., L. O. Jones, O. E. Houck, Sam Melick."

Prince's new quarters of steel and stone, which were almost double the size of the regular cells, had taken on an unusual air of domesticity. A bed had been moved in to go with his makeshift writing desk, and he was allowed books from the prison library. With the few dollars credited to his prison account, Prince had purchased horsehair, which he used to make braided watch fobs that were sold to souvenir seekers at the cigar stand. Unlike the other convicts, who were limited to writing letters once a week, Prince was permitted to correspond whenever he wished. Several of his letters contained poems written to occupy his time and, as often happened to men caught in death's shadow, he asked for a Bible and met regularly with Chaplain Johnson, a most sympathetic listener. His stepbrother, William Hyde, who looked more like Prince's twin, arrived from New York and found work as a waiter at a local hotel. They met often in the presence of a guard, who carefully inspected the fruit Hyde brought along and listened closely to their every word.

———◇——◇◉◇——◇———

Governor Chester Hardy Aldrich not only looked like a relic of the nineteenth century, he sounded like one. Atop his bull neck sat a square, granite head whose dimensions were magnified by a balding pate, across which a few wispy strands of dark hair were making their last stand, like shriveling leaves in windrows. With wide-set eyes and a prizefighter's iron jaw, Nebraska's chief executive spoke with conviction, and in a deep baritone capable of rattling windows. Little wonder that he counted the mercurial Theodore Roosevelt among his closest friends; the maverick leader of the Bull Moose party stayed at the Aldrich residence whenever he visited Lincoln.

The governor had been on the defensive ever since the prison stabbing nearly a month earlier, and now, with a Saturday- afternoon meeting at the capitol scheduled with half a dozen members of the Prison Reform Association and the Social Service Club, he knew exactly the kind of weekend it was going to be. To make matters worse, he had also agreed to see Chaplain Johnson, a staunch critic of Warden James Delahunty, Aldrich's handpicked man.

Johnson had barely entered the governor's office and closed the heavy oak door when a reporter waiting for developments in the anteroom heard the sound of raised voices. The shouting continued for two or three minutes as Aldrich upbraided the chaplain for disloyalty, and for not coming to him earlier, and with proof, to back up his claims of misconduct. Some said Aldrich resorted to profanity, but only his last words, uttered as he showed Johnson out, were intelligible: "I do not want to hear this kind of talk from you. If you have any specific charge to make, I'll listen to it, and if you can

**Governor Chester Hardy Aldrich (Used by permission of
The Nebraska State Historical Society)**

prove anything wrong I'll rip things open." Adding insult to injury,
he concluded, "I will do the preaching at the penitentiary myself if
I cannot get anyone else to do it. There's the door!" On the governor's desk lay Johnson's hastily scrawled letter of resignation.

An hour later the delegation of reformers, led by retired district court judge Lincoln Frost, was shown in. A few minutes before their arrival, Aldrich told reporters that the "next bunch" was
part of a conspiracy out to claim Delahunty's scalp. Still smarting
from his set-to with Johnson, Aldrich took the offensive and never
let go. He was willing to hear what his visitors had to say, but he
would not entertain charges against anyone connected with the
running of the penitentiary unless they were specific and supported by facts. He had heard more than enough so-called "gener-
alities."

Having been told of Johnson's fate, no member of the delegation felt emboldened enough to broach the subject of the warden. The discussion was confined to such matters as cell house ventilation, the inadequate pay of guards, the "dope" problem, and the need of a reformatory in which less hardened inmates could be segregated from the "old pros," all concerns of the governor as well. Before the meeting ended, Aldrich asked those present for their opinion of his decision to bar women Sunday school teachers from the prison. Almost everyone thought it a good idea, although no action would be taken until men were found to replace the ladies. As to the matter of Johnson's replacement, the governor wanted to think it over for a while. Recalling that his record clerk, J. H. Presson, was an ordained Methodist preacher, Aldrich had already prevailed upon him to conduct the next day's service.

Of all the problems associated with the running of Lancaster, none had proved more intractable than the use of drugs. Like Albert Prince, many inmates were addicted before they arrived, while others, unable to put up with the despair of confinement, sought out those who could supply them with opium or its derivatives, laudanum and morphine. Much of it was smuggled in by alcoholic guards who worked twelve-hour shifts in return for thirty dollars a month, a hard cot in a stuffy dormitory, and unappetizing meals. The rest arrived in hollowed-out shoe heels, in smoking tobacco, and in coal cars bearing coded chalk marks. One enterprising female visitor left some English walnuts whose shells had been hulled, filled with gum opium, and then glued back together.

On a cold night, less than a week before the meeting with Governor Aldrich, five well-respected citizens of Lincoln, including Judge Frost of the Prison Reform Association and Pastor I. F. Roach of St. Paul's Church, joined forces with ex-convict Charles Burns, who had just been released from the penitentiary after serving a year for breaking and entering. With a reporter from the

Nebraska State Journal filling the role of documentary witness, the reformers reached a darkened Lancaster just before ten o'clock. The guard towers were deserted, as always after sunset, there being no outdoor lighting to illuminate the grounds. The men made their way along the wall to a place where stone gave way to wood. Minutes later, a disembodied hand reached through an opening and took the bottle of morphine Burns was carrying without a word being spoken.

In a sensational story that appeared the next day, it was revealed that the hand was that of inmate Jack Crawford, a trusty and erstwhile friend of Burns's on the inside. This so-called "test" had been undertaken in response to charges "that a bad condition of affairs exists at the penitentiary at the present time." Crawford, it was alleged, could never have gotten the morphine without the direct involvement of the guards and the possession of one or more keys.

When reporters asked the warden to comment, Delahunty stated that his administration had been as successful as any in suppressing the pernicious traffic in dope. He went on to point out that the bottle of morphine could just as easily have been thrown over the fence.

Such lame reasoning did nothing to appease the deeply embarrassed governor, who responded by drafting a lengthy document in which he outlined the steps the warden must take to remedy the situation. Convict Crawford and all other trusties were to be locked up at five p.m., the same time as the other inmates. All guards accused of drunkenness were to be dismissed at once, and Dr. Spradling, the part-time prison physician, was to spend no less than two hours a day treating the prisoners and seeing to it that "hygienic conditions may be established as nearly perfect as possible." After supper, when all guards were normally off the wall, one of their number was to be stationed outside in the prison yard.

The muckraking investigation had resulted in other, more serious, allegations. Judge Frost had become convinced that Frank Dinsmore was the cunning mastermind behind Lancaster's dope trade. Though the governor was skeptical, he directed Delahunty to relieve Dinsmore of his duties as hospital trusty: "He is to have nothing whatever, either directly or indirectly, to do with the handling of drugs; that you are to find other employment for him absolutely; and he is to cell alone." Left unexplained for the time being was Aldrich's reference to what he described as other "charges of a character so heinous that they are unspeakable." These, too, pertained to Frank Dinsmore.

His pummeling in the papers only made the governor more combative. When he was asked about Charles Burns's claim that he had witnessed Prince being tortured in the hole, Aldrich stated that he had been able to account for the convict's whereabouts from the moment he had taken office. "The man has been subjected to no such treatment during that time." He went on to charge that such stories were being circulated in an attempt to secure a wave of popular sentiment favorable to a ruthless murderer. Aldrich had been carrying out his own investigation of the prison for the past two weeks, and no other official action was called for. Prince was certain to be convicted, and when that day came the unwarranted controversy involving both the prison and the prisoner would be laid to rest in short order.

Meanwhile, the *Lincoln Daily Star* noted that an unnamed Omaha newspaper was sending a reporter to interview P. C. Johnson at his home in Tecumseh. "It is generally understood here that the outside critics of the penitentiary management have been receiving a good deal of their information from the ex-chaplain."

The heaviest snowstorm of the season slammed into Lincoln in the early afternoon of Wednesday, March thirteenth. Sweeping across Nebraska from west to east, the blizzard forced the closing of schools, stores, offices, and most public facilities within hours of its onset. Railroad lines and roads running in all four directions from the city were clogged by massive drifts that filled cuts and buried landmarks, making travel impossible. Within the city itself public transportation was shut down after two streetcars headed for the suburbs disappeared into the white void and others jumped the tracks. The special car used by the local traction company to handle derailments was itself helplessly stuck in a drift in the nearby town of Havelock. On crowded street corners stranded passengers, shivering and caked in snow, were left to fend for themselves.

Adding to what the newspaper characterized as "the general demoralization" were warnings by local coal dealers that their supplies were running dangerously low. There had been so many winter storms—sixty inches of snow thus far versus a normal thirty-five—that stockpiles had dwindled to almost nothing. The anthracite was already gone, and the amount of Kansas steam coal was on "the ragged edge." Dealers were keeping the telegraph lines humming in an effort to get the tracks cleared, no matter the cost to the railroads in men and machinery.

The blizzard increased in fury as the day wore on. And instead of abating at nightfall, as predicted by forecasters in Washington, D.C., it grew still worse, owing to the high winds. Warden Delahunty came downstairs to his office about seven o'clock Thursday morning. It was his fifty-fifth birthday, and Walter Wilson wished him many more happy years. He thanked the deputy clerk and went straight to his desk where he worked until eleven, occasionally getting up to peer out the frosted windows in the hope that the streetcars were running again. He had planned to go into town for a meeting with the publisher of the *Lincoln Herald,* but the conditions were such that he had no choice other than to reschedule the appointment. He tried to reach the paper via the newly installed telephone, only to discover that the line was dead. After working another hour, Delahunty went upstairs to have lunch with his mother in their private quarters.

Although the disruption of streetcar service left the penitentiary shorthanded, work in the shops continued as usual. At about two in the afternoon, a convict named Charles Taylor, better known by the alias "Shorty Gray," and his cell mate, John Dowd, were working at their stations in West Shop A when they asked for permission to get a drink. Dennis McMahon, the cell keeper, told them to go ahead, and the two quickly disappeared. Instead of going to the faucet, Gray and Dowd crossed the snow-covered yard in the direction of the main building. When they reached the south door leading to the deputy warden's office and the chapel, the men raised their right hands, a signal to C. A. Eckley, the armed guard stationed in a cubicle overhead, that they were on an authorized errand. Eckley motioned them to proceed. Trudging through the snow only yards behind was convict Charles Morley, who had slipped away undetected from his station in West Shop B. Morley signaled his peaceful intentions as well and moments later rendezvoused with Gray and Dowd inside the chapel.

Endowed with the lanky build and rugged looks of a plainsman, Deputy Warden Charles Wagner, who had held his position for less than a month, was standing at his office basin washing his hands when the door suddenly burst open. Gray and Dowd both had six-shooters.

"Throw up your hands!" Gray exclaimed.

"Give me that gun!" Dowd commanded.

Acting on an impulse that some later called bravery, others foolishness, Wagner went for his pistol. He was instantly cut down, falling to the floor face first.

Usher E. G. Heilman, whose thick spectacles framed a white mustache and matching beard, stepped out of his office to investigate, not thinking to arm himself in advance. Accounts differ as to what happened next, but it was probably Gray who fired the two shots that struck Heilman in the left side below the heart. Though mortally wounded, the usher managed to stay on his feet long enough to stagger into the clerk's office, where he collapsed on the floor. Wilson and Chief Clerk T. J. Ward picked him up and gently placed him in a chair as more gunfire erupted. An unnerved Ward then made a beeline for the walk-in vault, pulling the doors shut behind him.

Shorty Gray ran across the chapel to the steel door at one end of the metal cage occupied by Claus Pahl. The turnkey could usually be seen through a barred window located about ten feet west of the door, but on hearing the shots he had plastered himself against an interior wall just out of the convicts' sight. Gray had no sooner begun working on the lock than cell keeper Thomas Doody, who heard the firing from the west cell house, entered the chapel by the south door. Morley saw him first and shouted, "Throw up your hands, you son of a bitch!"

Doody shouted back, "You don't get out of here except over my dead body, damn you," and fired at Morley. All three convicts returned fire as they jumped behind iron pillars supporting the chapel ceiling. On the wall nearest them was a scroll recognizing the inmates who had perfect Sunday school attendance; Shorty Gray's name topped the list.

With no cover of his own, Doody dropped to his stomach and emptied his revolver as bullets whizzed by his head. He reloaded once but could not get a clear shot at the blur of darting heads

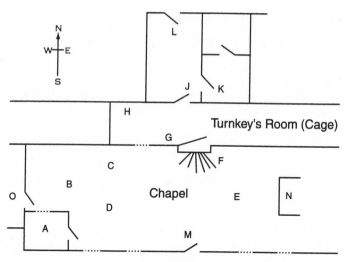

DIAGRAM OF SCENE OF BATTLE

Ground floor of the state penitentiary, showing chapel, turnkey's room, corridor, and offices in which the fight took place.

A. Deputy Warden Wagner was killed in his office.
B. Guard Doody during the fusillade.
C. Convict Gray.
D. Convict Dowd.
E. Convict Morley.
F. Cage door blown open by convicts.
G. Turnkey Pahl during fusillade.
H. Turnkey beaten and robbed of keys.
J. Door into corridor where Heilman was killed.
K. Where Warden Delahunty was killed.
L. North door of prison.
M. South door of prison.
N. Rostrum in prison chapel.
O. West cell house.
. . . . Windows with bars.

and hands. The first bullet to hit him passed between his arm and body, inflicting a slight flesh wound. The second struck him in the left leg below the knee, severing an artery and unleashing a gusher of blood. With only two bullets left, and no indication that help was on the way, he feared being rushed at any moment: "I figured it was time to go," he later said. Doody rolled out the door and dragged himself back to the cell house. Taking his time, a deliberate Morley broke open his gun, threw the spent cartridges on the floor, and reloaded. Dowd nervously did the same.

Inmate Frank Henry, a blue-eyed youth with brilliant red hair, had come up to the west chapel door intending to ask John Thomas, the Negro trusty in charge of the cigar stand, to go into the library and get him some paper. Thursday was "letter-writing day." Henry saw Thomas, who had been in the chapel when the three convicts first entered the door, with his hands raised, backed up against the glass case containing pictures of all the current inmates. At that point the gunfight with Doody had broken out. When it was over, Henry heard Dowd shout, "My God, Shorty, hurry up! We've wasted enough time!"

Gray returned to the lock, and seconds later Henry saw a flash followed by an explosion. Gray shook the door twice; the second time the lock fell to the floor and the door swung open, allowing the convicts to rush in, their weapons trained on Pahl. The elderly turnkey, who had been dodging ricocheting bullets and falling plaster, was ordered to raise his hands. Then they grabbed him and threw him into a corner before stealing the keys to the other end of the cage as well as the main door beyond. Pahl, who had become apoplectic, remained crouched on the floor unable to speak. His drained faced had taken on the pallor of a corpse and his eyes were fixed and protruding from his head. It was thought by some that he had gone berserk and had fired the shots himself, but the sounds of more gunplay quickly dispelled that notion.

Delahunty had come rushing downstairs to his office, grabbed a pistol, and entered the fray. Wilson had never before seen the warden, normally a deliberate, self-contained man, move so quickly. "There was a strange look upon his face—to me he looked many years younger." Delahunty suddenly stepped into the corridor, got off a shot, and ducked back into his office, a bullet splintering the door casing above his head. When he attempted to fire a second time, they were waiting. A bullet tore into his right side the moment he showed himself. Wilson watched as he spun around and doubled over for a minute, as if he was about to collapse. To the clerk's amazement, he suddenly straightened up and fired another shot or two. Then gravity took over and he fell to the floor.

By now the convicts were charging down the hallway toward the main entrance, the warden's office the last obstacle to freedom. Wilson had just managed to drag Delahunty, who was sitting upright, to the middle of the room when the trio passed by, firing away. One bullet plowed across a large calendar hanging on the wall, neatly slicing it in two. Another found its mark, causing Delahunty to clasp his hands to his chest and cry out, "Oh, my Lord." In the meantime, Ward had left his hiding place in the vault and had entered the office; kneeling down, he cradled the fallen warden in his arms. "Are you hurt?" he shouted, but the warden did not answer.

Cell keeper McMahon had an uneasy feeling. Gray and Dowd had not returned from their water break, and now Morley, who had been in and out of West Shop A delivering supplies, had disappeared. Someone reported seeing him leave through the door leading to the yard, which no convict was allowed to do without first gaining permission. The keeper decided to send a guard over to the deputy warden's office with instructions to report the three missing, a report that Charles Wagner would never get the chance to act upon. The messenger reached the south door in the middle of the gun battle between Doody and the inmates. After seeing what was going on, he rushed back across the yard to warn McMahon that an insurrection was under way.

About the same time, a guard named Smith assigned to the east cell house was alerted to the gunfight by the prison barber Kennison, who had headed upstairs for safety. Smith ran down the steps two at a time and exited the chapel door, shouting a warning to the shivering guards on the snowcapped wall. He had no gun, and told Eckley to hand him his rifle, but the guard refused; nor would he leave his post for fear a general mutiny was "breaking loose."

An identical scene was unfolding in the west cell house, where night guard Henry Evans, an ex-soldier with the reputation of being a crack shot, was asleep in the dormitory. Awakened by the gunfight, he dressed hurriedly and came downstairs on his way to the chapel. Evans saw what was happening at a glance, but he, too, was inexplicably unarmed. He made for the guard station, where Eckley proved no more willing to hand over his gun than before.

John Delahunty, the night yardmaster and the warden's brother, came down moments after the last shots were fired. He was barefoot and entered the office just as the revolver fell from the warden's hand. Delahunty picked up the gun and left in search of turnkey Pahl, but he was nowhere to be found. Once the old man had regained his senses, he headed for the protection of the basement. Delahunty finally located an extra key and locked the door leading from the chapel to the yard, preventing anyone else from going in or out.

When the handle to the telephone was cranked, the previously dead line miraculously crackled to life. The Bell operator was told to notify the governor, the county sheriff, the chief of police, and William B. Hughes of the Nebraska Bankers Association, whose members had been relieved of thousands of dollars by

Shorty Gray and his various accomplices through the years. In the meantime, Henry Evans gathered several men, including convicts Frank Dinsmore and John Thomas, for the purpose of carrying the warden up to his apartment on the second floor.

Delahunty was laid on his bed. At his side were Dr. Welch, the assistant surgeon, and Dinsmore. The warden had lost relatively little blood, which those present took as a sign of encouragement. Wilson, who was holding his hand, asked the doctor if there was any hope. Welch replied that he thought the patient had a chance. He injected some kind of fluid into Delahunty's left arm, causing him to stir. The warden opened his eyes for a minute, squeezed Wilson's hand, and died without speaking.

Although the entire episode, from the firing of the first shots to the exchange of bullets with the warden, had taken no more than five or six minutes, three men lay dead and another was seriously wounded. Their shooters had vanished into the blizzard. So incredulous were the cell keepers that they counted the inmate population not once but three times that evening. In each instance the diagonal slash marks in the "Daily Journal" added up to the same thing: Convicts Morley, Gray, and Dowd were armed and on the loose.

Still, there was something for which the authorities were thankful. Albert Prince, whom some believed to be a member of the conspiracy, remained locked securely in his cell.

THE DESPERADOES

Those stranded in downtown Lincoln by the blizzard became witnesses to a ritual not seen or heard since the beginning of the Spanish-American War, fourteen years earlier. At three in the afternoon, the bugler from Company F of the Nebraska State Militia suddenly appeared in uniform on a wind-blown street corner and sounded assembly, the staccato notes reverberating off the brick walls of office buildings and stores. When he had finished, he trudged through the snow to the corner of the next block and repeated the blood-stirring call to arms. He continued wending his way through the city streets for the better part of an hour, the ranks of the curious swelling in the wake of this modern-day pied piper. Members of the militia rushed from their offices and places of business to the armory, where they quickly donned uniforms and readied their weapons for action.

The bugler had been issued his orders by Adjutant General Ernest H. Phelps, who had been in direct contact with Governor Aldrich by long-distance telephone. The chief executive had left the capital to visit the normal school at Peru and had become stranded in the town of Auburn while trying to return, the engine of his train held fast by drifts so deep that its giant drive wheels spun helplessly, like a toy. In the absence of any signs that the storm was weakening, railroad executives were predicting that it would be many hours, possibly days, before the tracks could be cleared. Having been told that the prisoners in Lancaster had mutinied and that many were dead, Aldrich ordered Phelps to take all necessary steps to restore order. With Warden Delahunty tragically slain, he appointed Phelps military governor of the state penitentiary, then issued a proclamation declaring "a part of the convicts in a state of insurrection."

Lincoln Chief of Police Ernest Hunger, a native of Prussia and veteran of the 1866 war with Austria, during which he lost a finger in the battle of Metz, left for Lancaster a little before three o'clock in the fire chief's auto, accompanied by five patrolmen. At this same hour Lancaster County Sheriff Gus Hyers deputized enough men to fill a sleigh, including a reporter for the *Lincoln Daily Star,* and also set out for the penitentiary, the horses struggling under the whip. When the two parties reached the penitentiary, the body of usher E. G. Heilman was still lying in the main office where he had fallen. Not wanting to provide additional fuel for the anticipated journalistic frenzy, someone gave the order and the body was carried upstairs, beyond the prying eyes of reporters.

Although the breakout had occurred less than an hour earlier, rumors were already flying like the very snowflakes. Anywhere from one to thirteen men were believed to have been killed, and two hundred convicts were supposedly on the loose, many of them armed and headed directly for Lincoln. The telephone lines of the law-enforcement agencies and the newspapers were overwhelmed, lending further credence to the belief that mayhem was about to be visited on the snowbound community of innocents. By a little after three o'clock, dozens of citizens had armed themselves and were fighting their way south through the storm by any means available to keep an appointment with the Devil at Lancaster.

For the moment, the only members of the state militia on hand were Adjutant General Phelps and his orderly. The rest of

Company F was back at headquarters awaiting the arrival of the special train that would deliver them to the penitentiary. Until then, the prison staff would have to do its best to control some dangerously unpredictable convicts while placating the swelling ranks of zealous Lincolnites.

Despite the fact that official control of the prison had been delegated to Phelps, it was Gus Hyers who took over. The thirty-six-year-old sheriff was no stranger to the institution; not only had he delivered many prisoners to the facility, his father, Reuben W. Hyers, had served as its warden in the late 1880s. The younger Hyers had lived in the main building with his parents as an adolescent. Slight of build like his father, Hyers was partial to three-piece suits, well-crafted cowboy boots, and a Stetson that rested low on his brow, shadowing his spare countenance and dark, nervous eyes that seemed to take in everything. Like Shorty Gray, he loved horses but disliked the vehicle that was replacing them, and never used an automobile in his work if he could help it. Yet Hyers was fascinated by trains and had worked as a machinist for ten years in the railroad shops at Havelock just east of Lincoln. He later served as postmaster of the town from 1904 to 1911, before running for sheriff on the Republican ticket. There were those, including Hyers himself, who believed that he was destined for even bigger things, and suddenly he had a chance to prove it.

Aided by his deputy, Crawford Eikenbary, Hyers first posted additional guards atop the walls and along the corridors of the empty cell houses. Being short of men, he deputized some of the citizens who had rushed to the prison with visions of frustrating mayhem. When this was done, he sent word to the shop foreman to begin the process of returning the prisoners to their cells. The first line of men came from shop A, where Gray and Dowd had spent the better part of the day waiting for the most opportune time to make a break for it. Snaking northward in a line through

Sheriff Gus Hyers (Used by permission of Jack R. Haber)

the prison yard, the men walked with their heads up in the driving snow, intently scanning the gray wall for confirmation of the rumor that the warden and others were indeed dead. As they drew opposite the south door of the chapel, through which the escaped trio had launched their bloody foray, the line stiffened and a chorus of spontaneous whoops filled the air. The cries kept up as the line turned and entered the west cell house. That the men pretty much knew what had happened was evident from their remarks. Some of them even expressed their pleasure in "no uncertain terms."

What they didn't expect to see when they filed in was Sheriff Hyers, a deputized newspaperman, and several prison guards, none of whom was carrying a gun. Not yet knowing the extent of the conspiracy, Hyers did not want to risk being overwhelmed by the convicts and disarmed. Other than the guards walking the ramparts with their rifles, the only weapons visible to the prisoners were the dual revolvers in the hands of three men stationed at the chapel door. Though the whooping and the catcalls continued, the convicts passed into their cells without incident, and the other shops were soon cleared in the same manner. Still, the rowdiness persisted until an exasperated Chief Hunger took a horse thief named Scott from his cell and clamped him in solitary. This act had the desired effect, and a hush settled over the cell houses.

Shortly after six o'clock, as darkness fell, the Burlington special, carrying fifty men from Company F, finally reached the penitentiary, bringing with them a squad of the hospital corps. The militiamen were a mixed lot; some were young and inexperienced, engaged in their first special duty; others had served in the Spanish-American War and could remember a time when the Sioux roamed the Black Hills and buffalo covered the plains like a moving robe. While their superiors debated the logistics of how best to feed and handle the prisoners in the days to come, the troops were assigned to round-the-clock guard duty, the first shift to begin immediately. The rest spread their bedrolls on the floor of the bullet-riddled chapel and prepared to settle in for the duration.

Attorney E. J. Maggi, a member of the State Board of Pardons and Paroles, had been among the first to reach the prison after the alarm was raised. He talked on the phone to the governor, who further undercut the authority he had vested in General Phelps by placing Maggi in charge of the kitchen. The lawyer, who seemed to know nothing of prison routine, at first decided to leave the convicts unfed rather than risk a violent confrontation in the dining room. But when Maggi was reminded that not feeding them might have the opposite effect and spark a riot, he backed down and ordered that a cold supper be delivered to the cells.

The telephone calls never stopped coming. Practically every man employed at the penitentiary received one or more queries concerning his safety from anxious wives, children, and friends. Sandwiched between these countless nuisance calls were those from the helpless governor, who could see his political career dissolving only months into his first term. Mrs. Aldrich, who had remained in Lincoln, phoned to ask if anyone was looking after the murdered warden's elderly mother, and insisted on coming out to the prison to be with her—blizzard or no blizzard. Meanwhile, one of several reporters on the scene was supplied with detailed descriptions of the escapees and told to telephone the police departments and sheriffs' offices of all nearby cities and towns.

———⋄——⋄●⋄——⋄———

Charles A. Morley was born in Missouri, and as an adolescent had daydreamed of taking his place alongside the leading characters of the popular dime novels—Wild Bill Hickok, Kit Carson, Texas Jack, Buffalo Bill Cody, and Ned Buntline—mostly good men with some bad habits. But in time, his loyalties shifted to the outlaw heroes of the frontier, the first great crucible of American crime.

Morley, also spelled "Marley," was born on January 22, 1877, in Clay County, some twenty miles northeast of Kansas City. He claimed that his father, John H. Morley, was a prosperous cattleman, with substantial holdings outside the town of Kearney, and that he, Charles, had been born in the farm home of neighbors Frank and Jesse James, who were undergoing a transformation from renegades, with a melodramatic flair, to national heroes. Not surprisingly, the county historical atlas, local newspapers, and other records contain no entries for such a Morley. Neither do they make mention of a well-regarded physician of the same name, another of the incarnations that Charles attributed to his obscure father.

In a handwritten legal document filed with the Nebraska Board of Pardons and Paroles, in December of 1932, after he had been imprisoned more than twenty years, Morley stated that his formal education had ended after the third grade. When he was five, he moved with his family to the village of Knoxville, in neighboring Ray County, "where I remained until I was twenty—with the exception of one year in Oklahoma with my grandparents. After that I never had a permanent address until I landed in prison."

Yet eight years later, on the eve of his pardon hearing, he told a reporter that his father's prosperity had given him "advantages other kids didn't have." He completed eighth grade and was sent to Kemper Military School in Boonville, Missouri. One of his classmates was the budding humorist Will Rogers, who, coincidentally, had been born into a well-off family and had spent his youth as a cowboy in Indian Territory before it became the state of Oklahoma. All of this was recounted by Rogers in his oft-reprinted *Autobiography*. About the only thing Morley, an avid reader, didn't purloin from Rogers was his Cherokee blood.

To hear Morley tell it, this was not the end of his educational odyssey. Before the turn of the century, while he was in his early twenties, he came into a little money and invested in a coal mine near Knoxville. Not wanting to waste his time managing the property himself, he left the task to others and headed back to school in answer to "a calling." His choice of institutions was William Jewell College, in Liberty, Missouri, only miles from his birthplace. Intent on becoming a Baptist preacher, Morley saw his plans run aground one day when he "differed violently with the instructor on the point of whether Christ was mortal and stalked out of the classroom," leaving no trace of himself or his theological stance behind. He abandoned not only the seminary but also the idea of serving God, and took up with a traveling acrobatic troupe. While knocking around the country, he met Buster Keaton "and some other folks who have since seen their names in big lights."

There was still more. During an interview granted shortly before his death, the verbal escape artist—now you have him, now you don't—spoke of the origins of what he called his "Jesse-Jimmy" career, which allegedly began on the right side of the law. He was a kid of seventeen riding fence on his uncle's ranch near New Orleans when he was fired upon by a U.S. marshal wielding a rifle. One of the shots killed his mount and another wounded Morley in the heel. Using the dead animal for cover, the youth pulled a Winchester from its scabbard and returned fire, wounding the bushwhacking lawman. Morley was subsequently tried and acquitted of felonious assault, but the episode left him with the unwanted reputation as a kid who had shot a peace officer, later rendering him a "marked man."

The truth about Morley's childhood, or at least a part of it, is contained in a document that lay buried in the Clay County courthouse for nearly 120 years. On March 16, 1881, Alice Marley filed a petition for a divorce from her wayward husband, John H. Marley, who was nowhere to be found. Before issuing the final decree, the judge gave the defendant until the next term of district court to put in an appearance and explain himself.

Alice's complaint was as straightforward as it was painful. The couple, who had wed on December 13, 1869, when the bride was only fifteen, had not lived together since that terrible day in April of 1880, when John stormed out of the house never to return: "The Defendant was addicted to habitual drunkenness," and "guilty of such cruel and barbarian treatment of Plaintiff as to endanger her life." Marley's three children undoubtedly bore witness to their father's fits of rage and suffered from his lack of financial support, another of the grievances cited in Alice's petition. When the defendant, "although duly summoned and three times solemnly called," did not appear, Alice was granted her divorce. The children, "James Richard Marley, born October 11th

1870; Lennie Marley, born September 6th 1873; and Charles Marley, born January 22nd 1877," were placed in the sole custody of their mother, and John was "forever enjoined from interfering with the said Plaintiff and his offspring."

When Alice married for the second time, she married surprisingly well. The town of Knoxville, indeed all of Ray County, had no more prominent citizen than Dr. John C. Tiffin, who, together with his grown sons and daughters, owned more than twenty-seven hundred acres of rolling farmland, in addition to livestock and a considerable amount of commercial property. The marriage took place on June 18, 1885, at the Ray County seat of Richmond, before Justice of the Peace J. S. De Master. It was a quiet affair, in part because it was Tiffin's third marriage and Alice's second, and in part because the groom was seventy-three, the bride but thirty-one. There was the additional consideration that Tiffin's second wife, Elizabeth, had passed away the previous September, only nine months and a day before his third marriage. Elizabeth, who had borne Tiffin two daughters and three sons, had wed her husband just seven months after the death of the doctor's first wife, Margaret, the mother of three other Tiffin boys, several of whom followed in their father's footsteps and became physicians.

One Sunday afternoon in December of 1888, the good doctor was planning to visit one of his daughters. Before leaving home, he decided to eat some beef cooked on the fireplace coals. A piece of meat lodged in his throat, which was swollen from having been sore for several days. According to the extensive obituary in the *Richmond Democrat:* "The shock to his system destroyed the vital forces in an instant."

That Tiffin's third marriage was one more of convenience than passion wasn't a complete surprise. To begin with, Alice, unlike her husband's two previous wives, was not so much as mentioned in the doctor's obituary. Then, on the day of the funeral, his coffin was borne to Knoxville Cemetery, where it was buried next to his second wife beneath the most imposing monument around, a granite obelisk. Even more telling was the fact that Alice was not included in Tiffin's will, for the simple reason that there was none. Perhaps at the urging of his children, he had already deeded a major share of his property to each before his death, which may also explain why he died intestate, a fact that Alice herself swore to in one of several probate documents signed in her petite yet elegant hand. The embarrassed widow filed another document claiming that "she does not have on hand the provisions allowed by law for a year's support of herself and family and asks the court to make her an allowance for same out of the estate." The court concurred and for the next four years, while the case inched its way through probate, Alice received periodic payments that totaled $400—the same amount of cash each of Tiffin's children by his first two wives ultimately received. Of the remaining property, Alice got household goods worth an estimated $131.50, some seventy-seven acres of farmland, six lots in Knoxville, and another two acres adjoining the Knoxville city boundary. Richard, Lennie, and Charles were not mentioned by name in any of the legal documents, indeed, are referred to only once as "family." Alice was left with enough to get by on, but not much more. That some of the lots might have had commercial establishments on them is suggested by the fact that the widow listed her occupation as "income rents" in the census of 1900.

By the time Morley reached manhood, every self-respecting Missourian knew the words to the melancholy ballad condemning Robert Ford for having shot Jesse James in the back of the head. As if to make up for lost time, Morley soon began collecting his own scars of battle. Old wounds discovered during a medical examination, conducted while he was in prison, more or less confirmed Morley's claim that he had been shot twice, perhaps three times, not counting the dubious run-in with a U.S. marshal. The most serious injury had occurred in the early 1900s, when he supposedly got into a brawl with a "stool pigeon" in Kansas City and was creased over the left eye by a bullet from a cop's pistol. The wound resulted in partial blindness and, years later, the loss of the limited sight that had remained. Morley boasted that another scar had formed below one shoulder blade after he was shot though a window while playing poker in Little Rock, Arkansas.

The encounter with the Kansas City police was not the first and was far from the last. Morley spent many a night in the city jail, sentenced mostly to short terms for uncontrollable outbursts that resulted from his use of drugs or his lack of them. A self-described "hypo," he took opium and its derivatives by any means available, including the needle, the pipe, and laudanum from a bottle passed among friends. After being collared in St. Louis in 1910, Morley spent the first part of the year in a padded cell getting "the cure." Following his release, he saw the first and only airplane he would get close to for the next thirty years: "A fellow drove the thing under a bridge," he recalled wistfully.

Morley got out of St. Louis as quickly as he could, doubtless with some encouragement by the police. He rode the train to Omaha and settled for a time in the home of his "sister," a Mrs. Fred Walker. Standing almost six feet but weighing a scant 148 pounds (his appetite had been dulled by drugs), Morley was, nevertheless, a tough customer who knew how to use his dukes. On one arm was the dim letter tattoo, CM, making him feel that he could lick about anything but dope.

———— ◦ ◦━◦ ◦ ————

To a man constantly on opium, robbing a drugstore after dark on a Saturday must have seemed like a very good idea. Never mind the fact that Omaha's Walnut Hill Pharmacy was situated on the terminal branch of the Farnam Streetcar Company, whose passengers thronged the brightly illuminated intersection in the heart of the residential district. Witnesses to the crime described the robbers as "two youthful desperadoes . . . blessed by good fortune"—at least for the moment.

The men entered the store shortly before ten o'clock on the night of October 21, 1910. Gus Sandberg, the owner of a nearby confectionary shop, had just made some purchases and was leaving when he was confronted in the doorway. Two revolvers were stuck in his face, and he was told to "throw up his hands." Sandberg complied and backed into the pharmacy, where he was motioned to a corner by the robbers. When three boys drinking sodas at the counter saw the guns, they froze, wide-eyed.

Dr. F. A. Nelson, one of the establishment's owners, was busy behind the counter when the men entered, and he had paid them no mind. Nor did he respond when they ordered him to raise his hands. According to the crime reporter for the *Omaha World Herald*, "They did not pronounce their commands with sufficient fortissimo effect and Nelson did not understand them." One of the two men repeated the instructions in rather less polite language, and Nelson, thinking it was some kind of joke, started out from behind the counter. At that moment he saw the guns and reached for the ceiling as streetcars "buzzed merrily by."

While one of the men kept Sandberg covered, the other attempted to open the cash register. After anxiously pushing several keys, none of which released the drawer, he told the owner to step over and open it for him. Nelson did as he was told, and the register was emptied of cash totaling $28, about half the amount that was reported stolen in the next day's papers. The three boys, who were identified as Porter Durkee, and brothers Vito and Henry Pasacle, watched every move but made no sound.

Sandberg was thinking about his gold pocket watch and matching chain, fully expecting to be relieved of them together with his wallet. Nelson was no less worried about his merchandise, especially the stock of drugs. Both were surprised when the robbers started backing toward the door, pistols still leveled at them. After a hasty check of the street, the pair broke and ran. Nelson got to the door in time to see them go south on 40th Street and then east on Burt Street. He was startled when the three youths suddenly shot past him and took out after the robbers. They followed the men for a block or two before losing sight of them in the dark, which everyone agreed was just as well, though the boys were lauded for their bravery.

The police reached the scene within minutes of the robbery. They alerted other drugstores in the area and undertook a neighborhood search in the "emergency automobile," which yielded nothing. However, the felons had made no attempt to disguise their faces, and this fact enabled witnesses to provide excellent descriptions of the two. It was believed that they were the same pair responsible for several recent "jobs," during which both drugs and money were stolen. At least their general descriptions tallied: one man was about five feet six inches tall and considerably overweight; the other was taller by a head and thin as a rail. Both wore dark clothing, soft hats, and were clean shaven.

One of the policemen assigned to the robberies was a detective named Devereese. After gathering information on the perpetrators, he borrowed a picture from the rogues' gallery and paid a visit to Walnut Hill Pharmacy on a hunch. From the moment he was shown the photograph Dr. Nelson hadn't a doubt: The face was that of Charles A. Morley, also known by the alias Ed Craig. Devereese remembered Morley from an arrest the previous summer that had earned Morley ninety days in jail. The shameless hypo had been living off a crippled woman begging for alms in the streets.

Making quick use of the telephone, the Omaha police notified the authorities in the cities where Morley was known to hang out. They also got a line on two women—one of them a cripple—who were believed to be traveling to St. Joseph, Missouri, to rendezvous with the thieves. The police in St. Joseph undertook a search of all incoming trains, but they came up empty-handed. Then, about one o'clock in the afternoon of October twenty-third, just two days after the robbery, a hackman provided the break the police had been hoping for. Having spotted two men answering the descriptions being circulated by patrolmen, the driver headed for Central Station to tell Chief Haskell that the suspects were sauntering down 6th Street, as if they owned it, two women on their arms. Haskell and Detectives Duncan, Grable, and Linck jumped into the hackman's carriage and soon caught up with the foursome. The cops piled out, revolvers drawn, and confronted the suspects, who, at first, refused to raise their hands, but "were induced to do so." The men were searched and relieved of their loaded guns; then "the quartet," as the four were dubbed by the *St. Joseph News Press,* was marched down to Central Station to the stares of curious onlookers.

Marley, as he was still spelling his name, identified himself and so did his short, rotund partner James Evans, alias James Smith. The women gave their names as Marie Marley and Beatrice Evans, and stated that they were the wives of the suspects. Some cards used for begging were found on Marie. The four were carrying little money, but several watches, believed to have been stolen, were taken from them. The police also learned that the couples had been in St. Joseph a week before they went to Omaha, and had roomed above the Headlight Saloon. Knowing Morley, it would have been like him to pay homage to Jesse

James by visiting the nearby frame house where the outlaw had breathed his last.

Morley knew that he had no chance of dodging a lengthy prison sentence, and he also knew that he would be lucky if the law didn't nail him for crimes beyond the pharmacy stickup. While awaiting trial after his return to Omaha, he was questioned intensely about "a carnival of highway robbery" that began only nights before the heist on Walnut Hill. During one such encounter the tall and slender leader was in a playful mood. He joked with the victim and asked, half seriously, "Say, mister, how does it feel to be stuck up?" Then, the night the pharmacy was robbed, Louis Parsely's grocery store in South Omaha was hit, and the descriptions of the perpetrators roughly matched those of Morley and Evans. Police speculated that the two were after some extra cash before beating it to St. Joseph, and the ill-fated reunion with their wives. They were also suspected of holding up an Omaha streetcar conductor at 12th and Howard Streets with a third man, J. W. "Will" Connell, alias "the Indian," acting as a lookout—and the list went on. Ironically, the outlaws' one advantage sprang from their reputation for "gun play," which made potential witnesses extremely reluctant to confront them in open court. In the end, the state decided to base its prosecution on a single charge of armed robbery and to let the women, who had been cooperative, go free.

By the time the case went to trial before District Court Judge Lee S. Estelle, in early December, public interest in the defendants had ebbed to the point where very little of the proceedings made it into the Omaha papers. Nor does the trial record, which consists largely of subpoenas, witness lists, and lengthy jury instructions, shed much light on what transpired.

Morley and Evans both pleaded not guilty and signed the same affidavit attesting to their indigence. Thomas B. Murray, the lawyer appointed to defend them, was paid the usual $100 by the state. Needless to say, neither man was able to post the $1,500 bond that would have freed them until the trial. Prosecutor J. P. English called ten witnesses to testify—five of whom were in the pharmacy at the time of the robbery—among them, the three youths who had given chase. It appears as if the defendants, having nothing to lose, took the stand on their own behalf. Morley's presumed sister, Mrs. Fred Walker, also testified, and attempted to provide the wayward pair with a credible alibi.

If the jury, led by foreman A. J. Walsh, had any doubts concerning the defendants' guilt, these were instantly dispelled when Morley, during the testimony of one witness, leaned forward and whispered hoarsely into his attorney's ear: "He's a goddam liar. He couldn't have seen me from where he was." The remark was overheard by several of the jurors.

To the $28 the pair had gotten in the holdup, Judge Estelle added interest of fifteen years apiece. Sheriff E. F. Bailey delivered the convicted men to Lancaster on December 14, 1910, a year and a week after he had made the same trip with the manacled Albert Prince in tow. In the face of overwhelming evidence to the contrary, Morley never once strayed from the convict's lament: "I haven't led an entirely innocent life," he told a reporter decades after the robbery, "but I had nothing to do with that job."

Morley became convict 5569 and was assigned a cell whose walls were not padded. His craving for dope had gone unfulfilled during his imprisonment in Omaha, and he arrived at Lancaster an ill man. "The place was filthy," he recounted. "If you'd lean back against a bench, it was so greasy it would leave a mark on your shirt. And cockroaches! You could sweep them off the walls with a broom any time."

**Charles Morley, 1910 (Used by permission of The
Nebraska State Historical Society)**

Brooms were one thing Lancaster had in plenty. Morley was
immediately put to work in the broom shop, where he recognized
a "colored boy" he'd known in Mississippi.

"What's the matter? You sick?" the young man asked.

"Sure as hell am," Morley replied.

"I'll get you a drink."

"Of what?" Morley wanted to know.

"Why brandy, man, brandy!"

Without so much as batting an eye, he reached around and pulled out a bottle from behind one of the machines and handed it to Morley, who stood there and drank openly with a guard only twenty steps away. Morley recalled: "In those days, you could get morphine for $3 and whisky for $5 a quart right here." As for the supplier: "We usually got it from one of the guards."

Morley owned up to being "far from a model prisoner," an admission borne out by the frequency with which his name appeared in the penitentiary's "Day Journal." On May 25, 1911, Guard John McNeil wrote him up for using a flint in his cell, earning the convict a night in the hole. The following July found Morley back in solitary for a longer stay because he had been overheard "threatening violence to a foreman." He was next written up for "loafing behind a corn pile," the serious and the comic interwoven as the weeks and months dragged on.

———— ◇ ◦●◦ ◇ ————

The galvanizing news anxious authorities had been waiting for came well after dark when someone phoned the penitentiary to report that he had not only seen the fugitives but knew exactly where they were holed up in the storm. Sheriff Hyers's hand-picked posse, composed of eight men, two sleighs, and a carriage, was ready to go within minutes. Among its members were former sheriff Sam Melick, a city detective named Schmidt, and Charles Albright, superintendent of the prison farm. According to the informant, whose name never appeared in the newspapers, the convicts had burrowed into a couple of haystacks about two miles northeast of Lancaster, on the outer fringes of the city. Struggling through drifts that scraped against the heaving bellies of their horses, the posse reached its destination about nine-thirty p.m., the looming shapes outlined against the fresh snow. Leaving their vehicles behind, the men quietly approached on foot and surrounded the haystacks. When all was ready, Hyers commanded the fugitives to come out with their hands up, but nothing stirred, save the wind. He shouted the order a second time. Silence. At this point, the sheriff ordered his men to open fire with their Winchesters and to rush the haystacks. After emptying their rifles they drew their pistols and continued firing into the hay, setting up some unsuspecting cattle for a nasty dose of lead poisoning. The fusillade temporarily overcame the muffling effect of snow on wind, and the sound carried far enough to prompt some phone calls from frightened citizens who entertained the false hope that the ordeal must have come to a just, if bloody, end. The posse spent another half hour searching for signs of their quarry in the empty haystacks before deciding to call it quits for the night.

Homes in the area were few and scattered. Nearby, at the crest of a hill, was the residence of John Henry Tihen, bishop of the Lincoln Catholic diocese. Not far away, and just visible against the dark skyline, stood the Victorian-style Catholic orphanage, the largest building on the southeast side of the city. Both structures overlooked the home of Joseph Dickman, a secretary for Pioneer Insurance, and a dairy farmer on the side.

The horses were so played out that Hyers decided not to retrace the posse's route. It was known that Bishop Tihen had a telephone, and the light from his windows indicated that he had not yet gone to bed. When the exhausted, half-frozen men knocked on the cleric's front door they were met by his housekeeper, who promptly invited them in. Hyers placed a call to Rock Island freight agent H. B. Thompson and told him to dispatch an engine to the nearest crossing, where the posse would be waiting to be picked up.

Meanwhile, three reporters had somehow gotten wind of the posse's mission and had set out after the men in a sleigh, hoping to witness one of the fiercest gun battles in memory. They were headed down 27th Street when the light from the Dickman home came into view, leading them to conclude that Hyers was probably using it as his headquarters. Just then the sleigh came to a jarring halt, its runners embedded in a six-foot drift. After a futile attempt to free the rig, the men unhitched the team and watched as the horses bolted down the road in the direction of the city. A debate then took place as to whether they should continue on to the Dickman farm or head over to the bishop's residence, whose windows were also lit up. Like the posse, they opted for the bishop's, certain that he had a telephone. When they arrived to find that the sheriff and his men had recently come and gone, they began plunging through waist-deep snowdrifts in an effort to catch up. The three reached the crossing just in time to board the engine for the trip downtown. Not until two days later would the newsmen learn just how close they had come to a premature demise.

———— ◇ ◦◖◗◦ ◇ ————

Somewhere along the line, Morley had gotten to know a tough little "Mick" named Shorty Gray, though nobody dared use that slur to Gray's prison-hardened face. Charles Taylor, alias Shorty Gray, alias Dublin Shorty, alias Tom Murray, alias Tom Forbes, alias Tom Rogers, alias—you name it. The little that is known about Shorty Gray was gathered by prison officials each time he began serving another sentence. He was born about 1868, in Dublin, to a father named Mike Taylor and a mother who had since died, and whose name "he refuses to state." Gray had one sister, and also a brother, the latter having emigrated to Melbourne, Australia, to undertake the missionary's calling.

One of the few things Gray came by honestly was his nickname. Weighing some 132 pounds and standing just five feet three inches tall, he was a small man even by nineteenth-century standards. A gun in hand made him feel, and appear, considerably larger than he was, as did his sharp, angular features, fierce blue eyes, thick coal-black hair, and expansive mustache. He bore scars on his left elbow, neck, and wrist. Hidden beneath his clothing was an old scar on the front of his upper right leg, the trophy of a furious shootout in the Black Hills outside Deadwood, South Dakota. Taylor almost certainly spoke with a brogue familiar to the many Lancaster inmates of Irish extraction. On his first trip to the penitentiary, he gave as his occupation "horse trader"; on his second, he claimed to be an "upholsterer," although few had ever head of Shorty Gray doing any interior decorating beyond rearranging the steel doors of a bank safe with dynamite or nitroglycerine. Fewer still were aware of how well he could read and write.

Gray's true identity surfaced only after many years of criminal activity, which could have begun almost anywhere. It was said that he was arrested in Minnesota and served time in one of the state's two prisons—Stillwater or St. Cloud—but records are so sketchy, and his aliases so numerous, that he cannot be traced to either institution. Neither can the claim that he did time in the state of Kansas be verified.

The crime that sent Shorty Gray to Lancaster involved the Giltner Citizens Bank, to which Shorty applied a broad interpretation of the word *citizen*. The burglars had not acted with a light hand. The explosion, which occurred during the small hours of a Tuesday morning, in April of 1911, was heard by several residents of the Nebraska village, but nobody thought it worthy of raising an alarm. One person mistook it for a gunshot, still another credited it to her dreams. The blast was probably preceded by four or

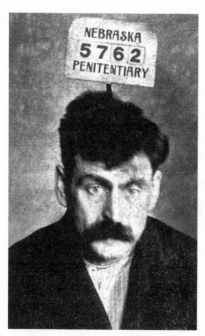

Charles Taylor, alias Shorty Gray, 1911 (Used by permission of The Nebraska State Historical Society)

five smaller explosions that yielded the burglars nothing except broken dials and door handles. Frustrated and working against the clock, they set off a charge so powerful that the safe became airborne, leveling the teller's cage and caving in a wall eighteen feet away. Large holes were blown in the ceiling and nearly every pane of glass in the building was cracked or shattered. Yet a reporter for the *Grand Island Daily Independent* noted that the burglars "were considerate and kind enough to move some of the fixtures out of the way, the adding machine being removed to a place of safety."

After tallying up the loss, bank vice-president Wagner announced that some $2,000 was missing. "It's a cinch," he proclaimed, "that the [burglars] will be loaded down proper." Of the money taken, almost half was in silver together with a thousand pennies; the balance was in bills of various denominations. Also broken into were the local blacksmith shop, where the thieves procured tools used in the burglary, and, more ominously, the hardware store, whose owner reported a shotgun missing.

On the night of the crime, a team of horses and a buggy were stolen from the Giles Perry farm located a few miles northwest of Giltner. Word was telegraphed to the prairie city of Grand Island that the burglars were headed that way, making for a section of the Platte River known as the nine bridges. Led by Chief of Police Marion D. Arbogast and Deputy Sheriff Bowers, several lawmen and dozens of deputized citizens scrambled into automobiles and began scouring the Platte Valley at speeds approaching sixty miles an hour on the downhill, rifles and shotguns sticking out the windows. A team of gray horses was found running loose on an island in the shallow Platte. Later in the morning, the missing buggy was discovered on another island pushed up against the bank to conceal it from sight, leading pursuers to conclude that the fugitives were now afoot and close by.

A search of the two islands proved fruitless, and the decision was made to divide the men into squads and station them at intervals along both sides of the river that had pointed pioneers west to the Oregon Trail. Anyone catching a glimpse of the outlaws was to fire his gun. As they fought their way through the heavy brush and undergrowth, someone discovered the footprints of three men in the sand leading toward yet a third island, which was immediately surrounded by the posse. Tensions mounted as the searchers began closing the circle amid the tangled flora; they were as fearful of shooting each other, by accident, as of being shot by the desperadoes.

Chief Arbogast was keeping an eye on an open space ahead to guard against the possibility that the men night attempt to cross from one stand of timber to another. As he inched forward, he heard a noise to his right. He turned and spied two hats bobbing about in the underbrush. Three men suddenly stepped into the open and started toward some trees farther on. Arbogast emerged from behind a bush, his Winchester leveled at the trio. "Hands up!" he commanded the startled men, and threatened to drop the first one who made a move. They were told to line up against a wire fence while keeping their hands in the air. Holding his rifle with one hand, a finger on the trigger, Arbogast searched them. He found no arms. Moments later, Deputy Sheriff Sass of Hamilton County appeared on the scene and undertook a more thorough search. Sass turned up a small bottle of nitroglycerine and cash totaling about $20, none of it traceable to the burglary. Nor were the men carrying anything on their persons by which they could be identified. It appeared that they had done all they could to separate themselves from the recent crime, and that the nitro had simply been overlooked in the rush to elude capture.

Arbogast fired into the air, and, within minutes, the captives were surrounded by at least fifty men. An attempt was made to question them about the burglary, but they refused to provide any information. They were handcuffed, loaded into separate automobiles, and then driven to Grand Island. Word of the triumph raced through the city and a crowd began to gather at the county jail. Although one of the men attempted to cover his face, jailer Bowers recognized all three, having seen them in Grand Island on more than one occasion. Some curious members of the crowd had driven in from Giltner, and were certain that they had observed the prisoners on the streets of their village. Giving in to pleas for a closer look at the men, Bowers permitted those assembled to file past their cells until the numbers became so great that he was forced to close the door.

Standing six feet and weighing 165 pounds, thirty-eight-year-old John Evans, alias "Slim Martin," was the tallest of the three. He was born in Canada but later emigrated to Milwaukee, where he became a machinist whose knowledge of metals was a distinct asset when it came to cracking safes. One of Evans's two accomplices was his fellow Canadian Harry Quincy Forbes, a short, slightly balding, and overweight railroad man of Scotch-Irish descent, who had a rose tattoo on his right forearm. Forbes, who was thirty-seven, had worked as a yardmaster and a conductor on the Canadian Pacific for several years before taking a job with a plumbing contractor in Sioux City, Iowa.

The tacit leader of the gang was the diminutive Shorty Gray, who at age forty-four was so well known to Nebraska authorities that any further attempt to use one of his many aliases was pointless. However, he added the occupation of "switchman" to his list of other callings, and claimed to have a wife and thirteen-year-old child in Chicago.

With the trio safely under lock and key, lawmen from Hall and Hamilton Counties turned their attention to the stolen money, a subject that none of the prisoners was willing to discuss. Wagner, the banker, was of the opinion that others had taken part in the crime and had made off with the plunder. Most were not so sure.

Sheriffs Young and Dunkle decided to go back over the fugitives' trail, beginning in the vicinity of nine bridges. Because the men had been on the move almost constantly from the moment the safe was blown until their capture, they could not have had more than a half hour or so to conceal the bulky loot. Moreover, they had no shovel or other tools with which to dig a hole of any consequence. A day was spent combing the three islands and riverbanks for any sign of freshly turned earth. Particularly close attention was paid to the areas near where the buggy was concealed and the horses were freed. In the back of everyone's mind was the thought that some enterprising citizen might be tempted to conduct a surreptitious search of his own and, if successful, conceal his discovery from the authorities. The possibility seemed all the more likely given the fact that the reward offered by the Citizens Bank and the Nebraska Bankers Association was half that of the missing cash.

The suspects were transferred from Grand Island to the jail in Aurora, the seat of Hamilton County where the crime had occurred. They were held there only long enough to be arraigned before County Judge George F. Washburn. After listening to the testimony of several witnesses, the judge found sufficient cause to bind them over for trial. Lacking the resources needed to post the $3,500 bond set by the court for each defendant, the men were taken by train to the penitentiary for safekeeping until their trial. They arrived in Lancaster in chains and were immediately put to work in the broom factory, an all-too-familiar routine to Shorty Gray, who suddenly appeared to be very religious, never once missing Bible class. Evans and Forbes, for whom prison officials could discover no prior convictions, despite the latter's use of an alias, minded their own business and blended in soon enough.

The trial, which did not begin until August seventeenth—four months after the burglary—involved the highest stakes that Shorty and his accomplices had yet faced. The good citizens of small-town Nebraska had grown weary of having the insides of their tidy banks blown to smithereens on what seemed to them a nightly basis. This, added to intense lobbying by the Nebraska Bankers Association and much lurid reporting by a sensationalistic press, had caused the state legislature to undertake a draconian revision of the sentencing laws. Anyone convicted of burglary with explosives, whether for the first time or the fifth, faced a mandatory prison term of twenty years to life at hard labor. Even under the best of circumstances, with maximum time off for good behavior, a guilty man would not see the light of day for fifteen years or more, unless he could somehow convince the Board of Pardons and Paroles that he was worthy of another crack at freedom.

The courthouse was packed and every inch of standing room taken when Judge Corcoran of Hamilton County District Court raised his gavel and hammered the proceedings to order. The prosecution was led by County Attorney Marion F. Stanley, who admitted in his opening remarks that the case against the defendants was based on circumstantial evidence, but evidence so powerful that it could withstand any challenge by the defense. Stanley then yielded the floor to his esteemed adversary, James Caldwell, of Lincoln, who asserted that his clients had been nowhere near the village of Giltner on the night of the said burglary; moreover, the defendants had the alibi to prove it.

The prosecution first called Chief Arbogast to the stand. The policeman related the details of a conversation he had entered into with Evans in the kitchen of the Hall County jail while in the presence of Sheriff Dunkle. Evans told the chief that on the Sunday evening previous to the burglary, he had eaten supper at the Vienna Cafe, in Grand Island, before spending the night in a boxcar in the Union Pacific yards. Evans further revealed that a night or two before the robbery all three of the accused had gone down to the river together to wash up.

Prosecutor Stanley next asked for Dr. C. E. Browne of Giltner. The grizzled physician told of walking home late on the night of the crime after paying a professional call. "Suddenly, and in a place where he could get a good view, he ran against a man into whose face he looked with such earnestness and who, in return, scrutinized the doctor so closely that the latter remarked to himself, 'If I ever see that man again I will certainly know him.'" As Browne finished describing the encounter, he turned around in his chair, raised a bony finger, and dramatically pointed to Forbes, exclaiming: "And there sits the man!"

C. O. Glover, a cashier at Giltner's other bank, swore that the prisoner known as Shorty Gray had been in on the Friday before the burglary, asking if he knew of any area farms where a fellow might find some work. More incriminating still was the testimony of Rufus Wilson, a Giltner merchant. A few days prior to the crime, Gray had come into his store and bought some White Russian soap. Afterward, Wilson saw Gray on the street with Forbes and, later still, observed the two talking to yet another stranger, presumably Evans, who was a head taller than either of them.

During this and much of the previous testimony, it was reported that the defendants were giving vent "to the vilest epithets against the witnesses, hissing out under their breath terms and names that would not look well in print."

On the morning after the burglary, sunlight was seen glinting off a round object in the stable yard at Giles Perry's place, where the team of grays had been stolen. It was identified as a crystal belonging to a small watch. When the suspects were captured, one of them was carrying a little silver watch, its crystal missing. The one found near the Perry stables turned out to be a perfect fit.

Having placed the defendants at Giltner, and at least one of them at the scene of the horse theft, the prosecution entered several more exhibits into the record. These included the stolen shotgun and shells, some fuse exactly like that used by the burglars, the remains of a bar of White Russian soap, and pieces of the broken safe, all discovered in a shallow hole near the stolen buggy. Also introduced into evidence was the nitroglycerine bottle found on one of the accused, its explosive contents presumably removed in advance of the trial.

The reporter covering the proceedings for the *Hamilton County Register* described Taylor, Forbes, and Evans as "not bad looking though they have the look of those whom circumstances or the choices of an early life has made bad." They were further characterized as men "of more than ordinary intelligence. Forbes and the other one called Shorty Gray being well versed in law and possessed of great ability." Surprising to many was their lawyer's claim that Gray "is a notable writer on socialism and that for their leading papers has written many strong articles"—a revelation that must have spawned more than one wisecrack about sharing the wealth. Forbes subscribed to Gray's political philosophy, and "while in prison made at least one convert by his presentation of unjust present conditions." What Caldwell did not reveal, indeed might not have known, is that Gray had recently broken with the faith of his fathers by renouncing his Catholic heritage to embrace deism and a clockwork universe.

Among those attending the trial were two women who became the focus of much speculation. One was Evelyn Forbes, the wife of Harry, and the other, described as "an older woman," was said to be a relative of Gray's wife, although her name was never set in print. They took great interest in the trial and were keenly aware of the negative feelings regarding their men. Still, they conducted themselves with a dignity that inspired compassion even as the evidence against the defendants mounted.

The time had come for the defense to try to score some points. The first came when Judge Corcoran ruled that the state would not be permitted to introduce into evidence any record of the defendants' criminal history, which would have convicted Gray on the spot. The proceedings must rest on the ability of the prosecution to tie these men—"captured without [stolen] money and unarmed at an unusual place"—to the crime. When Dr. Browne was recalled to the stand for cross-examination, he allowed that he might have been mistaken when he so confidently identified Forbes as the man he had encountered on the night of the burglary. And a prisoner who was supposed to have heard the three admit to the crime while sharing a cell with them did not testify, as the newspapers had indicated he would. The defense also called attention to the fact that the footprints allegedly left on the islands were never measured and therefore could not, as the prosecution claimed, be linked to the defendants.

The problem for the defense ultimately boiled down to the lack of the credible alibi it had promised to deliver during opening arguments. All three claimed to have been in Grand Island when the bank was blown. But, rather than allow his clients to take the stand and subject themselves to a rigorous cross-examination, Caldwell summoned the two women to testify. Both swore that they had seen the defendants' train off, in Denver, only a day or so before the burglary. The men could have just made it to Grand Island, but it would not have been possible for them to have reached Giltner in time to commit the theft. The prosecution hastened to challenge this testimony, arguing that the witnesses' close relationship to the accused cast profound doubts on their credibility.

The trial began on a Wednesday, and the case went to the jury two days later. Believing that a verdict would be swift in coming, the hundreds in attendance did not stray, and their perseverence was rewarded. By one account the jury returned in half an hour; by another it took them eight minutes longer to reach a guilty verdict. The prisoners were removed to the Aurora jail to await sentencing on Monday. Taking no chances, Judge Corcoran ordered that additional guards be posted around the clock.

Caldwell spent much of the weekend drafting a motion for a new trial, which, as he anticipated, was promptly overruled when court reconvened. Judge Corcoran then ordered the convicted men to rise as he pronounced sentence. Each was to be imprisoned in the state penitentiary for a period of twenty-eight years, "and there kept at hard labor, Sundays and Legal Holidays excepted, and on the 25th day of April each year, that being the anniversary of their crime, they and each of them be kept in solitary confinement."

The *Grand Island Daily Independent* speculated that these same three were responsible for a spate of other burglaries in the area that included Gibbon, Cushing, Ceresco, and Hadar. None of the money, including that stolen at Giltner, had ever been recovered. "With these men removed to a place of safe keeping for a while, the banking world breathes easier." "A while" translated into a minimum of nineteen years, with time off for good behavior, a virtual life sentence for men of middle age. The reporter added that there was a point in the trial when it was thought that the man named Taylor would break down and tell all he knew about the gang's operations, but "he never wilted."

———— ⊗ ⊛⬤⊚ ⊚ ————

The gray-and-white clouds parted during the night to reveal the blue roof of the Nebraska sky. Lincoln, its suburbs, and the prairie beyond were draped beneath a pristine mantle two feet deep, with drifts three or four times that. Snowfields encrusted with diamonds stretched far and away into the distance, magnifying the landscape as if it were being refracted through a giant telescope. Nothing, not even a wayward field mouse, could move unseen across the earth's corrugated surface.

Friday's single-sentence forecast promised clear skies and slowly rising temperatures, the best that could be hoped for. Sheriff Hyers, who had risen before dawn after a sleepless night, swore in twenty deputies early that morning, recruiting his posse from among penitentiary guards, "attaches" of the state militia, and members of the Lincoln Police Department, two of whom were selected for their skill with a rifle at long range. His objective was to conduct a systematic search of all Lancaster County, including every vacant house, barn, abandoned building, culvert, railroad viaduct, and haystack, a tall order even in the best of conditions. The men fanned out in all directions, on horseback, in sleighs, and on foot. Keepers of rooming houses of "a doubtful character" were told to watch out for anyone matching the descriptions of the convicts, whose pictures were already on thousands of wanted posters, and also in the morning editions of the Lincoln and Omaha papers. Interest in the capture was heightened by the posting of rewards totaling $2,100—the maximum allowed—and no statute prohibited the sheriff or any other lawman from collecting the money should destiny extend a friendly hand.

The newspapers were already enjoying a heyday printing five-cent extras in which they predicted, indeed were clearly hoping for, what the *Lincoln Daily Star* termed "a bloody affray." The *Nebraska State Journal,* one of several rivals, waxed equally graphic: "No peace officer expects to take them without a gun fight. The surety of blood spilling when they are found is impressed on every man connected with the chase." The papers, in turn, took their cue from the lawmen. Hyers made little secret of the fact that he had told the members of the posse to give the fugitives no quarter; they should "shoot to kill" on sight. He speculated that the only chance for a peaceful capture had to do with the prison garb worn by the convicts. Exposure to snow and cold might result in their becoming ill and "taken easily." But it could just as well drive them to take part in desperate acts too horrible to mention.

The search continued until nightfall, with some members of the posse traveling as far as the village of Cheney to the southeast, where the giant snowdrifts, like cresting waves, forced them to turn back. Deputy Sheriff Fetter, thinking that the search the previous night might have been directed at the wrong haystacks, returned to the area and inspected every mound of fodder in sight. The footsteps of the posse were clearly visible around the stacks described by Hyers, for the storm had begun to abate around midnight. Much to the deputy's chagrin, "there was not a trace of a human foot" anywhere near the rest. Hyers and the men with him enjoyed no more success than the other members of the posse, and his frustration showed at the end of the day when he responded to a query from a reporter with the *Lincoln Daily Star:* "There has been not a single statement from an eyewitness that has led to a trace of one of the fugitives," he snapped.

Some others involved in the manhunt had a more exciting time. A stranger supposedly fitting Morley's description was spotted loafing near the Burlington viaduct downtown. When a police officer named Heaton attempted to approach him, the man bolted. A foot chase ensued, during which Heaton fired once into the air. When that did no good he fired directly at the suspect, who went down. Thinking he had gotten his man, the officer slowed to a walk, only to see the fugitive miraculously leap to his feet and disappear into an alley. Heaton immediately called for assistance, which arrived in the form of sheriff's deputies from the courthouse, every policeman on duty, and a contingent of militiamen dispatched from the penitentiary by streetcar on the recently opened line. The block was sealed off and a foot-by-foot search undertaken. Minutes later, the suspect ignominiously emerged from behind a privy and gave himself up. After it was determined that he had not been shot, he was spirited off to police headquarters, where his pockets were emptied of three handkerchiefs, two of which were clean, a button, and a prayer book. It turned out that the poor fellow was a terrified vagrant named William Armstrong, whose resemblance to Morley required the overactive imagination of an impetuous officer.

On a more bizarre note, police were summoned by suspicious neighbors to a mysterious house marked by what they described as the "peculiar behavior" of its inhabitants. The dwellers were never seen to leave by the front door, kept the curtains drawn, and shunned any attempt at social contact. When the officers burst in, they discovered two men, a boy, and two parrots. According to the newspaper, "The man who was the head of this strange menage resented the interference of officers." What the paper did not report until later is that the person in question was an attorney, who subsequently filed suit against the city for splintering his door and invading his home without benefit of a search warrant.

◇———◇●◇———◇

In 1935 an old-time horse thief and safecracker named Eugene Lee published a memoir of his criminal days titled *Yeggman in the Shadows*. Lee told of traveling through the Dakotas in a covered wagon with two other men, King Brady and Shorty Gray. The fact that Lee was born in 1868, as was Gray, and later operated in the upper Midwest, in and around Omaha and Sioux City, makes it likely that the "Gray" he knew was the same man who had just shot his way out of prison.

On becoming a criminal, Shorty Gray entered a profession that had many branches and specialties, each with its own pecking order, argot, and symbols. Not that a man was precluded from taking advantage of a promising situation outside his field—so long as he didn't step on anyone's toes. In the parlance of the time, Shorty and his fellow burglars were yeggmen, a word of disputed etymology that has disappeared from some dictionaries and has been classified by most others as archaic.

One theory holds that *yegg* or *yeggman* derived from John Yegg, the reputed leader of a burglary ring, and the first to use nitroglycerine to blow a safe. William Pinkerton, brother and partner of the noted railroad detective Allan Pinkerton (who foiled a plot to assassinate Abraham Lincoln just days before his inauguration, in 1861), attributed the term to gypsies: "When a particulary clever thief is found among a gypsy tribe, he is selected as the 'Yegg' or chief thief." Other versions of its origins are that it was a corruption of the Chinese word *yekk*, meaning beggar or *yekkman*, or that it came from the German word *jaeger*, a hunter.

Operating in small gangs numbering four or less, yeggmen spent much of their time on the road, often riding the freights illegally or, when they took passenger trains, disguised to conceal their identity. Their bible was a publication called *Russell's Railroad Guide*, which contained such invaluable information as the distances between stations, timetables, and connecting lines. Their preference ran to banks in small but prosperous towns whose safes contained at least a thousand dollars in gold, silver, and bills; if they were lucky, a good deal more.

To the youngest and least experienced member of the gang, the so-called "gay cat," fell the responsibility for scouting the Promised Land. He went forth into the country under orders to size up the terrain from every angle, including the layout of the bank, the type of safe it contained, the best means of gaining entrance, the composition of the police force, and whether the main street was illuminated by electric lights. This meant that he usually had to visit the bank in question more than once, marking him as a stranger who was easily identifiable if the job was bungled. (It was for this very reason that Allan Pinkerton created the first rogues' gallery, which also allowed prison officials to exchange photographs of inmates, making it easier to trace the Shorty Grays of the criminal underworld.) Most important of all, though, was the formulation of a getaway plan. Those who had friends in the area could stay in a barn or an attic until the posse gave up in frustration. Others simply walked out of town, laid low by the railroad tracks, and swung aboard a slow-moving freight before dawn. Yeggman often added insult to injury by stealing a team of horses and a buggy in advance of the burglary, later abandoning the rig once they had made it to safety. As an added precaution in the event of capture, some burglars sewed a small cloth package to the inside of an undershirt so that it rested in the small of the back, undetectable even to the experienced eye. Inside were the finest of "jigs," or hacksaw blades.

The burgling of banks, like pickpocketing and rustling, had its seasons. It began in earnest in late autumn, when the nights grew long and chilly and most people began sleeping with their windows closed, and continued into early spring. So much the better if the moon was full to assist the gang's passage in the dark. Each yeggman had his favorite method of cracking a safe or vault, but all strategies were subject to modifications based on the changing technology employed by the manufacturers. By the turn of the century, hundreds of safes were being built in factories on a weekly basis while their various designs, aimed at eliminating every possible flaw, were changing almost as rapidly.

Certain burglars were known as "mechanical thieves," and each had an arsenal of specialty tools. Some employed a blowpipe and a spirit lamp to soften the metals, thus enabling them to peel back the hinges with a crowbar and remove the doors. But this was an arduous, time-consuming process that became more difficult to apply as cheaper, high-tempered steel came onto the market. A cruder but more effective method involved the use of the cumbersome jackscrew, which had the advantage of being both powerful and quiet. Operated by two men, the tip of the implement was aligned with the vertical crack in the safe door. A knife-thin metal wedge was inserted into the crack and the noiseless screw was turned, forcing the wedge into the narrow opening. As more wedges of increasing thickness were added, the mounting pressure on the hinges eventually reached the point at which they gave way, yielding the treasure within.

The jackscrew and similar devices were gradually abandoned in favor of dynamite and nitroglycerine—the inventions of the Swedish chemist Alfred Nobel and his associates. While these powerful explosives had the advantage of being quick and efficient, their users risked serious injury, or even death, as testified to by the graphic monikers attached to yeggmen like Two-Fingered Red, One-Armed Louie, and Kansas City Stubby.

Dynamite was commonly sold without a permit at hardware stores, no questions asked. If a yeggman was busted after a spree or an unlucky run of cards, he could easily steal it from the supply shed on a construction site. But nitro, or "soup" in the criminal lexicon, was an entirely different matter. Because of its great volatility when heated or jarred, the explosive had to be custom-made in a basin or similar container from ingredients that included distilled water, table salt, sodium bicarbonate, nitric acid, sulfuric acid, and a small measure of glycerine, which was added a drop at a time.

The well schooled knew that soup began to thicken at the freezing point, rendering its effectiveness uncertain. They also knew that at ninety degrees or above it was likely to ignite and blow one's head off. Of course, it could do the same at any temperature in between, if jostled or dropped. To protect themselves, some burglars transported their nitro in rubber water bags; others used padded cases similar to those containing a brace of fine pistols or delicate instruments. The more daring poured the mixture into a small glass bottle and placed it in an inside coat pocket, as they would a flask. Eugene Lee told the story of how he once crawled under a railroad passenger car and settled himself on the two narrow beams or "rods" that crossed each other. He stretched out lengthwise, his pockets containing bundles of dynamite and soup, which he liked to use in combination on more complex jobs. He fell asleep without intending to, and the train was doing an estimated forty miles an hour when he suddenly awoke in a sweat: "I had enough [explosives] on me to blow the whole train to Kingdom Come, and me with it; and often when jumping around the freight trains, a bottle of soup has fallen out of my pocket."

Access to a bank was usually gained by forcing the back door or side window with a crowbar. To minimize the chance of detection by a night watchman or some restless insomniac out for a stroll, a single candle provided the only source of light. After stationing an accomplice at a window, the lead burglar took a bar of common hand soap from his kit and plastered up the narrow cracks around the door of the safe, leaving a small opening at the top. Then he fashioned the remaining soap into a crude little cup and stuck it to the door. Next came the soup, which was poured into the cup, causing it to pass through the tiny opening and around the seal until the soap was saturated. Once this was done the burglar had a choice as to how he wanted to set off the nitro. Lee used what yeggmen called a "cigarette," a little finger-shaped bundle of cloth stuffed with dynamite. It was placed in the cup and attached to a length of fuse together with a fulminating cap. The other method dispensed with the dynamite; the fulminating cap, with fuse attached, was simply inserted into the cup. When all was ready, the fuse was lit with the candle and the burglars made for the farthest corner of the bank, where they ducked down, pulses racing. Depending on the skill of the safecracker, the resulting explosion ranged from a thud to a resounding blast that brought down plaster and temporarily deafened the perpetrators. But if the nitro had done its job, one need only kneel down, pull open the door, and bag the loot. It was when the steel doors refused to budge that the burglars faced the dilemma of either trying again and risking detection or leaving town whipped, their tails between their legs.

Morley knew how to pick his accomplices. Shorty knew the ropes as well as anyone, and he had the convict numbers (5762 and 4231, his first stint at Lancaster for another bank burglary) to prove it. The two got to commiserating about how they had been wronged by their fellow man, and how they were being treated "as less than animals." Almost inevitably the subject of escape came up, at first in hypothetical terms but then, later on, in actual planning and execution. Morley was further motivated by his appetite for drugs, which could only be purchased with what little he earned at the broom shop, not nearly enough to quiet his demons. "It was narcotics or die," he said of a habit that had lasted eight years. What was needed were some guns, a quantity of nitro, and a third man who wasn't afraid to use them.

In June of 1913, Frank McCann, thirty-four years old and Irish-born, filed an unsuccessful application asking the Board of Pardons and Paroles to commute the remainder of his twenty-year sentence on humanitarian grounds. He claimed to be a sick man whose chances of recovery behind Lancaster's stone walls were virtually nil. Under item fifteen of the application—"Tell your story of the crime"—the convict offered this semi-literate version of the events that had seen him sentenced to the penitentiary in December of 1911.

> I met John Douwd in Plattsmouth and we got to drinking and he proposed that we go to Louisvill, Nebr. to work in the stone quaries. We failed to find any

> implyment however so we went into Louisvill and
> went into Jerry McHugh saloon where we drank some
> liquor also where I met Geo. Lyttle. This was the saloon
> where Johm Douwd proposed to me and Lyttle to Bur-
> gle with Explosive which deed was committed at
> Louisvill in M. Trisch store on the night of Sept. 28th
> 1911 by Douwd, Lyttle, and McCann.

McCann wrote that he had been twice jailed in Chicago for disturbing the peace, and had served a year in Lancaster for the crime of burglary. That was in 1909, when he was going by the name of Frank Dixon. Cass County Attorney Calvin H. Taylor, who prosecuted McCann for the Louisville burglary, wrote a letter opposing his early release. Taylor also included some details that McCann had conveniently omitted. Contrary to the applicant's claim that he had been respectably employed as an electrician before his temporary fall from grace, Taylor noted: "I do not think he has followed any legitimate occupation for a number of years. The detectives connected with the Nebraska and Iowa Bankers Ass'n tell me that McCann has been operating with the bank-blowing gang [out of Omaha] for some time." Taylor's version of McCann's past was bolstered by the fact that the convict was missing three fingers from his left hand, the telltale mark of a yeggman.

When it came to physical appearance, Frank McCann was hard to overlook. Two of his front teeth had gone the way of his fingers, while two others were capped by gold, lending the immigrant a double air of mystery and menace that his hulking frame and thick brogue did nothing to dispel. John Dowd, the alleged instigator of the crime spree, could not have been more different. At only twenty-four, he resembled a young Ralph Waldo Emerson, his long slender face accented by low-set ears and light, close-cropped hair. In photographs, Dowd's dreamy eyes are suggestive of intellectuality and abstraction, but in appearance he was the essence of the materialism ushered in during the Gilded Age, or as close to it as a onetime fireman could be. A flashy presence on the streets of Omaha, Dowd was known as a "boulevardier," silk hat and all. Never without a comb and pocket mirror, he draped his slender six-foot frame in fine suits, fastened his shirts with diamond studs, and wore a gleaming stickpin in his perfectly knotted tie, a dandy in the truest sense of the word.

While the idea of burglarizing a place of business in Louisville may have taken shape in a smoke-filled tavern, there was far more to the story than McCann had seen fit to divulge, starting with the trio's choice of targets. When J. M. Teegarden, cashier of the City National Bank in Weeping Water, a village of one hundred souls some twenty-five miles south of Omaha, entered the premises on the morning of September 28, 1911, he met with an unpleasant surprise. The small ornamental knobs on the hinges of the vault had been unscrewed and left lying on the floor. How the would-be thieves had gained access to the bank was never determined, but it was thought that they had been frightened off by someone or something before they could get down to the serious business of blowing the doors.

Bent on pushing their luck, the burglars moved their operations to the nearby village of Wabash, where they broke into the Farmer's State Bank the very next night. All that lay between them and $5,000 in gold, silver, and bills was a vault that seemed susceptible to a proper charge of nitroglycerine. About two-twenty a.m., H. T. Hinds, keeper of the Wabash Hotel just a door down from the bank, heard a muffled explosion and went to the window to investigate. Seeing nothing, he returned to his seat behind the desk. A second explosion followed a few minutes later, and still Hinds had no inkling that the bank was under assault. Then came a third blast, this one much louder than the first two. All three explosions had occurred within the span of half an hour. When Hinds attempted to account for his

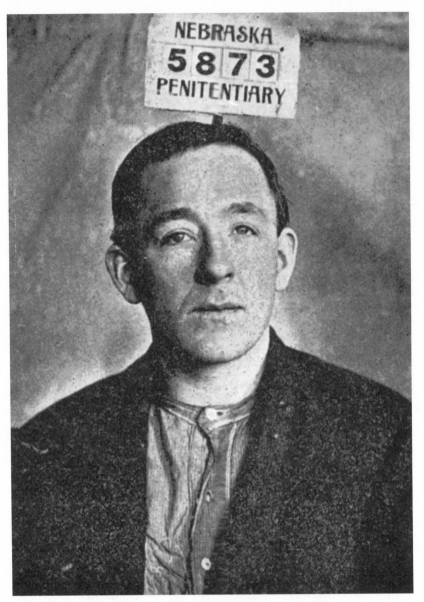

**John Dowd, 1912 (Used by permission of
The Nebraska State Historical Society)**

inaction the next morning, he meekly explained that "the sounds
did not seem to him to be nearby and he did not raise the alarm."

The steel doors of the battered vault were closed when the
cashier arrived at the litter-strewn bank the next morning. How-

ever, they would not yield to the combination, leading bank officials to conclude that they had been jammed on purpose by the yeggmen after the money had been removed, a common ploy when trying to buy more getaway time. It took until two-thirty in the afternoon for an expert to arrive from Omaha, but the wait proved well worth it. When the dramatic moment came and the vault doors parted at last, the money was still inside, undamaged.

The thieves had gained entrance to the bank by using a crowbar on the back window. This they had stolen, in classic fashion, by first breaking into the local blacksmith shop. They had come to Wabash from the Platte River village of South Bend, where they had stolen a team and harness from the barn of farmer Gus Thimgan, then went to the home of Charles Hill and appropriated a buggy. After the failed attempt on the bank, the men drove back to South Bend and returned the horses to their owner's barn. When Thimgan went out to feed his animals at six in the morning, he found them heavily lathered and covered with dirt. The tack was in disarray, and he noticed that the thieves had used the harness for the right horse from two different sets, an indication that the culprits were no farmers. Trailing a pack of baying hounds brought in from Lincoln, Sheriff Quinton, of Cass County, and a posse armed with shotguns scoured the countryside between Louisville and South Bend, but they turned up nothing out of the ordinary.

A third night brought a third village, and thoughts of an easier conquest drifted to the top of the outlaws' improvised menu. They headed for Louisville after returning the horses, and reached town in plenty of time to purchase some food and also the supplies needed for their next burglary attempt. Two of the three strangers were seen and remembered by several store owners, but nobody added up the score and tried to contact the authorities at Wabash, only eight miles away.

Their target was Mike Tritsch's jewelry shop, located in a back corner of F. H. Nichols's general store on Main Street. Harry Thompson, a clerk in the employ of Nichols, sold one of the three men, whom he later identified as Dowd, a ten-cent can of tomatoes, little realizing that his unfamiliar customer was sizing up the place. The fellow then crossed the street and purchased a loaf of bread from the grocery owned by T. C. Amick, who also remembered him. One of the others, probably George Lytle, bought a bar of Sunda Munda soap from a clerk named Fred Ossenkop, while Tim Schlater, a local bartender, told of selling beer to the three men, but he was able to identify only Dowd and McCann. For the most part, the trio spent the day loafing in the shadows of the grain elevator and finalizing their plans while they awaited nightfall. Miss Rosa Masters, whose father's house was nearby, took note of the strangers as they passed back and forth, but what mischief they were up to she could not tell.

Fred Nichols locked the front door of his business at seven-forty-five in the evening of September twenty-eighth while his clerk, F. F. Ross, locked the back door, after which both left for home and a late supper. About two a.m., an explosion rocked the building, tearing the door off the hinges of Trisch's 1,880-pound safe and hurling it an estimated ten to twelve feet. The rest of the safe, composed of "iron fireclay," was scattered about in pieces, as was plaster, fuse, and the remains of a bar of Sunda Munda soap. An estimated $1,000 in jewelry was missing, including watches, rings, lockets, stickpins, and gold chains. Also gone was Tritsch's stock of fine safety razors.

The perpetrators were on foot and headed north toward their base in Omaha, following the railroad tracks. Incautious to the point of arrogance, they discarded price tags, display trays, and even some of the cheaper pieces of jewelry along the right-of-way—"clews," the reporters called them, though they might as well have been semaphores. McCann decided to practice his handwriting and scrawled his name on a gravel car with some chalk—a signature that would not go unnoticed. Trusting more to luck than to planning, the three came upon a handcar just outside Louisville. They rode it across the long railroad bridge spanning the Platte and all the way to Albright, a village near Omaha, then disappeared into the city.

It took the law less than a week to catch up with two of the three fugitives. Sheriff Quinton arrested McCann in front of Sargent's Saloon, in Omaha, on September thirtieth, easily recognizing him by his missing fingers and his jack-o'-lantern face. McCann was wearing a fancy stickpin, and when he was taken up to his rented room, at gunpoint, a suitcase containing jewelry of all descriptions was found in plain view. Quinton sent word of the arrest to Louisville, requesting Tritsch come at once to Plattsmouth, the county seat where McCann was being held. The jeweler arrived the next day and was able to identify a diamond ring, a lady's gold watch, and other objects as part of the stolen merchandise. The stickpin worn by McCann looked very much like one he had in stock the night of the theft, but he could not swear to it. A ten-man delegation from Louisville followed, all of whom were potential witnesses at the upcoming trial. McCann foolishly reached his damaged hand through the cell bars and asked the visitors if they knew who he was. Several of them instantly identified him as one of the three strangers seen in town the day of the burglary.

Dowd was spotted within a day or two of McCann, dressed to the nines and carrying a new safety razor from Tritsch's decimated shop. He told the authorities that he was from Aberdeen, South Dakota, and "only a country boy." He had never been out of the county where he was reared until he jumped a freight that he thought was headed from Sioux City to Omaha. But he got on the wrong train and would up in South Bend. Dowd admitted to being in the area at the time of the burglary, but swore that he had heard nothing about it until his arrest.

Sheriff Quinton had a few problems with Dowd's claim of mistaken identity. To begin with, police officers in Aberdeen could find no record of his ever having lived there. Nor were the names of his grown brother and sisters, whom he claimed were still living in Aberdeen, to be found in the city directory. The suspect had also been seen in Omaha weeks, if not months, prior to the crime, and word had it that he had been consorting with some of its more disreputable citizens. Most damaging of all to Dowd's credibility was a visit paid to his cell by a Minnesota sheriff who, somehow, had gotten wind of his arrest. The lawman recognized Dowd as one of two men who had torn the legs off a jail table and then used them to beat him senseless, thus gaining their liberty. According to the *Nebraska State Journal,* "Dowd turned pale when he saw the sheriff, but professed not to know him."

The obscure and elusive Lytle was still on the loose when County Attorney Taylor filed charges in district court against Dowd and McCann. They were accused of committing the jewelry store theft and of the failed attempt to blow the safe of the Farmer's State Bank, at Wabash, the night before. Both men pleaded innocent, and their court-appointed attorney, faced with a list of prosecution witnesses a mile long, and enough circumstantial evidence to convict a dozen men, successfully petitioned for separate trials. Until his identity could be established beyond doubt following an arrest, Lytle was referred to as "John Doe" throughout the proceedings. Bond was fixed at $5,000 each, but it might as well have been five million so far as the defendants were concerned.

McCann was the first to go on trial. His appearance had undergone a change in the two months since his arrest: He had grown a mustache. This attempt at subterfuge seemed to have no effect on the witnesses, twenty-five of whom offered damaging testimony against the defendant. There were those like Tim Schlater, who had sold McCann beer while looking him square in the face; and others, like Mrs. Gus Thimgan, who swore that McCann was one of the three men she had seen skulking around the barn before her husband's team and harness were stolen. Rosa Masters stuck to her story that McCann had been loitering by the elevator, where she last saw him at ten-thirty on the night of the burglary, though she never explained how she could tell who he was in the dark. The jewelry found in McCann's suitcase was brought in next. Mike Tritsch was called to the stand and once more identified much of it as his. Then an enterprising Sheriff Quinton testified that he had measured McCann's foot, as well as that of Dowd, by placing the shoes they were believed to have been wearing on a piece of paper and running a lead pencil around the soles. A stick that Gus Thimgan had used to measure the footprints of the horse thieves was placed next to the drawings, and they "corresponded very nearly." Lastly, there was the unanswered question of how McCann's name came to be scrawled on that railroad car.

The case relating to the Louisville burglary was proving so strong that the prosecutor, confident of gaining a conviction, moved to drop the second charge. McCann's attorney, C. W. Britt, was grateful for any help he could get and offered no objection, leading Judge Harvey D. Travis to grant the motion. Testimony was completed on December seventeenth, and closing arguments were scheduled for the following morning at ten o'clock. Having precious little to work with, the defense kept its remarks to a minimum, relying on the timeworn strategy of mistaken identity based on whether the defendant was wearing a slouch hat or one with a stiff brim.

The jury was out less than an hour before convicting McCann. When asked whether he wished to have the jurors polled, attorney

Britt declined, doubtless wishing to get the proceedings over with as soon as possible, for he still had Dowd to defend. When Mc-Cann was brought up for sentencing a few days later, Judge Travis had no choice but to commit him to the state penitentiary for a period of twenty years to life at hard labor. Remaining silent all the while, McCann resumed his seat but then unexpectedly turned to the jury and said, "You have convicted an innocent man." Judge Travis countered by asking McCann if he had not passed sentence on the prisoner once before, in Otoe County. McCann lamely replied: "That is true."

Dowd was just about to go on trial when the Omaha police arrested a young George Lytle. Like McCann, he had attempted to change his appearance by growing a full beard. Lytle's color was bad and he looked ill, which the authorities attributed to an appetite for drugs. His trial was set for January of 1912, and he was given the same attorney as his alleged co-conspirators.

The trial of John Dowd took no unusual twists. He was confronted by virtually the same procession of witnesses, all of whom tied him to the crime in one way or another. With the fates fast closing around him, Dowd decided to take the stand on his own behalf. He told his country boy story one more time, but it struck no tonic chord with the all-male jurors of English, German, and Scandinavian descent. Neither was he able to give a credible account of how he came to have one of Mike Tritsch's safety razors in his pocket when arrested. It may have been Dowd's very narcissism that kept him from altering his looks in an effort to confuse the witnesses, not that it would have done him any good.

After both sides had rested, Britt took the floor and began his summation, which he had already tried out on the McCann jury. The skillful orator brought many in the courtroom to the verge of tears by picturing "liberty and freedom in all its attractiveness, weaving into his oratory touches of nature, and here and there a bit of poetry."

As good as Britt was, the prosecution was even better. A lawyer and former judge named Slabaugh, who had joined the county attorney's office, began his address by telling the jurors that freedom and liberty were not license, and that the liberty given to every citizen under the Constitution was not the sort that permitted the "midnight assassin to prowl in the midnight hour and with terrible explosives destroy property and maybe life." Then Slabaugh struck the chord that had eluded Britt by playing on the jury's deep-seated feelings about the Sodom and Gomorrah to the north: "Omaha was the home of the alibi; alibis could be had there for any price, for half price, for no price at all. When a man was tried in Omaha he had no trouble in getting alibi witnesses; when one was tried in the country, Omaha furnished the alibi witnesses." He might as well have quoted Ezekiel: "The land is full of bloody crimes, and the city is full of violence." By the time Slabaugh had finished, he had not only laid Dowd low but also cast a shadow of suspicion over the defendant's counsel—a man who practiced law and made his home in the benighted city on the plains.

A verdict of guilty was returned at four a.m. on January twenty-fifth of the new year. Lytle, sickness and all, was adjudged to be the same a few days later, and both received the requisite sentence of twenty years to life at hard labor. A reporter for the *Louisville Weekly Courier* reflected: "Twenty years seems a long time to confine a man, but when a hard-working citizen has his property stolen, no punishment seems too severe to impose." Truth to tell, an uninsured Mike Tritsch had seen the last of his finest pieces of jewelry, a financial blow from which he was unable to recover. He announced that he was resigning his positions as village clerk, as clerk of the local Woodman camp, and as secretary of the

Odd Fellows lodge, and that he would be leaving town in the spring, after his children had completed the school year.

Meanwhile, the trio responsible for the jeweler's grief was escorted to Lancaster by Sheriff Quinton and his deputies. Once there, Dowd was assigned convict number 5873. Despite the fact that he had just turned twenty-five, he was placed in the same cell as the dangerous and unpredictable Shorty Gray, twenty years his senior and itching for a way out. Dowd had been in Lancaster barely a week when a Negro convict named Prince stabbed Deputy Warden Davis to death. What was more, Shorty had plans. Taking the Irish-Catholic Dowd into his confidence, Shorty told him that weapons were being smuggled into the prison and that he was partners with a savvy convict named Morley, who knew everything there was to know about guns. They needed a third man to guarantee their success, and Dowd could not have arrived at a better time. One might even look upon it as an act of providence. Whether Dowd had serious misgivings about Shorty's plot will never be known, but he soon decided to make it a conspiracy of three. From now on it was one from Missouri, one from Ireland, and one from God knows where.

VANISHED

Coroner Jack Matthews, who only a month earlier had been called to the penitentiary after the fatal stabbing of Deputy Warden Davis, took charge of the murdered men's bodies pending the inquest, which was scheduled for the following Monday. Matthews had the corpses delivered to the morgue, but not before removing certain personal effects, including some valuable diamonds worn by Delahunty. When the coroner opened the warden's automatic pistol, only three unspent cartridges fell out, causing him to revise his thinking about the number of shots the dead administrator had gotten off before being mortally wounded.

With public attention riveted on the triple murders and the "desperadoes" who had committed them, it was almost inevitable that some little-known facts about their past lives would surface. Under the headline WHERE GRAY LEARNED HOW, the *Nebraska State Journal* published an interview with R. T. Mara, who had met Shorty Gray back in 1890, when both were laboring on the Burlington line's extension into the Black Hills. Gray was "Billy" Murphy then, a raw Irish boy fresh from Dublin. Both he and Mara worked as "powder monkeys" under a fellow Irishman named John Fitzgerald, who taught them how to sunder rock with dynamite. ("Gray's later career," the reporter interjected, "points to a continuation of his education along this line.") Mara claimed that young Billy lived in Deadwood for some months, still the home of Calamity Jane and the burial place of Wild Bill Hickok. Nearby rested the king of all dime novel characters, Deadwood Dick. Gray had gotten into an altercation with a subcontractor named James. A gunfight ensued, landing Gray in the hospital with a serious wound in the right leg, the scar from which was noted in his Bertillon profile. How his adversary fared in the shootout Mara could not say.

Just as fascinating, if less romantic, was the story told to the *Lincoln Daily Star* by a local police officer named Overton. Some thirteen years earlier, while Overton was involved in the horse trading business, he had gone to Omaha to purchase some stock. He ran into a fellow trader named Harvey Bartlett, who also hailed from Lincoln. One afternoon, Bartlett was approached by a short, well-dressed man who asked him for a job. Bartlett hired "Shorty" Murphy on the spot, and he quickly became a familiar figure on Lincoln's Hay Market Square, where the traders camped overnight while bartering their animals. "He appeared to be fairly well educated," Overton recalled, "and did a large part of Bartlett's work."

Murphy had not been with Bartlett long when the latter decided to drive a string of horses to Denver in hopes of selling them at a high price. After telling the younger man of his intentions, Murphy spoke of how he had "railroaded considerably" and was acquainted with the West. He also knew the best overland route to Denver. Bartlett was impressed enough to take Murphy along with him in addition to $900 in cash. "That was the last seen of Bartlett," Overton mused. Where he disappeared to no one knew. The search went on for months, reaching as far as Colorado's prisons and those of other western states. The trader had simply vanished for good. The years passed and Overton had all but forgotten about his lost friend until the prison break thrust its undersized leader into the limelight: "I would swear that 'Shorty' Gray was no other than Murphy the horseman who started for Denver with Bartlett."

Gray seems to have continued "horse trading" for several years after Bartlett's disappearance. Mara saw him briefly again sometime in 1908, when he passed through Ceresco, Nebraska, with a number of animals. Later, horses stolen near the town were chalked up to Gray, as was the burglary of the local bank.

While Gray was still convict 4231 and imprisoned for burglarizing the First National Bank at Lyons, Nebraska, he had broken the penitentiary rules near the end of his term, resulting in the loss of all of his "good time." His Lincoln attorney, William Buchanan Price, contended that only his client's good time for the previous year could be lawfully taken away, an argument that ultimately prevailed. After getting to know Gray, Price concluded that he was "a natural criminal," and a desperate one at that. He warned Delahunty that Gray would have to be watched; indeed, they had entered into several conversations on the matter. "The warden said that he was taking no chances with the man," a downcast Price recalled. "He admitted that he was afraid of him as a prisoner because of what he might conjure up while serving time."

Yet the thing that stuck in Price's mind was a letter that Gray had written him decrying the efforts of prison officials to extend his sentence, and which he had signed "Thomas Gray." Reprinted in the *Omaha World Herald,* the letter was drafted in impeccable English, showed an excellent command of vocabulary, and offered evidence of a more than casual knowledge of the ins and outs of the American legal system. Nor was it absent a touch of paranoia:

> Dear Sir:
>   In compliance with your request, I herein set forth the major facts in my case, but having given the matter considerable thought since our consultation, I have reached the conclusion that under no consideration will I attach my signature, under oath, to any paper. I would not even swear to the incontrovertible fact that I am Nebraska State convict No. 4231.

Gray went on to tell of how he had been treated while in prison:

> I have been deprived of every one of my legal and constitutional rights; I have been subjected to brutal and inhuman punishment by one of the ex-officials and one of the present officials of this prison, solely for the reason that I dared to lift my voice in protest against conditions so dehumanizing in their nature and character that when made public they will horrify the people of this state; that I have seen men paroled from this prison who had 'lost' all of their 'good-time' for exactly the same offense (attempting to escape), for which I had my 'good-time' taken from me illegally.
>   I cannot here explain the reason for my refusal to sign the paper which you intended to present to Governor Shallenburger in my behalf, and trusting you will not misconstrue it to mean an attack on your integrity, I remain yours very truly . . .

No less a figure than William B. Hughes, secretary of the Nebraska Bankers Association, admitted to a grudging admiration for Gray, who had been the nemesis of his organization for years. Hughes characterized him as "a man of much force and a thinker.

He [is] a socialist and would argue on socialistic lines with anyone who would attempt to controvert him." That Gray had committed many more burglaries than those he had been convicted of was further testament to his cunning. If reporters didn't want to take Hughes's word for it, they need only ask the victimized citizens of Meadow Grove, Ceresco, Oakdale, Randolph, and a dozen other Nebraska towns.

Hughes was in the process of forming a second posse, to be funded by the Bankers Association, and he also knew something about John Dowd. Though the document was never made public, Hughes claimed to possess a letter written by the young peacock "that would do credit to a literary genius." However, another of Dowd's letters, dated March 3, 1912, and probably the last one he wrote before his escape, did find its way into the *Omaha World Herald*. It was addressed to C. W. Britt, the lawyer who had defended him against the charge of blowing the jewelry shop safe at Louisville. Dowd was having a hard time adjusting to prison life and wanted to know about his chances of filing an appeal. Like the letter drafted by Gray, this one was impressive for qualities not often seen in a criminal with such an obscure background. It also hinted of things to come:

> What I desire to know is if it is not possible for me to have my case reviewed by the supreme court, as I am certain that [the] court would not affirm the judgment rendered against me by the trial court. While I have no means at present to pay an attorney, I will not always be in this condition.
>
> I will make a showing stating that I have no means to prosecute an appeal and ask the court to order a transcript and bill of exceptions at the expense of the county.
>
> Let me hear from you at once what the prospects are, or if you could come and see me, as this is a matter of almost life and death to me.

There was another side to Dowd that Britt remembered equally well. Throughout the trial, he swore that Sheriff Quinton had testified falsely against him. After sentence was pronounced, when Dowd was being led from the courtroom, he paused, turned to Quinton, and said: "I hope I'll never die until I get you." This brought to mind the Minnesota's sheriff's claim that he had been beaten senseless with table legs wielded by Dowd and his accomplice.

It turned out that Dowd had some slender connections to South Dakota after all. When his picture was published in the *Tecumseh Chieftain* and sent to Aberdeen, several residents of the town claimed that they recognized him. A. J. Giedl, a streetcar conductor, was certain that Dowd had once worked for Giedl's brother as a member of his threshing crew. "I used to see him hanging around the European hotel," Giedl said. "I think he lived there when in Aberdeen. I never knew anything wrong about Dowd"—but then that had been three years earlier.

The only other credible information on Dowd's background was supplied by C. T. Bowen, brother of John Bowen, Lincoln's former city clerk. C. T. owned a farm in Pottawatamie County, Iowa, and claimed that Dowd had worked for him about ten weeks in the spring of 1911. "He was the best hired hand I ever had," the farmer unhesitatingly declared. "He left one Saturday night without telling me where he was going. I had not seen him since. When he left he had $8 in wages due him. He went by the name of Charley Hansen then." Not only was Dowd the best hand Bowen ever had, "he was the kindest. He loved horses. I never knew anyone to take as good care of them as he did," which explains why the stolen team was returned to Gus Thimgan's barn once it was no longer needed.

There was one more thing. Dowd was no great rebel; indeed, he seemed to be just the opposite. "He never drank, but he was an inveterate cigarette smoker. When he came to the farm I told him he could not smoke around the place and I never knew him to break the rule."

Morley had written no letters that anyone knew about, but he was suddenly being blamed for every armed robbery committed on both sides of the Missouri. He was wanted by the police in Kansas City, St. Louis, St. Joseph, and as many points in between. Back in Omaha, where a dozen or more unsolved stick-ups were thought to be his handiwork, most witnesses had shied away from testifying against him, truly believing that, sooner or later, he would come calling with a gun. Two days after the escape, a police captain named Dunn swore that "Morley will not come to Omaha for some time, unless he has less cunning than we have given him credit for. He has been on the inspection block several times in our department and every man on the police force would know him. He is a marked man in Omaha." Still, just to be sure, several policemen were concealed near the home of Mrs. Fred Walker, who was not Morley's sister after all, but the wife of an ex-convict with a ready alibi whenever a confederate needed one.

What most shocked the public about Morley's conduct, aside from the murders themselves, was the revelation made by Patrick Ryan, superintendent of the identification bureau of the Lincoln police: "Morley is an opium fiend and was goaded to rebellion by the desire for the drug after activity on the part of prison officials had cut off his supply." Now that he was on the loose, there was absolutely no telling what the half-crazed convict might do. With lawmen running ragged all over the place, it was the duty of the male citizens of Nebraska to step forward and protect the virtue of their mothers, their wives, and above all their innocent daughters.

The train bearing Governor Aldrich finally lumbered into the state capital at three o'clock Saturday morning, going on two days after the jailbreak. On another set of tracks, within sight of his Pullman, stood a black leviathan, hissing and smoking and straining to be loosed. Aldrich was informed that it was the backup engine for use by the posse once the convicts were flushed from their hiding place, which was still as much a mystery as it had been from the moment they vanished. The only good thing about the cold and the ungodly hour was the absence of reporters. They had been told not to expect the chief executive's train until sometime after dawn. Aldrich got only a couple of hours of troubled sleep before rising early and driving out to the penitentiary with the first lady, where he undertook an inspection of the scene of battle.

He reached Lancaster at eight and stayed until eleven, listening to the stories of the participants firsthand. Turnkey Claus Pahl and Guard Thomas Doody were among those who spoke, the latter from a hospital cot where his throbbing leg remained in the balance. The governor viewed the bullet-scarred walls and the places where the murdered men had fallen; together with Mrs. Aldrich he consoled the slain warden's gritty mother, who insisted on continuing with her duties as matron until Jim's funeral in the coming week.

When the visit was over and a reporter asked the governor if he had reached any conclusions, Aldrich replied that he was in no position to comment at the present time. But he promised, "A thorough, systematic investigation will be conducted; until that is finished I can say nothing."

Meanwhile, General Phelps would remain in overall command, but now that the facility was secure, Aldrich was appointing former warden Reuben Hyers to the post of acting warden. The governor had already turned down T. W. Smith's offer to take over for "ten or twenty days," wanting nothing to do with the man accused of having Prince trussed up and hosed into submission—issues that were about to resurface at the convict's murder trial. He also announced that chapel services would be held on Sunday, but that otherwise the men would remain locked in their cells, where they were eating cold meals on their bunks. If all went well, the shops and the dining room would reopen on the coming Monday.

How long the militia would remain on duty had not yet been decided. Some of the troops had already lost their patience during long hours of inactivity, and tempers had flared. The more inexperienced among them were sick of being taunted by the caged inmates, who delighted in calling the outsiders "play soldiers," and worse. It was the old story of some men taking themselves too seriously and of others not taking themselves seriously enough, of obedience versus rebellion. Rumors had begun to circulate that scores were being settled with rifle butts and fists. Yet to stand down prematurely might open the way for another, even bloodier, confrontation. Phelps promised the governor that he would tighten up on discipline and mete out swift punishment to any militia member who failed to toe the line.

It did not help matters when a shot rang out late Friday night, echoing down the stone corridors like an electric shock and wakening the entire building. Bleary-eyed militiamen, harboring visions of bloodshed and another uprising, reached for their loaded rifles and scrambled from warm blankets. Convicts lying breathless in their bunks remained perfectly still as they listened for the sound of more shots, but all was eerily silent. It seemed that a militiaman had just come off guard duty and was preparing to turn in when his gun accidentally discharged in the semidarkness. The source of the firing was quickly determined, and the grumbling soldiers returned to their makeshift beds.

If the governor held out any hope that the press would grant him some breathing room until the escapees were captured and things could be sorted out, he was quickly disabused of it. The drumbeat of criticism had already begun with his firing of Chaplain Johnson shortly before the fatal shootout, and with Judge Frost's nocturnal foray in search of evidence that Lancaster's dope trade was thriving. On Sunday, March tenth, when the Reverend J. H. Presson, Johnson's temporary replacement as chaplain, rose to preach his first sermon, he had made the mistake of asking that divine providence watch over Warden Delahunty and the other prison officials. The hostile reaction was reported in the *Lincoln Daily Star:* "A groan, not riotous, but even grimmer because of its stealthy utterance, swept over the congregation of the prison-garbed men." The article went on to explain, "Friends of the prisoners declare that the groans were not meant . . . as a sacrilege . . . [but] it cannot be denied that [they were] aimed at the officials."

Ironically, it was Delahunty, more than anyone, who had welcomed the change of pastors. Just before the service, Deputy Clerk Wilson noticed that the warden was not carrying his usual copy of the *Star,* and made mention of the fact. "No, my boy," the warden replied with a smile on his face, "this young preacher looks good to me and I am going to listen to his sermon. . . . He will do no underhanded work against us."

Delahunty had been dead only a matter of hours before the first phone call from a reporter reached Johnson at his home in Tecumseh. While the preacher was understandably cautious, he exercised less restraint in answering the newsman's questions than might have been anticipated under the circumstances. "I was not surprised by the trouble at the penitentiary, although I had not expected it to come in such a violent form," Johnson remarked. He had observed "a certain bitterness of feeling" among the convicts toward the penitentiary officials. While he could not say that lax discipline was the rule, "I believe a certain freedom inconsistent with conditions did prevail." When he was asked about the men who had shot their way out, he replied: "I never heard of any of the three escaped convicts making any threats, nor do I know of any action on their part that indicated a desperate tendency." What, if anything, Prince had to do with the fugitive trio he could not say.

Johnson became a bolder critic of the governor and deceased warden with each passing day, as did the press. At Aurora, where Shorty Gray had been convicted of burglarizing the bank at Giltner, the *Hamilton County Register* excoriated Aldrich for his "plumb foolishness." He "has been terribly mistaken. It was not a general mutiny fomented by reformers and criticisms of himself and his officials. It was a break for liberty of three desperate men," the result of "incompetency and persistence in error of those who were being justly censured." The *Nebraska State Journal* was less scathing, but equally adamant: "In the shadow of this tragedy it becomes the duty of the governor to reorganize the staff of the institution. There can be no disagreement over what the state needs—a wise, humane management that will make this a place of correction when reform is possible, and of punishment without brutality when punishment is necessary. The governor cannot afford to go on with this work without . . . the best thought and experience of the world on the subject."

Pressure on Aldrich was compounded when newspapers from around the country picked up the story. The March fifteenth headline in the *New York Times* read: CONVICTS MUTINY: KILL THREE OFFICERS. The author of the ensuing article claimed that unrest had been "prevalent" among the prisoners for more than a month, the result of the fatal stabbing of Deputy Warden Davis during chapel services.

With the press in full cry and his credibility with the public on the line, Aldrich felt that he had no choice but to fight back, exercising the politician's natural instinct. He scheduled a meeting with several reporters during the noon hour, at his office in the capitol, in an attempt to set the record straight. Of the many charges he wished to refute, none distressed him more than the criticism that he had recklessly called out the militia while declaring the penitentiary to be in a state of insurrection, thus sparking a general panic.

He reminded those assembled that he was snowbound in Auburn when the call came that an uprising was in progress. Only later was it revealed that Chief Clerk Ward had gotten on the phone with an operator, telling her that the prison was in chaos and that a murderous gun battle was under way. She, in turn, raised the alarm. When convict Frank Dinsmore overheard Ward's part of the agitated conversation, he went over to the chief clerk and assured him that "the boys were quiet as mice," but by then the damage had already been done. The real blame, according to Aldrich, rested with the publishers of the *Omaha World Herald,* the *Nebraska State Journal,* and the *Omaha Daily News,* all of whom refused to acknowledge that the guards had quickly regained control of the facility. Instead, they proceeded to "gild the lily" by creating visions of a ruthless convict army on the march, then played the grossly overblown story for all it was worth by publishing extras at a nickel a copy. By the following day, only the *Journal* had altered its reporting to conform to the facts: "The poison has been spread," Aldrich declared in his most vigorous window-rattling baritone, thumping the table with his huge fist, "and it is too late to correct it!"

The governor next addressed the charge that the prison administration had been too lenient in its treatment of the inmates: "The present regime," he observed, "is a continuation of the management during the past twenty years so far as methods are concerned." Over time discipline had undergone a gradual relaxation, a policy that had been initiated by Warden A. D. Beemer back in the 1890s. For that, almost every citizen was accountable, but especially those "who think no one should be punished. No person outside of the penitentiary has any idea of how difficult the work of the warden is. . . . I had full confidence in Jim Delahunty, and nothing I have found . . . has shaken it."

Taking a backhanded swipe at Johnson and his allies, Aldrich charged Delahunty's critics with blaming the warden for mistreating convicts like Prince, "while in the same interview and the very next breath they would assert that prison discipline had been destroyed and the men were being allowed too many liberties. The lives of three men are a high price to pay for stopping this foolish crusade."

Aldrich concluded by pointing out that two decades of neglect had suddenly toppled into his lap after only a few months as chief executive. The penitentiary buildings were old-fashioned and poorly ventilated; two, sometimes three, prisoners were crowded into a single cell; and it was impossible to segregate first-time offenders from lifelong miscreants. "Men such as the three desperados who escaped and committed murder in fact should be in a class by themselves and . . . not allowed to associate with other prisoners." The situation "will never be what it ought to be until the state spends more money to modernize the prison. . . . There ought to be an intermediate prison, a separate institution."

With that, the interview was over. Whether the governor had done himself any good he did not know, but at least he felt better for having gotten a month's accumulation of grievances off his chest.

One of the reporters who questioned General Phelps the morning after the escape wanted to know if Albert Prince was aware of what had happened. Phelps replied that he had no idea, but then he paused for a moment's reflection. Considering the fact that Prince was in solitary and not allowed to speak with anyone but his attorney, Phelps believed that he was ignorant of the previous day's events. The commander had apparently forgotten that the convict named Scott had been locked in the hole for whooping it up after the killings, and that he might well have told Prince what had taken place.

Two days later, with the conspiracy mills grinding away at full speed, a former Lincoln detective and confidant of the murdered warden put forth an intriguing theory, which was picked up by *Lincoln Daily Star.* C. M. Franklin believed that Prince was a member of the plot to break out of Lancaster, and that his stabbing of Deputy Warden Davis had been a diversion. In the congregation that day was a Mrs. May Woodworth, the "sweetheart" of Shorty Gray, who always dressed in black, as if in perpetual mourning. During the excitement following the tragedy, the large, dark-haired woman had somehow managed to slip a bundle containing weapons and ammunition to her paramour. What became of them was now crystal clear. There was also the fact that Gray had come from Dublin, the city where Prince claimed his white father had been born.

A story told by a convict named Dales, who was imprisoned for murder, seemed to support Franklin's theory, though Dales believed that the woman seen at chapel was none other than Mrs. Gray. He recalled sitting next to Dowd in Sunday school class only four days before the escape. Mrs. Gray was seated in the back corner of the chapel, with a clear view of the class. At one point Shorty turned around and looked at her: "She held up her hand and arm as if to shoot a pistol, and Shorty nodded his head."

Creative as Franklin's hypothesis was, most of those present on the Sunday of the murder gave it little credence, including the wife of the slain deputy warden. Mrs. Davis noticed that Mrs. Woodworth had attended practically every weekly service for months prior to her husband's death, but that she never occupied a seat near Gray. More important still was the fact that Prince's attack raised little commotion, certainly not enough to allow a person to leave her place in the chapel, walk a considerable distance with a heavy bundle in her arms, and then make the exchange, all undetected. Still, what Dales said about the signaling between Gray and the woman may have been true, regardless of how the guns were smuggled in. None of the other convicts offered any information to the authorities save one: "Go to Kansas City and find Shorty Gray's woman," he whispered to Deputy Sheriff Eikenbary as he walked down a corridor at the penitentiary. "She can tell you how the guns and stuff got into the prison."

The more the police learned about the dark lady, the more suspicious they became. She had been staying at a rooming house favored by newly released convicts attempting to regain their bearings. But it was not by the name of Woodworth that she was known, but by "Mrs. Mary Brown," another mundane selection from a whole coloring box of aliases, and one almost certainly concocted by Gray, who claimed to have a mother-in-law by that name.

The woman had been working as a helper in a shirt factory for the previous six months, and, according to the manager, a man named Nelson, she had seemed "nervous and worried about something." Looking as if she had missed several nights' sleep, she drew her pay Wednesday afternoon, the day before the escape, and told Nelson she was leaving the city. A fellow worker informed the police that Mary's brother had supposedly arrived in Lincoln, and she told her that she was going to Kansas City with him.

Instead, Mrs. Brown put a twelve-year-old youth, thought to be her son, on the Burlington train at two p.m., and then returned to South 11th Street to collect her things. Thoughtful, as always, she gave her magazine subscription to another boarder and even asked the landlady to have the name changed at the post office to avoid a mixup. At four-thirty-six that afternoon, she climbed aboard the Rock Island train to Omaha without so much as leaving a forwarding address.

Those living at the rooming house refused to believe that the kindly lodger they had befriended had any knowledge of the escape plan. Rather, they were of the opinion that Gray had convinced her to leave town at once, but had told her little else. She was a hardworking woman whose conduct was beyond reproach, and nothing, including her use of an alias, was about to convince them otherwise.

The police took a rather more jaundiced view, speculating that a rendezvous had been arranged between Mrs. Brown and the convicts. Once together, she would supply them with food, changes of clothing, additional ammunition, and, possibly, horses. The authorities were also told that she was not the wife of Gray but a married woman, who planned to divorce her husband and wed the convict, if Gray succeeded in getting a reversal of his case in the state supreme court, thus adding one more layer of mystery to the many others.

When Major Antles, chief of staff to General Phelps, asked Walter Wilson if he had an idea as to how the guns had gotten in, the deputy clerk went into the vaults and brought out the convicts' bank ledger. Among the entries were those of a safe-blower whose identity Wilson did not reveal in print. The convict had sent two money orders to a female relative of Gray's living in Lincoln. The ledger also showed that this same convict had given another inmate, who happened to be a trusty, a check for $8. Wilson believed that the first two sums had paid for the pistols, ammunition, and nitroglycerine while the latter amount had greased the skids and gotten them smuggled in. The major asked several questions, then fell silent as he sat with the book before him, deep in thought. When Antles finally stirred, Wilson watched as he headed inside to pursue the matter further, but before he could do so the officer was distracted by yet another report that the escaped convicts had been sighted.

———— ◇ ◦◗◦ ◇ ————

Two days and more of squinting into a shimmering landscape had deepened the creases around a bone-tired Hyers's dark eyes. Though the sheriff was sticking to his pronouncement that the convicts were still in hiding somewhere in or around Lincoln, he was beginning to have his private doubts, especially in light of the information gathered on the shady Mrs. Brown.

Another theory had the trio headed for Grand Island and the river bottoms, where Gray and his former accomplices were believed to have hidden the loot from the Giltner robbery. The money had never been found—at least so far as anyone knew—although the amount taken had been reduced from $2,000 to $1,200 after a more thorough audit of the accounts.

Calls, theories, and clues continued pouring into the various headquarters all day Saturday. From Alliance, to the west, and Omaha, to the east; from Valentine, to the north, and Marysville, Kansas, to the south, came rumors of the convicts' presence.

Acting on a tip received late Saturday afternoon, Hyers and a posse of eleven men headed out to the farmstead of an ex-convict named J. Gould Fadewa. As they rode in, Fadewa's aged mother, one of Nebraska's early pioneers, poked her head out the door: "Are you looking for them fellows?" she asked, and she was told that they were.

Neither Mrs. Fadewa nor her son objected to having the place searched without a warrant, but two female relatives raised a ruckus, first by shouting at the men, and then wailing while they went through every room in the house, including the garret. When the posse had finished inside, eight of the twelve stood lookout, with rifles and pistols drawn, while the other four checked out the barn and both privies. Mrs. Fadewa finally had enough of the caterwauling and, in a harsh voice, told the young women to shush. The crusty matriarch admitted that she was no friend of the law, but never would she give shelter to such men as the three desperadoes: "I was born in the north of Ireland," she proudly explained, "and Jim Delahunty was a big-hearted Irishman." After following the men to the road, she declared in parting: "I hope you get 'em."

The posse had no sooner returned to Lincoln when word was received that a side-loading .38-caliber pistol had been found near a bridge only blocks from the Fadewa place. The gun was free of rust and gave signs of having been fired recently, though it had a broken spring. It was surmised that the weapon had been used during the breakout and was later discarded as no good by the convicts, who had probably spent Friday night in the area.

A peculiar deal at a pawnshop had also piqued the interest of lawmen. Just prior to the escape, two strangers claiming to be detectives had purchased a Colt revolver after much dickering and allegations that the weapon had been stolen from them. At first, they had demanded that the gun be returned to them free of charge. When the proprietor refused to be intimidated, the men began to haggle, finally agreeing on a price of $8. After the sale, the two asked the pawnbroker if he had another gun like the first, but he had grown wary and ushered them out of the store as quickly as possible, then watched as they headed east. They were later traced to a downtown hotel, where they stayed in their room for just two hours before checking out at two a.m. on Wednesday, the day before the escape. It so happened that two men had visited Mrs. Brown on Wednesday, and their descriptions generally matched those supplied by the pawnbroker.

Another posse of five sheriff's deputies, accompanied by a reporter, headed for nearby College View, in sleighs, on Saturday, around noon, after having received a call that a party of three men had been seen riding east out of town. The alarm had been raised by a boy on the Bixby farm, who had phoned his mother, who had, in turn, called the sheriff's office. The deputies intercepted the men, all headed into Lincoln, only to be disappointed when none of their faces matched the convict posters. In the distance could be seen the youth who had first spotted them, playing sheriff while staying out of firing range.

Meanwhile, a "strange young man" entered the barbershop at College View and joined in the local gossip about the murders. Suddenly, his demeanor changed, and he began to express sympathy for the wanted men "in no uncertain terms," stating that "he would like to see them get away." Then he left in a huff. By the time the aghast customers recovered and phoned the sheriff's office, the suspicious character had disappeared.

A discouraged Hyers returned to his office to find two young men, brothers Solomon and Simon Harris, under arrest. They had gone to a livery and secured horses, stating that they were deputy sheriffs. One had produced a game warden's star to back up their contention. When the father of the two discovered they had left home with guns and extra clothing, he tracked them to the livery, fearing that they had taken the horses to the convicts without explaining why they would do such a thing. Two deputies and the manager of the stable set out after them. In the meantime the brothers, who simply wanted to gain a share of the reward money and attendant glory, telephoned from the insane asylum and informed the livery employees that the horses were there. The two were soon collected and brought to the Hyers's office, where they were subjected to some hard questioning. Both denied any intention of assisting the criminals, and they were finally turned loose. It turned out that Solomon Harris had been involved in another recent brush with the law, having been arrested for adultery and desertion, only to be acquitted.

The medieval gloom hanging over the penitentiary's gray walls only deepened on Saturday afternoon when the widowed Mrs. Davis arrived by carriage, still dressed in mourning clothes. Waiting for her in the warden's office were the mother and sister of Jim Delahunty. The women embraced in a scene described as "pathetic in its sadness," while Acting Warden Hyers looked on, utterly helpless against the flood of tears.

The grim mood was not made any better by the backtracking of an embarrassed General Phelps earlier in the day. One of the first things the militia had done on the evening of the escape was to strip every cell of its furniture and other nonessential possessions, further angering the convicts, who deeply resented this outside presence. Their things were carelessly stacked at one end of the chapel, where they would remain pending a search for weapons. Phelps had first told the press that only a single, bone-handled pocketknife had been discovered, but a reporter with an ear to the ground had heard otherwise. When confronted, Phelps admitted that more weapons had turned up, but that they were part of a collection that had been accumulating in the desks of the slain deputy warden and his murdered predecessor for some time. Still not satisfied, the reporters continued to press Phelps on the matter until he finally conceded that many weapons, perhaps as many as sixty all told, had surfaced during the shakedown, resulting in one more black mark against Delahunty and Governor Aldrich.

Much to Phelps's relief, the press became distracted when a call was received that the convicts had been surrounded near the town of Eagle, twenty miles due east of Lincoln. So certain were the authorities of a capture that the *Lincoln Daily Star* put out an extra, but to no avail. It was another of a score of false alarms, yet one long remembered by a youth whose parents farmed near the town. Rudolph Umland, who served as editor of the Nebraska Writers' Project, an offshoot of the Depression-era Works Progress Administration, and later published in *Esquire* magazine, recalled how his older brothers first loaded the family shotgun and rifle, then took the almost unheard-of precaution of locking up the house before they went to bed.

Years later, Umland met a tall and brooding young poet while both were freshmen at the University of Nebraska. His name was Loren Eiseley, and, if anything, his memories of the desperate escape were even more vivid than Umland's. Loren's father, Clyde, an itinerant hardware salesman, kept his son abreast of the dark adventure by reading him the long newspaper accounts after returning home of an evening. One night, after he had put down the paper with a sigh, Clyde remarked: "Someday when you are grown up you may remember this."

Eiseley later went to work for Umland at the W.P.A., penning essays on the geology, paleontology, and prehistoric Indian culture of the state. He eventually found his voice as a literary naturalist, becoming one of the more original and evocative essayists of the twentieth century; one who occupied the night country of the insomniac, ever alert to the midnight knock on the door. As the decades passed he never forgot the words spoken to a five-year-old by his father. When composing his elegiac autobiography, *All the Strange Hours,* a world-weary Eiseley reentered that winter of snow and arctic wind, joining forces with Gray, Morley, and Dowd. Together, they fled in his imagination through the howling blizzard, their ammunition running desperately low, Death's posse fast closing around them.

———◇——◇●◇——◇———

The snow was so deep by midafternoon that Chandler, the Dickmans' hired man, had brought up a horse from the barn so that Mrs. Dickman could ride it back and help him out with the chores. While the two were standing at the kitchen door, mesmerized by the storm, three insubstantial figures slowly emerged from out of the white mantle, like birthing ghosts.

"Look," Chandler exclaimed, "there are some men lost in the snow." He ran out into the yard and began struggling toward them through the sea of drifts. When he was close enough to be heard over the wind, he called to them to come over if they were lost. At first, they shouted back that they were not lost and only wanted directions to town. Then something changed their minds and they turned toward the house. Chandler retreated to wait for them by the door with Mrs. Dickman. As the staggering shapes came into focus, he suddenly recognized the gray clothing and turned to her, exclaiming, "My God, I believe they're convicts."

They had trudged almost two miles as the crow flies, though there were no crows or birds of any other feather aloft on such a miserable day. At first, they had the drifts and blowing snow to contend with, which was plenty enough. But then the land began to rise, forming a series of hills that added to the heavy going until they stumbled onto the Dickman place. Had Chandler not waved them in, they could have easily missed Lincoln altogether and frozen to death in the little ice age.

They came into the house soaked and trembling, a "pitiful looking sight" in Mrs. Dickman's eyes. The face of the convict she would come to know as Shorty Gray was deathly pale. Neither he nor Morley could speak coherently at first. Dowd, who was both younger and stronger, was fatigued, but in much better shape than the other two. Just then the telephone rang; the caller was Mrs. Benham, a neighbor. The convicts believed that Mrs. Dickman was attempting to notify the law and ordered her to drop the receiver.

"We know you are afraid of us," one of them said.

"I can tell you I am not," Mrs. Dickman replied, pretending to be calm. Not knowing about the jailbreak, she assumed the men were trusties who had simply taken advantage of the foul weather and walked away, giving her reason to hope.

By the time the intruders settled in, it was well past chore time, and Mrs. Dickman announced that she was going to the barn and could use some help. Morley and Dowd agreed to go with her, while Gray was left to stand guard at the windows. When they entered the barn she asked them if they knew how to milk, and both shook their heads no—a curious admission for men who had been on farms and around livestock much of their lives. Dowd climbed up into the silo and began pitching fodder to the animals below while Morley did various chores around the barn, all the while keeping a close eye on Mrs. Dickman and the hired man, who together did the milking. While Morley stood watching, Mrs. Dickman remarked that her sons had gone out in the blizzard to deliver milk against her wishes, and her concern for them was growing what with nightfall coming on. "I think all boys ought to mind their mothers," she added, looking up at her captor.

"I would not be here if I had," Morley replied. For the briefest of moments he seemed "somewhat affected," as if on the verge of tears, and turned away.

Morley was a tall man, but it seemed to Mrs. Dickman that his strength had been undermined by cigarettes, which he smoked one after the other. She thought him rather nice looking, but for his shifty eyes.

By this time Dowd, whom Mrs. Dickman called "the big convict" and credited with being the most gentlemanly of the three, had climbed down and was filling the mangers. While they were at work, he asked her if she and the hired man were alone. When she told him that she had two sons who should have been home hours ago, he asked their ages and was told that one was twenty-four, the other seventeen. He then wanted to know what kind of boys they were. Puzzled by the question, she replied that they were "all right."

Dowd tried again: "Would any trouble be caused by their appearance?"

"Oh no," she replied, "[you] need have no fear of that."

Taking in his surroundings, Dowd said something that softened Mrs. Dickman's heart: "I wish I could stay at a place like this. That is a great way they have of reforming men in the penitentiary. The way they treat men down there will never do them any good." She was tempted to believe him, if just for the moment, mostly because Dowd was the only one of the three who looked her in the eye the entire time he was speaking.

When the chores were finished they returned to the house, plowing through drifts that stood them upright. The convicts offered to carry Mrs. Dickman, but she declined the favor. She had barely removed her coat before Gray ordered her to draw the curtains. It was then that she took note of the cruelty in his face as well as his extreme nervousness: "He paced the floor between the two windows like a hyena."

A short time later the Dickman brothers walked in, compliant and respectful as their mother promised Dowd they would be. One of the convicts asked about the news in town. Donald, the older of the two, told them what he had heard, the first intimation Mrs. Dickman had that the men under her roof were no wayward trusties but hunted murderers.

The phone rang again and this time Lloyd, the younger brother, answered it while Gray stood on one side of him and Dowd on the other, listening in. It was Mr. Sisson, another neighbor, wanting to know if the Dickmans had seen anything of the escaped convicts. The youth answered in the negative and hung up, but not before being told to telephone the sheriff's office if they saw them and a posse would come right out. Gray then admitted that three men most likely lay dead back at the prison.

Mrs. Benham phoned again to ask about the outlaws, but she was not to be so easily dismissed as the previous caller. The fury of the storm and the whereabouts of the killers notwithstanding, she was sending her son over to pick up the family milk. To refuse her might arouse suspicion, but if the boy came ahead and noticed anything unusual the consequences could be tragic. Thinking quickly, Mrs. Dickman persuaded the men to hide in return for her promise that she would "get the boy away" as soon as possible. Once he arrived, she kept the youth in the kitchen, and he never removed his heavy winter clothing. Mrs. Dickman ushered him out minutes later, a pail of fresh milk in hand and none the wiser.

Gray's incessant pacing, a telltale habit formed behind bars, began to take its toll on the matron's nerves. She decided to help move the clock along by preparing supper. When it was ready, she called out and everyone but Gray gathered around the large oak dining table. It was a "peculiar situation," one that Mrs. Dickman would long remember. They sat in the lamplight, the two murderers, the hired hand, and the three family members, their elongated shadows crossing and uncrossing on papered walls, like a gathering of dark spirits. No one spoke; the only sounds were those of softly ringing utensils and the footfalls of the third killer keeping vigil in the next room. The strange spell was broken when Dowd abruptly rose from his chair and stalked out. Moments later, they could hear him telling Gray to settle down.

After Dowd and Morley had finished, Gray came in and took a seat. Unlike the other two, he ate slowly, as if chewing over his thoughts as well as his food. He, too, was a heavy smoker and, like Morley, averted his eyes when talking. Yet when he spoke, which was not often, he "hissed" his words as if to give them a reptilian force.

The phone rang once again and Mrs. Dickman picked up the receiver. It was her husband, Joseph, a bookkeeper who was stranded in downtown Lincoln. He wanted to be sure that she and the boys were all right, and to alert them to the fact that three convicts were on the loose after killing Warden Delahunty and two other members of the prison staff.

About nine-thirty, the sound of distant gunfire brought everyone to instant attention. With the wind whipping up a gale, it was difficult to tell from which direction the shots had come, but they were too close for comfort. Little did they know that Sheriff Hyers and his men were firing into the dark corners of some haystacks in which the convicts were believed to be hiding. Things soon quieted down and remained that way until an hour or so later when they heard what sounded like a steam-powered automobile. In truth, it was the spinning drive wheels of the locomotive sent out to collect the posse and the three incautious reporters, who had nearly walked into a disaster.

After promising not to flee, Mrs. Dickman was allowed to go to the dairy by herself to take care of the afternoon's milk. She had been there only a few minutes when Chandler showed up and told her she was wanted back at the house. When she walked in and asked if something were the matter, it was Dowd who spoke. He apologized for imposing on her good nature after all she had done for them, but they had decided to leave. She could barely contain her joy, a feeling that was all too short-lived. The convicts would be taking her youngest son Lloyd with them, and they wanted to know the best way to proceed.

Believing that Lloyd's chances of survival would improve if she cooperated, the heartbroken woman suggested that they use the milk wagon. Dowd agreed and offered to help get it ready. When the team was led from barn he patted one of the animals on the neck, remarking: "I hate to have these horses taken out in the storm on such a mission as this." Doing as she was told, Mrs. Dickman came up with three pairs of blue overalls, which the convicts donned over their prison garb. Then they shook hands with their involuntary hostess and told Lloyd to climb on board the wagon.

"Remember, your son is with us," Gray remarked as the wagon began to roll. They were not to telephone anyone for several days. Indeed, the best thing they could do was never to mention what had happened, or their lives could be in danger. "The first man who gets his is this boy of yours." A minute or so later, the wagon was swallowed up by the darkness and the swirling storm, leaving a sobbing Mrs. Dickman to wait and to wonder.

With Lloyd handling the reins, the four headed north toward downtown Lincoln along the eastern edge of the city. Things were going well when the wagon suddenly got hung up in a huge drift at 23rd and Randolph Streets. Lloyd was trying to decide what to do next when he looked up and saw a man standing on the sidewalk. The youth could hardly believe his eyes: It was none other than Ernest Hunger, Lincoln's chief of police.

The old Prussian was returning home about eleven o'clock after a long afternoon and evening of fruitless searching for the convicts, little suspecting that they were crouched under a blanket fifteen feet away, the barrel of Gray's pistol hard against the Dickman boy's ribs. The chief called out, wanting to know if Lloyd was a hackman. He replied that he was driving a milk wagon and had gotten stuck. Gray's voice could be heard from beneath the blanket, asking who the man was. When Lloyd told him it was the chief of police he could feel the convict's arm stiffen: "You tell him who we are or that we're here and you will go first and Hunger after that," Gray snarled.

Hunger walked over and took the horses by the bridles, then coaxed them through the worst of the drift. He told Lloyd to go up the next alley to the paved street beyond, which should be pretty much clear of major obstacles. Lloyd thanked the chief and the wagon lumbered off, the pressure on his ribs easing. They continued north along the paved route and finally reached a lumberyard at 20th and R Streets, on the eastern edge of downtown. At that point Lloyd was ordered to stop the wagon so that the men could get out. Once on the ground they paused to shake his hand, but not before repeating the warning issued at the Dickman home an hour earlier. As Lloyd turned the team around and headed back south, he cast a glance over his shoulder just in time to see the men vanish once more.

◇ ◦◗◖◦ ◇

It took the Dickmans two days to reveal their story and then only under duress. Instead of reporting for work on Saturday morning, Chandler, who was suffering from a troubled conscience, phoned the sheriff's office wanting to talk to Hyers. But the lawman was at the Fadewa place and didn't reach the dairy farm until early evening. At first, Mrs. Dickman refused to say a word. It wasn't until Hyers made it clear that she could either tell him what she knew in her own home, or she could do so at the county jail, that she decided to speak. Hyers was both stunned and embarrassed to learn just how frustratingly close he had come to a showdown with the fugitives. "We started to go to the Dickman home," he later told reporters. "We foundered about in the snow for a time and found it would be easier to get to the bishop's house. We depended too much on the telephone, and the telephone, where the conversation is censored by outlaws, is not a reliable institution. I have no doubt that had we gone up to the Dickman home, as we went to other places, that there would have been a pitched battle with the bandits."

If the sheriff was chagrined, the chief of police was doubly so. Hunger quickly become the butt of jokes among his own men. He tried to duck reporters, which only made matters worse. When he was finally cornered on the phone by a representative of the *Nebraska State Journal* and asked about the story, his large ears turned a deep red and he exploded like a time bomb: "I know nothing about it," he shouted. "You always print lies about me and I will tell you not one damn thing." Hunger slammed down the receiver before the reporter could ask another question.

It was Hunger's misfortune to have a "traitor" living under his very roof, a man with the Dickensian name of Buckstaff. The house guest was one of those to whom the chief had revealed his encounter with the milk wagon Thursday night. Buckstaff retold the story "with considerable pleasure" to Edward Friend, H. C. Lindsay, and several other acquaintances, all of whom relished a good joke on the staid old chief. Some minutes after denying that the incident had ever taken place, Hunger again answered the phone, but this time the caller asked for Buckstaff. The wary chief demanded to know the name of the party on the other end, who confessed that he was a reporter from the *Journal.* Down went the receiver again.

Once they decided to speak, the Dickmans became overnight celebrities, garnering the sympathy of almost everyone who tried to imagine what they would have done in similar circumstances. "You can never know how I felt as I saw that wagon leave," Mrs. Dickman recalled. "The last glimpse I had of it was . . . its faint outline as it turned north on the road leading toward Lincoln. There was my son in that fearful storm with three murderers."

Joseph Dickman had arrived home shortly after the kidnapping of his boy to find his wife "hysterical" and the rest of the family almost "crazed." He agreed with the others that to telephone the sheriff would almost certainly result in a death sentence for Lloyd. Two hours had gone by since the abduction, and Mrs. Dickman was experiencing the greatest agony of her life. Then, from out of the storm, came the apparition of a solitary driver, a team of spent horses, and a creaking milk wagon, all encased in a ghostly cocoon of white. Lloyd Dickman had made it home without so much as a scratch.

Yes, the convicts had treated him well, very well indeed. The three had talked to him quite a bit, mostly about the weather and "just common things." Dowd was easily the most sociable: "He seemed to be a very nice fellow. It was hard to realize that he was a desperate criminal." Morley did not say as much and Gray was silent most of the way.

A rumor had spread according to which Gray, the "darkest figure in the tragedy," had decided that Mrs. Dickman and her two sons must be shot together with the hired man. Dowd was said to have stood up to the ringleader, arguing that enough blood had been shed and that the prisoners were not to be harmed. But when the hostages were queried about this matter, not one of them remembered hearing anything of the kind. Indeed, Mrs. Dickman called their treatment at the hands of the convicts "gentlemanly." Never once had she or anyone else in the house been forced to do anything at the point of a gun; in fact, she never saw a pistol in the hands of a convict, and that included Shorty Gray, for whom she had no use whatsoever.

It was also being said that the men spoke of dynamiting the governor's mansion while they were being driven into town, and that they even asked young Dickman for directions to the stately residence. Lloyd supposedly talked them out of it by arguing that the drifts were too deep. But once again, the rumor was denied: "There isn't a word of truth in it," Lloyd declared.

The one thing all agreed on was the shared fear that a promise made would be a promise kept. The hostages had been told in no uncertain terms that the convicts had confederates and that their lives would be forfeited if they contacted the law. Mrs. Dickman spoke for everyone when she told a reporter: "I have spent three days the like of which I hope will never be repeated."

No one knew how the convicts felt, but in the span of an hour or so they had come within two blocks of shooting it out with a posse led by the county sheriff and far closer to a bloody encounter with the local chief of police; yet they had managed to slip away undetected, leaving a baffled constabulary without a hint as to their whereabouts. Some might have called it the luck of the Irish and maybe it was, it being St. Patrick's Day.

"THIS IS AWFUL"

A Sunday visitor to Lincoln might have taken the surging column of carriages, wagons, and sleighs as proof that the plains had given rise to its own Great Awakening. But it was not evangelical fervor that drew the multitude to services at the penitentiary chapel but the fevered headlines dominating the front pages on this the third morning after the escape: THREE CONVICT ASSASSINS ARE STILL AT LARGE; ALL SEARCH FAILS: BOY TELLS STORY OF THE RIDE WITH MURDERERS; TRAIL OF MURDERERS NOW LEADS TO OMAHA: THREATENED TO DYNAMITE GOVERNOR'S MANSION; and so on.

An incredulous General Phelps took one look at the oncoming deluge and promptly canceled services, nearly provoking a riot. His reasons were valid enough: The militia was still bivouacking on the chapel floor; the furniture and the other belongings of the prisoners remained stacked, helter-skelter, along the walls; and, most important, no one had any idea how the convicts would react in the presence of curious onlookers. The problem was that Phelps should have thought of all this beforehand. As late as Saturday evening he was assuring callers to the penitentiary that they would be most welcome at morning chapel. Now, only hours later, the guards in charge of turning people away had become the targets of verbal barbs while Lincoln's clergy were decrying the drop in attendance at their own services, and all for nothing.

The idea that the escapees were headed for Omaha came from Sheriff Hyers, who, in turn, got it from the bits of conversation Lloyd Dickman had overheard during the storm-tossed drive into Lincoln. Believing that the men were still together and following the railroad tracks, Hyers caught a train to Omaha, where he met with Douglas County Sheriff Felix McShane and several members of the Omaha Police Department. The authorities there were already searching every train coming into the city and had set up surveillance posts along the main roads. They had secreted additional men near the home of Mrs. Fred Walker on North 17th Street and were still conducting an extensive, but, so far, fruitless search for the mysterious Mrs. Brown, who, Hyers had learned, was given ten dollars by an ex-convict with which to depart Lincoln. As a final precaution, they decided to contact every household with a telephone in eastern Nebraska for the purpose of providing a description of the desperadoes now that they had donned other clothing. Individuals with information living on the east side of the Platte were to call the Omaha police; those living west of the river were to phone Sheriff Hyers.

Starved for copy in the fierce battle of journalistic one-upmanship, certain reporters had resorted to fabricating their own. According to the *Lincoln Daily Star*, the convicts had been sighted walking along the Burlington tracks on Saturday night, heading north toward Omaha. They were said to be terrorizing the residents of farm homes along the way, stealing additional food and clothing. "It is believed that the men imbibed freely of liquor during the day, and were made less secretive by it." A dubious Hyers sent some deputies to check out the report, only to have them run into yet another dead end.

The lawman had made no secret of the fact that he was as interested in collecting the large reward as the next fellow, but his prospects seemed to be slipping away. Not only did it appear that the men had left the city, interlopers of all sorts had entered the deadly game of hide-and-seek. At least six posses were in the field, the latest one organized by Special Agent James Malone of the Burlington Railroad. Together with six men, Malone was scouring the countryside around Eagle and had planted armed detectives on the Burlington lines leading to Kansas City, where Gray and Morley had numerous underworld contacts.

Even more unsettling to Hyers was word that the William J. Burns National Detective Agency had become interested in the case. The Burns organization, second only to the much older Pinkerton Agency in prestige and number of clients, operated as a kind of private police force, often in the employ of big business interests against organized labor. Its director and namesake was the famous private eye William J. Burns, the beefy but dapper son of Irish immigrants, who was not above using brutal tactics and illegal means to advance a difficult investigation. Two of his men had slipped in and out of Lincoln all but unrecognized over the weekend, their visit coinciding with a letter received by Governor Aldrich from J. A. Gustafson, the superintendent of Burns's Chicago agency. Gustafson noted that his office already had a file on the safecracker known as Shorty Gray, whom he suspected of having ties with one or more of the dynamiting gangs connected with the socialist labor movement. What he needed from the governor was a supply of photographs and the Bertillon measurements of the three convicts.

Of greater interest to Aldrich was Gustafson's reference to an informant who "will be in a position to furnish us with information thru which we will be able to effect the arrest of the three men who escaped, . . . also the persons who assisted in their escape." Gustafson dared not disclose his informant's line of work "for fear of his identity becoming known in the matter." But he could guarantee that the person in the agency's employ would go directly to the places where the fugitives would most likely conceal themselves, for he knew their habits well. All the governor had to do was wire the requested information.

By the time of the inquest the next day, the bodies of Delahunty and Heilman had been released to their families, while that of Wagner remained in the morgue as officials attempted to locate his relatives. Fourteen witnesses were called by Coroner Jack Matthews, who must have had a sense of déjà vu, having gone through this same procedure after the recent murder of Deputy Warden Davis. All who had seen Delahunty fall agreed that he had been shot down by Shorty Gray, and several also placed the blame for Heilman's death on the reputed ringleader.

Cell keeper Dennis McMahon told of how Gray and Dowd, after receiving permission to get a drink, had passed a large load of broomcorn standing on the scales, keeping it between them and the keeper's line of sight. They then walked by the toilet room and emerged from the building undetected. When the runner he had sent to report them missing returned with the news that a gun battle had broken out, McMahon had his hands full controlling the prisoners in his charge. The cell keeper believed that Morley, who had also disappeared, must have been killed during the fighting and did not realize that he had escaped until after Sheriff Hyers returned the convicts to their cells later in the afternoon.

Claus Pahl, the apoplectic turnkey, presented himself to the coroner's jury as considerably braver and quicker thinking than most remembered. He said that when he first heard shots he rushed to his desk in search of a revolver. A bullet struck the ceiling above his head, showering him with plaster, and he ducked under a barred window where a safe was located in the wall. He opened it, took out a gun, and braced for a fight. It was then that the explosion came, and Gray was on him like a cat. Forced to drop his gun, Pahl was thrown to the floor and kicked by one of the men. As the convicts left the turnkey's room Gray fired another shot into the body of Heilman, who was lying back in a chair in the clerk's office.

According to Pahl and Chief Clerk T. J. Ward, the warden may have already been dying by this time. They had seen Delahunty come down the stairs and enter his office. He emerged with a gun moments later and began firing at the convicts through the bars of the turnkey's cage. A single shot from Gray's pistol struck home and Delahunty staggered back into his office.

Cell house keeper Doody was the last to testify. The jury visited him as he lay on his cot in the guards' room above the chapel, his stiff, heavily bandaged leg resting on a pillow. He spoke of how he had come into the chapel just as the convicts were emerging from the deputy warden's office after gunning down Wagner. Doody immediately opened fire, as did the other three, who jumped behind pillars, making them difficult targets. He remembered getting off nine shots while each of the convicts had fired just as many rounds and thought that the battle had lasted between ten and twelve minutes. Whether Doody, who had emerged from the affray a hero, was consciously exaggerating is difficult to say, but others testified that no more than a total of twenty shots were fired during an exchange that had lasted only two or three minutes.

Before leaving the coroner's jury to deliberate in the prison library, Matthews instructed the six men to base their verdict on the sole issue of assigning responsibility for the murders. As he later told reporters, he had taken this action to prevent them from considering penitentiary discipline as a factor in the escape. There were those who believed that the administration's conduct toward the prisoners should be reviewed, but "that is not the business of [coroner's] juries." Given this simple charge, it took the panel no more than half an hour to credit the three convicts with the deaths.

The odor of cigarette smoke put farmer Elmer Hall on notice that something was wrong even before he entered the barn to do his Saturday-morning chores. He swung the door open and found himself standing face-to-face with John Dowd, who ordered him to come in and shut the door. "Have you heard of the convicts who escaped from the penitentiary?" Dowd asked.

Hall replied that he had.

"Well, we are the three," Dowd declared.

Gray and Morley hadn't yet shown themselves, but they soon emerged from the oat bin, where they had been resting and smoking. Dowd announced that they intended to stay at the house a while and ordered Hall to lead them in, a revolver pointed at his back. They entered the kitchen and informed Mrs. Hall who they were before telling her to prepare them breakfast. While she nervously busied herself at the stove, Dowd followed her husband back to the barn and stood guard as he did the chores. Then they returned to the house, where everyone but Gray sat down to a breakfast of wheat cakes, bacon, and coffee. Although the convicts had eaten little in the two days since dining at the Dickman farm, no one seemed to have much of an appetite. Morley hardly ate anything and said he was sick, an indication that he may have been suffering withdrawal symptoms from a lack of dope.

The men were heavily armed and made no attempt to keep their guns out of sight as they had at the Dickman place. They bragged to Hall of having six revolvers, and he actually saw five of them. He later described the pistols as .44 caliber, with barrels of blue steel about eight inches long. Dowd's weapon had a fancy pearl handle.

The day passed with one of the convicts stationed at the parlor window and another watching the back of the place from the kitchen. The third "shadowed" the farmer's every move, but Mrs. Hall was given her freedom to the point of being allowed to go into the farmyard alone to feed the chickens and gather eggs from the henhouse. Once it was clear that the young couple posed no threat the men became almost apologetic: "We don't want to impose on you," one of them told her, "but we must protect ourselves. If you do as we say you'll not be harmed." There was no rough language, no threats of violence.

The Halls were the first to learn what had happened to the convicts after they were dropped off in downtown Lincoln shortly before midnight on Thursday. According to Morley, the three had trudged northeast toward the Rock Island yards at Havelock, with the idea of jumping an outgoing freight. But the weather had blocked all the tracks and the sun was beginning to come up, so they made for a barn on the south side of town, concealing themselves in the loft. They did not know it at the time, but the building was rented by a local coal company to house its team of horses. During the next day and a half, driver H. J. Hoss regularly came by to feed "Billy" and "Grace," whose names Morley recounted to the Halls with a smile. Each time the driver climbed up into the loft the convicts were forced to burrow deeper into the hay, and the unsuspecting Hoss once came within inches of stabbing Morley in the leg with his pitchfork. It was going on eleven o'clock Saturday night when the trio set out once again, following the Rock Island tracks some five miles east to the Hall farm near the village of Prairie Home, where they passed another freezing night before surprising the farmer.

The more the weary convicts relaxed the better their appetites became until they were eating everything Mrs. Hall could put on the table. They also talked a good deal and made no attempt to hide their disdain for the men they had gunned down, with the exception of the aging Heilman, against whom they bore no grudge. They were especially critical of Delahunty, blaming him for the poor quality and meager amounts of food. Much of their harsh talk was a reaction to the accounts of the escape in the *Lincoln Daily Star*, which was delivered to the farm every morning. "The men would read the story over and over again," Hall recounted.

Another frequent topic of conversation was their escape plan. They made it clear that they were headed for Omaha and expected to proceed to Chicago from there. Morley revealed that his wife was in Omaha, while Gray said that his was in Lincoln, a statement authorities would later dispute given what they knew of Mrs. Brown's recent peregrinations.

The five were all seated in the living about ten-thirty Saturday night when Mrs. Hall turned to Gray and bluntly asked him what he was planning to do next.

"Your husband is going to drive us to Ashland tonight," he calmly replied.

"I can't do it," a surprised Hall interjected, "my team would not be able to make it the way the roads are."

"Then you'll have to take us as far as you can before daylight," Gray replied. "We'll stay at a farm house just as we have yours." He ordered Hall to hitch up the team, and the four men met in the yard a short while later. They were about to climb aboard the sled when Mrs. Hall came running out of the house to protest being left behind. After a brief debate, the convicts agreed to take her with them, and all five piled into the sled.

In making the sharp turn onto the main road, which was still covered by three-foot drifts in many places, the tongue of the sled let loose. It was soon replaced by a chain and the unlikely party started out again. They had traveled about two miles when one of the runners dropped into a rut and was wrenched off when Hall turned the horses too sharply in an attempt to free it. After some discussion about what to do next, a disgusted Shorty Gray declared: "We can't go anywhere tonight." The horses were unhitched and Hall held the reins while the men struggled mightily to turn the sled around, which the farmer took as a sign of their generally poor physical condition. The team was hitched up again and they limped home, not reaching the farmhouse until one o'clock Sunday morning.

The Halls were ordered to go upstairs to bed but neither came within a mile of nodding off. The men bedded down on quilts spread on the living room floor, one sleeping while the other two kept watch. They turned the lamps down low and kept them burning all night.

When Mrs. Hall came down at seven Sunday morning she found Gray and Dowd asleep on the floor and Morley dozing in a chair. Four large revolvers rested against the wall on one side of the room within easy reach of Gray. Even though it took several minutes for the men to stir, she never seriously thought about going for the guns.

Morley was at the kitchen table eating breakfast when Gray walked in, one shoe off and the other on. "That's bad luck," he exclaimed, looking down at Gray's swollen feet. Saying nothing, Shorty went back and put on his other shoe.

Later on in the morning, while everyone was gathered in the parlor, Gray reached over and opened the cover of a Bible lying in the middle of a table. Morley was watching and started a conversation about religion. Though he had claimed to be a Methodist when he was admitted to Lancaster, he spoke highly of Father Moran, a Catholic priest who visited the penitentiary several times a month. Gray, a lapsed Catholic and self-proclaimed Deist, also liked the cleric, and it was the Halls' impression that both men "seemed to favor the Catholic creed above all others." While Dowd also came from a Catholic background, he stated that he rarely attended prison chapel and did not appear to be what the Halls termed "religiously inclined."

The conversation was picked up later in the day when Dowd asked his hostage whom he thought the next president would be. Hall said that he had no idea. Morley spoke up and declared he was putting his money on Roosevelt. Gray immediately took issue with Morley, saying Roosevelt would not win, nor was he fit to be president. He applied the "shorter but uglier word [Teddy]" to the colonel. Dowd then brought up the subject of socialism, and for the next two hours talk centered on the principles of the party founded and led by Eugene V. Debs, who had served a six-month prison sentence for his part in the Pullman Strike of 1894. The labor leader was Gray's man; to him, socialism held the promise of creating the only just political system on the face of the earth. The convict might well have added that it provided as good an excuse as any for blowing the safes of capitalist-owned banks.

Gray asked Hall to play checkers with him several times during the day, but the farmer repeatedly declined, displaying a certain resolve. In frustration he turned to Morley, who also refused to join in: "I am past playing checkers," he glumly replied. From time to time, Morley would step to the kitchen window and gaze wistfully out into the bright sunlight. He once turned to Hall with a pathetic expression on his face and said: "This is awful." Hall said nothing, but he was left with the impression that Morley had a "bad case of the blues coupled with a certain foreboding."

Morley and Dowd became more agitated and downcast as evening approached. After dark, Mrs. Hall was told to phone the Burlington depot at Waverly and find out if the midnight train stopped there. When she was informed that it didn't they ordered her to call Havelock and ask if it picked up passengers there. She was again told that it passed right on through. The men entered into a discussion of their limited options, seemingly paying no mind to their attentive listeners. They finally decided to hike over to Waverly and break into the depot. Once inside, they would steal a switchman's lantern and flag the train. Despite her predicament, Mrs. Hall couldn't help but wince when she looked down at her captors' painfully frostbitten feet. All they had to protect them were the same low-cut prison shoes they had been wearing ever since their escape three days earlier.

After Mrs. Hall had fixed them sandwiches and cake to take along, she was ordered to seat herself in a rocking chair. A rope that had served as a halter line was used to bind her hands to the chair arms. Her husband was then placed in another rocker, but his hands were tied behind his back. As an added precaution the convicts split the rope, using one of the strands to further secure Mr. Hall. Nonetheless, Gray, whom the others addressed as "Shorty," was not satisfied. Fearing that Hall would work himself free, he checked the bindings three times, complaining all the while to Morley that Hall would get loose. Morley kept assuring him that the farmer wasn't going anywhere.

The men apologized once again for their treatment of the Halls, stating that they hated having to tie them up. After jerking the receiver from the telephone and cutting the line they asked the couple for the number of their nearest neighbor, promising to call and have them released once they had a good start. As they were about to leave one of the three picked up Hall's shotgun and a box of shells. Still wearing the Dickmans' blue overalls on top of their prison grays, the men bid their hostages good-bye and headed into the night.

Whether or not the fugitives were lying to throw the authorities off when they spoke of heading for Waverly is not known, but, instead, they settled for the tiny community of nearby Prairie Home, some four miles from the Hall place and fifteen miles northeast of Lincoln. By the time they reached the slumbering village it was early Monday morning, with not a light to be seen. The three were on the lookout for a team and wagon to steal when they glimpsed the silhouette of a handcar in the distance. Scarcely believing their good luck, they lifted the vehicle onto the Rock Island tracks and started pumping.

As the snow-covered fields slipped by to the sound of a low rumble, the land was transformed from flat to rolling in the brilliant moonlight. Pumping uphill for all they were worth and then coasting down, they reached Alvo in well under an hour, putting another seven or eight miles between themselves and Lincoln. The men paused briefly to nose around before pushing on six more miles to Murdock, where they found just what they were looking for in the brick-fronted buildings lining the main street.

Their first target was the hardware store owned by Louis Maxwell. After gaining entry by shattering a window with a piece of gas pipe, they stole a shotgun, a revolver, several knives, and a large quantity of ammunition. S. O. Beal's general store was next. Each man took a complete change of clothing, including overalls, a shirt, shoes, overshoes, and a cap. They also emptied the cash drawer of $3.66, mostly in pennies, which weighed them down. Though it was around three a.m. the local postmaster, who lived across from the general store, was up and about. When he saw light coming from the windows, it caused him no concern. He supposed that Beal had come down to stoke the furnace and get an early jump on the work week.

Back at the Hall farm Shorty Gray had been proven right. After struggling for twenty minutes, Hall was able to free a hand and grab a knife. He quickly cut his bonds and those of his wife, who was completely exhausted from the prolonged ordeal. Hall's father lived only a mile away, and Mrs. Hall's family also resided in the neighborhood. Even with the telephone out and the roads in poor condition, it would have taken no more than a half hour to raise the alarm. But Hall thought better of leaving his unnerved wife alone on the offhand chance that the convicts might return if they found the going too difficult. So the couple went to bed after deciding to report what had happened to them in the morning.

The convicts' charmed odyssey continued across the white sea, its surface broken only by two steep ridges of plowed snow reaching into the distance on both sides of the tracks. For the first time since their escape the men were exhilarated, knowing that they were moving ever closer to the swift-flowing Platte, more a psychological barrier than a physical one. They covered another five miles and glided into South Bend just as the first rays of the sun were spiking the eastern horizon. Seen by a few early risers, they were mistaken for members of a section gang that had been working in the area ever since the recent storm.

The river lay dead ahead, and they kept on through town to a point just short of the railroad bridge. Then they stopped to gaze across the swollen Platte, squinting into the pink-and-silver dawn as they scanned the woods on the opposite bank for any signs of movement. Seeing none, they decided to get rid of the conspicuous handcar and take their chances on foot. After collecting the guns and a few other things, they lifted the car off the tracks and sent it hurtling into a creek. Twenty minutes later found them safely across the broad waters and ready to continue their journey north and east along the right-of-way.

Paralleling the river, they walked no more than a mile through the heavily wooded landscape before veering off the tracks into a draw. They had not gone far when they spotted a cabin in the distance. Finding it to be uninhabited, they were about to build a fire and rest a while when one of them spied an approaching stranger carrying what appeared to be a set of carpenter's tools. The man stepped inside, took one look at the three convicts, and blanched. He explained that he had been hired to make some repairs, but that he would come back another time. For some reason Shorty decided to let him go.

It was at this point that the three had their first serious falling-out. Morley and Dowd accused Gray of pushing too hard. Omaha would still be there in another few days, and it was foolish to think that they wouldn't be spotted if they kept on in broad daylight. Dowd knew the quarries over by Louisville pretty well; there were at least half a dozen good places to hide, and they could always scrounge enough grub to see them through until things cooled down. They might even hop a train headed in the opposite direction of Omaha and throw the authorities off their trail.

Gray wasn't listening. Instead, he was for going back to the tracks and following them another mile or two, then turning "up into the country." That way they were certain to strike a road; and where there was a road there had to be a farmhouse and breakfast, Mrs. Hall's sandwiches and cake having been devoured long since. Sticking with their pledge that they wouldn't split up no matter what, the younger men reluctantly agreed and the trio set off back down the draw.

———————— ⋄ ●◗● ⋄ ————————

The requiem mass for fifty-five-year-old James Delahunty began promptly at nine-thirty Monday morning in Lincoln's Catholic cathedral at 14th and K Streets. Dressed in a surplice, black stole, and black cope, Father Moran, the Catholic chaplain at the state prison, met the body at the top of the steps and sprinkled it with holy water, intoning: *Aspérges me hyssópo, et mundábor: lavábis me, et super nivem dealbábor.* ("Thou shalt sprinkle me with hyssop, and I shall be cleansed: Thou shalt wash me, and I shall be made whiter than snow.")

The chanting priest led the solemn procession past the thronged pews and down the nave, the casket borne by employees of the penitentiary: *Réquiem aetérnam dona eis Dómine: et lux perpé-tua lúceat eis.* ("Eternal rest give unto them, O Lord: and let perpetual light shine upon them.") The fallen warden's mother, who wept uncontrollably throughout the service, was flanked by her three daughters and four sons, all of whom were dressed in black mourning clothes and dark suits. Governor and Mrs. Aldrich led the large delegation of state and local officials. Few of the priest's remarks made it into the papers, but he stressed the fact that Jim Delahunty was among the bravest of men, one who, as a devout Christian, had chosen to remain at his post in spite of mortal danger, not unlike the martyrs of old. Following the rosary, Moran recited the paternoster and passed twice around the body, sprinkling it with holy water and incensing it: *Et ne nos indúcas in tentationem. Sed líbera nos a malo. A porta inferi.* ("And lead us not into temptation. But deliver us from evil. From the gate of hell.")

The one person conspicuously absent from the funeral was Gus Hyers, and when the puzzled governor emerged from the cathedral he quickly learned the reason why. A young farm couple from near Prairie Home had called in early to report that they had been held hostage by the escaped convicts for upward of two days. And there was more: Two stores in Murdock had been relieved of clothing and arms in the middle of the night, while men fitting the fugitives' descriptions had passed through South Bend on a handcar about dawn, heading for the Platte. Most recently, a section gang, whose members had been cautioned by railroad detectives to stay clear of strangers, reported seeing the three men on the east side of the river.

Hyers, who had literally moved into his office and had taken nothing but catnaps for the past four days, knew just what to do. As soon as he received word of the burglaries in Murdock, he called a Mr. Pollock of the Plattsmouth Telephone Company and asked him to keep the lines to his Lincoln office open, so that reports of the criminals' movements could be sent at a moment's notice. He also requested that Pollock get in touch with every farm along the escape route and tell the residents to phone the minute anyone set eyes on the men. Hyers then called the authorities at Omaha and South Omaha to tell them to form posses and head for South Bend as fast as they could. Lastly, he phoned Burlington detective James Malone and told him that he had need of the waiting engine, and that he wanted the tracks cleared of all rolling stock between Lincoln and South Bend. The posse would be at the rail yard and ready to load up in no more than half an hour, possibly less. With any luck at all, Hyers would finally get his men before sunset—one way or the other.

DANSE MACABRE

Plunging through drifts reaching to their waists, the fugitive trio was in an area known locally as the "bottoms" or "fisheries." The frozen surface gave way with a loud crunching sound at every step, leaving a series of craters in their wake rather than footprints. They had followed the railroad tracks through the timber another two miles or so before veering off and heading north across the snowfields. There were a number of farms in the area, and while the alarm had not been raised locally as yet, the sight of three strangers crossing their land with shotguns more than piqued the curiosity of George Phelps and his neighbors, the Balls and the Jarmans. After walking another two miles, Gray made up his mind and started toward a smoking chimney on a hill directly ahead.

It was around nine o'clock and Carmellette Blunt was busy in her kitchen while her husband, Roy, lingered over coffee with his older brother Lloyd, who had stopped by to see how the newlyweds were faring. The wedding, which had taken place less than three months earlier, on December twenty-seventh, had created something of a stir in the local community, not least because Carmellette was just seventeen and needed the consent of her father, a respected immigrant farmer named Peter Anderson, to marry. She had been attending school in nearby Springfield, and according to the *Gretna Breeze*, "Friends of both the bride and the groom were somewhat surprised at the announcement of their marriage, but their congratulations are none the less hearty."

The couple posed self-consciously for a photograph after the ceremony, lightly touching shoulders: the twenty-one-year-old groom, blond and pale in his tailored suit and white tie; the petite bride elegantly dressed in a long gown of white lace and high button shoes, her chestnut hair swept back to highlight her pleasant features and youthful countenance. Whether it was due to the presence of the camera or to faint misgivings about what might lie ahead, the groom projected a certain reticence, as if staring into some destiny not quite decided. At the same time Carmellette, her fingers slightly curled, shoulders braced, and eyes sharply focused, appears to be a young woman of considerable resolve, a reflection of her sober Scandinavian heritage.

Peter Anderson, a slight, diminutive man who burned off his food almost before he ate it, had grown up in Denmark and had served as an officer in the army before immigrating to Nebraska. Carmellette's mother, Finia, was also the child of Danish parents but, unlike her husband, she had been born in the United States. Finia's inheritance consisted of some 360 acres of farmland divided into three parcels, all located in Sarpy County's Plattford Township, no more than two miles north of the river. It was on the largest of these that she gave birth to the couple's nine children during a span of nineteen years. Carmellette, pronounced "Carmelita," was the second youngest, and no one remembers why she alone among her siblings was given an exotic name while the others were christened Anna, Mary, Russell, Lucille, Jay, and so forth.

James and Effie Blunt rented a farm three miles to the northeast of the Andersons and were almost as prolific as their new inlaws. Of their seven children, all of whom were boys, Roy was the

**Roy and Carmellette Blunt on their wedding day, December 1911
(Used by permission of Jean Blunt Laughlin)**

middle son. After graduating from high school at eighteen, the
youth had left home to attend business college at York, not far
from the village of Giltner. While there he had likely heard talk
about the daring burglary and furious chase that had landed gang
leader Shorty Gray and his cohorts in the state penitentiary. Roy

completed the two-year commercial course and returned home, drawn by his heartstrings and feelings for the land. A year later, just before his marriage, he rented forty acres from W. H. Davidson, one of the most prosperous farmers in Plattford Township. There, amid family and childhood friends, he set up housekeeping with his pretty bride, both dreaming of the day when they could afford a farm of their own.

Dispensing with formalities, the winded convicts walked right into the Blunt kitchen, shotguns trained on Roy and Lloyd. After telling them who they were and that they would not harm anyone if their instructions were obeyed, they ordered Carmellette to fix them breakfast. Feigning obedience, she asked if the men could wait until she went out to the chicken coop to gather some fresh eggs. Having had no trouble with Mrs. Dickman and Mrs. Hall, Gray saw no reason why he shouldn't trust this slender young woman and told her to go ahead.

Once she was out of the house, Carmellette gathered up her skirts and broke into a run while attempting to dodge the graying snowdrifts. She had not gone far before a wagon appeared in the distance, driven by the Blunts' neighbor, Arthur Jarman. The prisoners had passed Jarman about a half mile from the Blunt house, and he immediately became suspicious. After dropping off a load of corn, he was coming over to check things out. Carmellette told him what was happening as she climbed onto the wagon seat and Jarman turned his team around. He drove her partway to her parents' home before leaving her with his son, then telephoned the sheriff's office in Papillion.

By this time the convicts realized that they had been tricked, but instead of leaving they ordered Roy to finish making their breakfast. When it was ready the three were so famished that they posted no guard but sat down together, leaning their shotguns against the wall and placing their revolvers in their laps. While they were distracted Lloyd drew his brother aside and told him that he was carrying a pistol. "I'll shoot two of them with my automatic," he whispered, "if you'll take the other with the shotgun."

According to Lloyd, Roy refused, stating that he could not shoot a man in the back who had done him no harm, especially one seated at his own table. They would be fine if they kept their heads and followed orders as they had promised to do. What most concerned him at the moment was the whereabouts of Carmellette.

The intruders ate hurriedly and then told the brothers to hitch up the team. Morley and Dowd followed them out to the barn while Gray remained behind. The massive wagon box, on whose side was stenciled the nickname OLD HICKORY, was mounted on the bobsled, but the convicts insisted that it be removed and placed on the running gears of the wagon, together with the tall end gate. With front wheels nearly as high as a man's chest, and rear ones even taller, the fully assembled wagon made a formidable vehicle. Taking into account the terrible state of the roads, and the considerable weight they would be pulling, Roy decided on his less experienced but more powerful team of gray colts.

In the meantime, Arthur Jarman had collected neighbors George Phelps and John Bartell and was heading back to the Blunt place. When the three got within sight of the buildings they saw Roy come around the corner of the cowshed and begin waving. Thinking that he wanted them to come over, they started forward, but he suddenly motioned them to stop and then disappeared. It was at this point that Lloyd unexpectedly showed up, having slipped away as his captors were harnessing the team. Roy had his chance to escape as well, but he had no idea where his wife was, and he would not leave, in the event that she was hiding in one of the outbuildings.

Gray strode out of the house moments later and ordered Roy to climb up on the spring seat of the wagon. The young man turned to the convict and begged to be left behind, giving Gray permission—as if he needed it—to take the team and go wherever he wished. The convict flatly refused; Blunt was their hostage and, knowing this, his bride would likely prevail upon the expected posse not to follow them. Were she to do otherwise, her husband's fate was sealed.

With the three fugitives hunkered down in the wagon, and Roy perched on the driver's seat high above, they pulled onto the narrow road and started north at a walk, the young farmer's neighbors and brother watching helplessly from a respectful distance. They had not gone far when they met a wagon coming from the opposite direction. Its driver was James Blunt, and when father and son pulled alongside one another Roy wanted to know whether Carmellette was at his father's house. The elder Blunt shook his head and could not help noticing the keen look of disappointment on his son's face.

"Well," said Roy, "I haven't any idea where she is, then."

James turned to the convicts and asked them to be careful with his son, at which point Roy interrupted him: "Father, I am not afraid of these men. They will not hurt me if I do as they tell me to." If the Blunts wished to say anything more they didn't get the chance; an anxious Gray cut them off, commanding Roy to drive on.

———— ◦ ◦●◦ ◦ ————

The fugitives had been eating breakfast about the time the locomotive carrying Sheriff Hyers steamed into South Bend. With him were twenty-five men, armed with Winchester long-range rifles and with pistols and shotguns for "close-range work." Accompanying them were six militiamen under the command of Lieutenant

Harry Gilhaar, all of whom were equipped with army rifles and Colt revolvers. Hyers was shown the piece of gas pipe the convicts used to break into the stores at Murdock, in addition to a discarded bag containing a pair of prison shoes and stained rags thought to have been used as foot bindings.

The plan had been to divide the thirty-odd men into four smaller posses and let them off at different locations to search every house, barn, and other hiding place between Murdock and South Bend. But everything changed when Hyers received a message that the convicts had been spotted passing through South Bend some three hours earlier and had already crossed the Platte.

Once everyone was off the train, Hyers picked twelve men who immediately climbed onto handcars and began crossing the river. When they reached the other side, a good half mile away, they followed the Rock Island tracks to the point where the fugitives had turned north. Waiting there for them with a team and bobsled was Dean Applegate, a local youth who reported that the men had been seen walking toward the Blunt place. Hyers debated whether to head directly for the farm or to search every wooded draw and culvert along the way. Anxious though he was to overtake them, he decided to err on the side of caution. After placing two men with rifles in the front seat of the sled, he ordered the others to fan out on both sides, making certain not to overlook a thing.

The posse advanced at a walk, having reached the road fronting the Preston, Overton, Phelps, Ball, and Jarman farms. They had not gone far before the first of several men rushed out to confirm Applegate's story. The convicts had passed by more than an hour earlier and had been seen at the Blunts. Everyone in the area had been alerted by telephone; indeed, the fugitives' progress was being reported farm by farm as the wagon went by.

Nor was there any mistaking the fact that the reins were in the hands of Roy Blunt.

After commandeering some additional vehicles, the posse charged up the waterlogged road, slush and mud flying. On reaching the Blunt place, the men surrounded the frame house and waited with their rifles raised as Hyers and Deputy Eikenbary cautiously approached the front door and knocked. There was no response, and the blinds were drawn, preventing the lawmen from peering inside. Eikenbary went around to the back door and forced it open. Entering the house alone with his revolver drawn, the deputy went from room to room, finally emerging with an unsigned note that was later determined to be in Shorty Gray's hand. The curt message had been written while the others were at the barn preparing Blunt's team: "To the Posse—We have taken your neighbor for a hostage. If you do not follow us or report the matter, he will not be injured." It seemed that Gray had eyes in the back of his head until the lawmen realized that he was expecting a posse of local farmers as opposed to a heavily armed delegation of professionals.

Even so, this was far from the worst of it, as the hunted were about to discover. Although Hyers and the dozen men with him had taken every available handcar on the west side of the Rock Island bridge, the rest of the posse and militiamen were determined not to be left behind. They crossed the bridge on foot and were able to secure handcars from a railroad camp on the other side. Led by Deputy Sheriff Robert Malone, they soon arrived at the place where the bobsled had been waiting for Hyers and the others. At this point they split up; half proceeding on down the line to the site of a second railroad bridge near Meadow in case the fugitives tried to double back; the rest, under Malone's command, following the bobsled tracks and oversized footprints across country. Wading through water that came almost to their knees in places, they walked a mile before straggling into the Phelps farm, where they were forced to wait another hour for wagons to carry them north.

Trailed by a divided posse from behind, the fugitives were on the verge of being hemmed in from the front and sides as well. Sarpy County Sheriff Grant Chase, a gaunt, sleepy-eyed man whose easy manner belied his name, had begun moving southwest from Papillion at the head of a posse made up of townsmen and farmers armed with everything from long-range rifles to single-shot pistols of pre–Civil War vintage. Chase and his men were headed for the Sarpy County town of Springfield, about two and a half miles north and three miles east of the scene of the kidnapping. So, too, was John Briggs, the chief of police of South Omaha. Having been informed by Hyers of the convicts' whereabouts, Briggs, a tall and powerfully built man with the shoulders of a bull, a huge head, and stern features that combined to create an intimidating aspect, first stationed several officers at the local Rock Island depot, then climbed aboard a chartered train and set out for Springfield, where he and his men would eventually join forces with Sheriff Chase. Following Briggs down these same tracks was another posse comprised of ten men from Omaha led by Douglas County Sheriff Felix McShane.

To Sheriff Quinton of Cass County it must have seemed like old times, which, in fact, were not so very old at all. Just the previous September, Quinton and a posse armed with shotguns had ranged the countryside between Louisville and South Bend searching for John Dowd and his accomplices, following their unsuccessful attempt to blow the vault of the Farmer's State Bank, at Wabash. Now, some six months later, the sheriff found himself and sixteen men, including the Plattsmouth chief of police, bound for Louisville in hopes of apprehending Dowd a second time. After reaching the village, Quinton and his posse climbed aboard a wagon and hastened across the Platte on the passenger bridge, which spanned the river next to the railroad bridge that was being guarded by some of Hyers's deputies and also the Lincoln militia, near Meadow. Once he determined that all was well, Quinton pushed on to the rock quarries that Dowd and Morley had favored as a hiding place. Nothing stirred in the warm March air, and from the absence of markings in the snow it appeared that no one had been near there since the recent storm. Nevertheless, Quinton left a few men to guard the area and departed with the rest of his posse and some soldiers for Ritchfield, a station on the Rock Island line. Word had come from a "telephone girl laboring under much suppressed excitement" that the fugitives were zigzagging north and west, and it seemed a good place to intercept them. Vying for the same honor was yet another posse of aroused citizens led by the police chief from the town of Gretna, almost directly in line with the fleeing wagon.

Officially, there were at least six posses in the field, and if the freelancers from Springfield and Chalco were counted, the number came to eight. This was on top of numerous farmers who had begun merging with the contingents of duly sworn lawmen along the escape route. A reporter for the *Omaha World Herald,* dazzled by the cavalcade, wrote of a "thousand or more men, with rifles and shotguns glistening in the sunlight"—a description that would have done justice to a medieval chronicler. The reporter for the *Lincoln Daily Star,* who was also on the scene, came up with a more modest estimate of 360, which was still too great by half. Before it was over, those participating directly in the chase probably numbered between 150 and 200, each a small part of a shifting mosaic subject to myriad retellings and interpretations, no two of which would ever be the same.

The one thing everyone would later agree on was the weather: March 18, 1912, was a beautiful late-winter day. A gentle wind stirred the naked branches of trees just beginning to swell in anticipation of spring. In the fields, melting snow was underlain by pools of standing water that had no place to go, with the earth still frozen solid. Creeks were filled even above the brim, fed by streamlets that followed the ditches like rivers in miniature. Their precarious situation notwithstanding, the exhausted convicts occasionally nodded off, started, and nodded off again—the warm sun, the fresh straw covering the wagon floor, and the rhythmic clip-clop of hoofs creating an irresistible soporific.

The rolling countryside of Sarpy County had been known as the Gretna Hills almost ever since the first settler's plow had turned the first furrow. Roy and Carmellette Blunt lived at the top of one such rise, and when the young man turned Old Hickory onto the county road from his lane the convicts were treated to a vista that extended for miles in every direction. To men used to being locked up it must have looked like eternity. After their brief encounter with Roy's father, they followed the undulating road through various combinations of mud, slush, snow, and water for the next two miles, past the Ossenkops, the Davidsons, the Addlemans, and the farmstead occupied by James Blunt. As they descended the first steep hill, the horses occasionally slipped while straining against the wagon's forward momentum. At the bottom, with mud rising almost to the hubs and water a foot and a half deep, they crossed a fork of Big Buffalo Creek and struggled up the opposite slope, the hooves of the big colts flailing as they attempted to gain a purchase, young Blunt urging them on in his calm farmer's voice.

On cresting the hill, the convicts sighted two rigs approaching from the north. Their hostage was ordered to keep going, and, within minutes, the self-appointed posse from Springfield was staring down the muzzles of three shotguns. At this point Blunt took over, as he had during the recent encounter with his father, establishing a kind of protocol of the road. These men mean business, he pleaded. They had warned him time and again that if anyone began shooting, he would be the first to die. Some of the dozen or so posse members knew Blunt personally and even those who didn't found him a convincing advocate, the tempting reward notwithstanding. After pausing for a few moments to talk things over, they reversed directions and headed for the nearest crossroad, where they turned east at the Pflug schoolhouse and drove another quarter of a mile before stopping. Once the wagon had passed, they fell in behind at a distance of about two hundred yards, prepared to dog the fugitives to the end. They were not alone. Witnessing the encounter on horseback from a few hundred feet away was George Phelps, Blunt's neighbor, who had armed himself with a Winchester and had been following the wagon ever since it left the farm.

It was going on eleven o'clock, and the phone lines kept humming as neighbor after neighbor called in to report the exact location of the slow-moving wagon. Back in Lincoln, Henry Miller, who was in charge of the telephone in Sheriff Hyers's office at the courthouse, kept track of the fugitives' movements by long-distance operator, then relayed the information to spellbound citizens. A call would be received locating the convicts at a certain point. Minutes later another would follow, stating that they had passed a farmhouse a little farther on. After a wait of several more minutes, yet another "bulletin" told just how far the posse was behind the trio. One of those caught up in the drama formed such a vivid mental image of it that he told a reporter: "It seemed like watching a moving picture."

By this time, Sheriff Chase and Police Chief Briggs had reached Springfield south of Omaha and were itching to go. Giving little thought to the men who had accompanied them, they pulled rank and hired local driver Charley Rose, an employee of Wade's Livery Barn. Together with John Trouton, the deputy state fire warden and onetime South Omaha fire chief, they scrambled into a buggy and headed west on Pflug Road. Meanwhile, Hyers had made the mistake of choosing a four-horse bobsled that was too slow, and he was passed up by several lighter rigs. With everyone else but a few deputies left pretty much to their own devices, it didn't take long for tempers to flare.

About two miles from the Blunt house, some posse members encountered a farmer named A. L. Graham, whom a reporter for the *Lincoln Daily Star* described as "a big German." Their team was too fatigued to go on, so they decided to "commandeer" Graham's fresh draft horses. He didn't seem to grasp what was happening and protested when they set about harnessing the animals. Only when one of the men pulled a gun and pointed it at the dazed immigrant's head did he back off. Other instances of threatening conduct were reported by farmers, who feared that their teams would be "driven into the ground" by men concerned only with the reward.

The farms and faces grew less familiar to Blunt the farther north he drove, but the pattern did not change. Waiting at every crossroad were buggies, sleds, and wagons occupied by tight-lipped men, rifles resting on their knees or pointed into the air in grudging recognition that the convicts had the upper hand, at least for the time being. Back home their wives, left alone with the children, were frantic with fear and clung to the phones; on the streets of every area town groups of men tense with anxiety waited for some word as to the outcome. Gray, his adrenaline pumping, sometimes stood up and eyed his pursuers with contempt, as if daring anyone to make a move. Some nodded or waved to Blunt, but most remained silent, and he returned these sympathetic gestures with a wan smile. Then, after the wagon was safely past, they joined the swelling force, being ever careful to keep well out of shotgun range. By noon, Henry Miller could report that the posse was strung out for the better part of two miles and growing in length almost by the minute. From time to time, Blunt was seen to turn in his seat and look back up the road, doubtless thinking of Carmellette and wondering at the large number of men and horses on his trail.

Ironically, each horseman and conveyance joining the pursuit became just one more impediment to the lawmen. Hemmed in on both sides by barbed-wire fence and snow-filled ditches running knee-high in freezing water, they were effectively trapped in an elongated funnel, with little prospect of breaking out. One reporter described the narrow road as "horse-killing," and for good reason. The more the muddy surface was stirred up the more the struggling animals bogged down, forcing passengers to exit their sinking vehicles at times and proceed on foot, adding greatly to the congestion.

Flashing their badges, Briggs, Chase, and Trouton gradually worked their way toward the head of the line, but they, too, had to get out and walk in places, icy water flowing in over their boot tops. Lagging well behind his fellow officers, a frustrated Hyers decided to abandon the bobsled, whose runners were continually hanging up in the mire. He began leapfrogging ahead, catching a ride with one buggy or carriage until another, faster vehicle came along, enabling him to change again. After an hour or so of this, he finally succeeded in overtaking a buggy containing one of Chase's officers, Deputy Denver Carpenter, and his driver Albert Empey, from which he could see the front of the snaking procession. Suddenly, his pulse began to race as he got his first glimpse of a large farm wagon and the outline of its slender driver just visible against the shuddering horizon. The sheriff was no stranger to the game of poker, and he was as certain now as were the men he was chasing that all the chips were on the table.

———◇——◦●◦——◇———

Laid out in squares with an exquisite precision, each section of Nebraska farmland contained exactly 640 acres bounded by mile-long dirt roads on all four sides. These were directly linked, creating a vast grid system interrupted only by natural barriers such as rivers and by man-made ones in the form of cities and towns. One could literally saddle up and ride for days in any of the cardinal directions without altering course, the landscape dotted by farmsteads settled well within the memory of the elderly, many of whom had come to Nebraska Territory as youngsters in covered wagons. As was true of most roads in the area, the one on which the procession was moving northward had no official name, although parts of it were known locally by the prosperous landowners whose property it skirted: Davidson, Pflug, Dallman, and Mowinkle. To others it was simply the Gretna-Chalco road.

About seven miles from where Blunt was taken hostage, the wagon passed Dallman schoolhouse, whose students and teacher had been evacuated by anxious parents. Patience, always the farmer's greatest asset, now seemed to be paying off as Blunt's young grays were visibly tiring. After covering another mile the buggy carrying Briggs, Chase, and Trouton was less than a hundred yards behind the fugitive wagon and closing in.

At this point, Lloyd Blunt galloped up on horseback and warned the trio not to shoot as long as his brother remained in the driver's seat. Briggs responded by telling him to phone South Omaha and alert his men that the convicts were headed their way. Constable Minurn, of Springfield, would later claim that he, too, cautioned the officers not to fire at the wagon, as an innocent

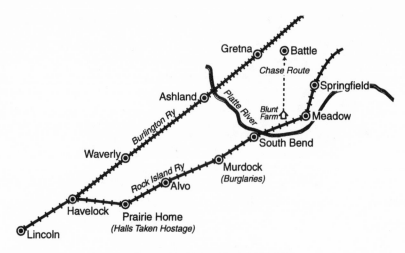

ROUTE OF ESCAPED CONVICTS

Leaving Lincoln late Thursday night, the men stayed in a barn at Havelock for a day and a half and then worked their way northeast through Prairie Home (taking the Halls hostage), Alvo, Murdock (burglarizing two stores), and South Bend. After crossing the Platte, they left the Rock Island tracks and struck north, arriving at the Blunt home Monday morning. After kidnapping Roy Blunt they continued north along the Gretna-Chalco road for some ten miles, until the battle ended their flight.

man was in danger. "To hell with Blunt," was Briggs's alleged reply. "We know our business."

His blood up, Briggs ordered Rose to begin "crowding" the fugitives, but the driver, who feared becoming involved in a running gun battle, had another idea. Instead of urging the team on, he stopped the buggy, handed the reins to Trouton, and jumped to the ground.

Mowinkle schoolhouse came into view, and its forty pupils were still in class as the wagon and posse drew near about one-thirty in the afternoon. Hoping to divert the convicts' attention, Briggs had Trouton stop the buggy while he got down and hailed the men, promising them no harm if they raised their hands and surrendered. Gray responded with a spate of unprintable epithets and turned toward Blunt, who leaned forward and began whipping his sweat-lathered team into a gallop. The wagon had barely passed the schoolhouse when the first shot rang out, the spray of lead pellets stinging the faces of the trailing men and horses.

A loyal George Phelps had followed his neighbor on horseback all the way from the scene of the kidnapping. He was nearing the front of the posse when a man wearing a Stetson and star suddenly leapt from a nearby buggy, rifle in hand. Believing the stranger be a U.S. marshal, Phelps surrendered his horse and climbed into the rig next to Carpenter and Empey. The lawman rode beside them for a few moments, with Phelps shouting at the top of his lungs: "For God's sake, men, don't shoot." He had barely spoken when a member of the posse fired. "It came from the wagon Briggs was in," Phelps later told reporters. The police chief's buggy was a little ahead of the one carrying Phelps, while the stranger who took his mount had left the road and was galloping like fury along the fence line.

Amid shouts and curses, the entire posse surged ahead like a moving churn, turning the road into a slurry that coated men, horses, and vehicles with a rank mixture of mud, dirty water, and fresh manure. Now that he was on horseback, Hyers had his first clear view of the fugitives, and he bolted into the lead as if propelled by the moral force of the universe. The buggy carrying Briggs was close behind, and the police chief stood up and called to the convicts a second time. His efforts were greeted by a double volley of profanity and buckshot from Shorty Gray, who was standing next to Blunt, literally daring Briggs to fire: "Go to Hell, you son of a bitch."

A nearly crazed Lloyd Blunt was still yelling at the officers not to shoot; failing that, he begged them to aim for the horses. Sheriff Chase obliged. Getting out of the buggy, he waded through mud and ditch water until he reached a barbed-wire fence. But when he raised his rifle to shoot one of the animals in the neck his vision was obstructed by a poor angle and the uneven terrain, making it impossible to hit anything but the wagon itself.

Not far beyond Mowinkle school, the road took one of its steepest drops in nine miles, causing the careening wagon to briefly disappear from sight. It was still descending when the first of the pursuers reached the top of the hill, providing them with their best target yet. Someone fired down at the wagon, and the large-caliber bullet passed clean through the heavy end gate concealing the prone convicts and tore into Roy Blunt, just above the left hip. It then exited his groin but not before severing a main artery. The youth clutched his side and cried out, "Oh, my God, I'm shot through the belly." His body began to sway as he lost consciousness and toppled backward into the wagon box, taking the driver's seat with him. A large crimson stain spread rapidly across the floorboards, and, by the time Morley reached Blunt's side, amid the continuing gunfire, the mortally wounded hostage was clearly dying.

From a distance, it appeared to members of the posse that Blunt had attempted to escape from his kidnappers by jumping out of the wagon, and that Gray had made good his promise to shoot him. Meanwhile, a kneeling Dowd grabbed the loose reins, while Morley threw the bloodstained seat overboard, further riling the hostile pursuers. Gray kept up a steady fire from behind the end gate, sometimes crouching and sometimes standing up in the plunging vehicle. When the heavily lathered horses faltered, he would run to the front and beat them with the butt of his shotgun.

Nobody knows how many rounds were fired by the posse, but the shootout was still in progress when word was received by a pacing Henry Miller that the sheriff had worked his way to head of the pack. A spontaneous cheer went up from those crowding Hyers's office when Miller announced the news, but the tension soon returned as the waiting continued. Miller recalled that it was during this time, "when we were listening with bated breath, that someone called up and wanted to know what color the horses were. Some of the most ridiculous inquiries were telephoned to us." Yet he had to admit that "these helped to remove the strain we were under."

While Dowd had his hands full wrestling the team, Morley and Gray showered their pursuers with no.-5 shot, which sounded like hail bouncing off the buggy tops. Several pellets became embedded under the skin of Briggs, Chase, and Trouton, but it was the stung and bleeding horses that were taking most of the punishment. The convicts had revolvers of various calibers, which they brought into play now that the posse was close enough to distinguish the features of individual men.

The headlong chase was into its tenth mile when the convicts and the trailing posses approached the overhead railroad bridge near the August Harriman farm. Gus Hyers reined in his horse next to a telephone pole whose very lines were carrying accounts of the unfolding story. The sheriff dismounted, rested his Winchester against the wooden pillar, and took aim. Seconds later a shot rang out and a standing Gray, who had been defying the odds all morning, keeled over with a bullet in the chest. Morley knelt down and asked him if he was hurt; Gray nodded his head yes but said nothing. Shorty died within a minute or two, blood pouring from his gaping wound and mingling with that still being shed by Blunt.

The sight of Gray's lifeless, blood-soaked body unnerved Dowd, whose hatred of prison was greater even than that of his more hardened accomplices. Morley turned around just in time to see him raise a pistol to his head. But before Dowd could fire he knocked the gun away, shouting: "We might as well fight it out." Morley got off another half a dozen shots with his revolver before looking around again. This time Dowd had the gun pressed firmly against his temple. He told Morley that he was going to die anyway and that it might as well be here: "It's hopeless." Then Dowd pulled the trigger, making him the sixth man to fall within four days.

Morley grabbed Gray's pistol, but it was empty, and he had no stomach for reaching into Shorty's bloody pockets for more shells. He gazed down at the three men, twitching like ashen ghosts of battle, as the jaded horses continued on without a driver. Unnerved and beaten, Morley jumped from the wagon and began staggering through the mud toward the oncoming posse, hands in the air.

Sheriff Chase remembered Morley's first words when the posse reached him: "For God's sake, don't shoot me, the others are all dead." A disbelieving Briggs replied with an oath, calling Morley a liar, then rushed up and gave him a rough frisking while he was being covered by Chase and Trouton. The trembling grays, their massive sides heaving and running with sweat, had come to a halt not far from where the party stood. Once Morley was pronounced clean the lawmen approached the wagon on cat's feet, little prepared for what they were about to see. In the bottom of the vehicle were three men, lying in pools of blood that saturated the straw in the box and oozed between the floorboards, staining the snow beneath a deep crimson like a freshly butchered animal. Gray was on his back with his head against the end gate, dead. Lying incongruously with his body between Gray's legs and his head resting on the convict's stomach was Roy Blunt, one hand raised and gasping for his last breath. Moments later his arm dropped and, as Chase described the scene, "it was all over in this world for him." In the front of the wagon, crouched on hands and knees, with his maimed head pressed against the sideboard, was Dowd, who drew a few more breaths before dying within seconds of Blunt.

Dozens of others had reached the scene by this time, adding to the confusion as things suddenly turned ugly. Morley found himself surrounded by what a reporter from the *Lincoln Daily Star* characterized as "dark looks . . . from intensely drawn faces." The men swore at him and issued violent threats. Someone yelled, "Shoot the son of a bitch," and one of the lawmen twice tried to strike him with the butt of a revolver, at which point J. C. Eikenbary, Hyers's ubiquitous deputy and a veteran of many manhunts, stepped in. He grabbed a cuffed Morley by the collar and leveled his revolver at the most threatening in the crowd: "This man is my prisoner," he shouted. "I'll shoot the first man that shoots him," and he meant it.

The lawmen now faced the grim task of dealing with the corpses. Hyers made the decision to haul the three of them into nearby Gretna so that the coroner of Sarpy County could undertake a postmortem examination of Blunt. Gray and Dowd, along with Morley, would be returned to the penitentiary on a special train.

At that moment Peter Anderson, Blunt's father-in-law, drove up, escorted by Roy's brother Lloyd, both of whom were stunned by the revelation of the young man's death. When they learned of Hyers's plan to take Roy's body into Gretna, Lloyd requested permission to carry his brother home. When Hyers refused, Lloyd slipped two shells into his double-barreled shotgun and trained it on the lawman. Anderson also drew a gun as some 150 men looked on in astonishment. The two demanded that the bodies of the dead murderers be taken from the wagon in which their own dead lay. Hyers complied, and the corpses were dragged out and thrown into the box of a sled like sacks of coal, blood still oozing from the wounds.

Hyers knew better than to argue when emotions were running at fever pitch and so instructed two militiamen to put Morley in a spring wagon. They set out for Gretna, followed by the sled and most of the mud-spattered posse, whose members were anxious to show off their trophies, both dead and alive. Once they were safely gone, Blunt's body, which had suddenly become that of a fallen hero, was shrouded in a horse blanket and gently removed from the wagon whose sickening interior wreaked of gore. It was placed in the vehicle in which a hopeful Peter Anderson had followed the posse ever since midmorning when Carmellette was delivered to his front door in tears. Then began the sad procession back over the same road where only hours before Roy Blunt had assured his father that he would come to no harm.

—————◇—— ◈●◈ ——◇—————

The five-and-a-half-mile ride into Gretna was permeated with a sense of foreboding. Whispered accusations and threats were being made about the killing of young Blunt, and it was not only Morley they were blaming but Hyers, whom many credited with firing the fatal shot. Tempers were further aggravated by the sheriff's statement to the effect that Sarpy County farmers and citizens were cowards, further muddying the waters of who to bless and who to blame for the day's dramatic turn of events. Morley's manacled hands trembled as he crouched down in the wagon bed, his shifting eyes full of fear. Sensing that trouble was brewing, Hyers ordered the driver to push the team as hard as possible.

By the time they reached Gretna, those ill disposed toward the sheriff and his prisoner could be counted in the hundreds, their numbers augmented by farm families who had joined the procession as it passed by. From the spectators who lined the streets on the way to the station came cries of "get a rope" and "lynch him." Never before, according to some of Gretna's older residents, had the town been so thoroughly aroused.

Everyone converged on the depot, where, on the heels of additional threats, Morley was hustled into the baggage room and made to crawl into a locker for his own safety. Several militiamen who had been in the posse were commanded to hold the swelling throng back while others carrying rifles, with bayonets fixed, stationed themselves at both ends of the platform, their muddy puttees and caked boots near eye-level with the crowd.

Word came that the train would be arriving soon. Summoned from his hiding place, his handcuffs loosened by Deputy Eikenbary, the convict rolled a cigarette and answered questions about the escape that were put to him by newsmen in a manner characterized by one reporter as "easy nonchalance."

"Yes," he said, "he was sorry that Blunt was killed." They had hoped to hold him until dark, after which they had planned to let him go. He also paid tribute to Deputy Warden Wagner, who in a rare display of courage drew his pistol after they had him covered. But Morley was contemptuous of turnkey Claus Pahl, whom he laughingly described as throwing his gun down and running rings around himself. Nor did he agree with the generally held belief that cell keeper Thomas Doody was a hero: "Doody came in shooting like a Chinaman. You know how they do with both eyes shut. He fired four wild shots."

To the repeated question as to where he and the others had gotten the guns and nitro, he denied having any knowledge of the source, stating only that Gray had made all the arrangements. In fact, he didn't even know of the escape plan "until it happened." Gray was a silver-tongued devil and at the center of everything. It was Shorty who gunned down the warden and the deputy warden; Shorty who blew the lock; Shorty who came up with the idea of taking hostages. Morning readers would need little imagination to figure out what legal strategy Morley intended to employ at his trial.

Though he didn't know their names, he credited Hyers and Eikenbary, both of whom were by his side, with saving his life after he surrendered. In answer to the question as to who killed Gray, he pointed to Hyers and said he was the man.

Gazing out the window at the unruly crowd, Morley said if he were free and had a revolver, he could scatter them like leaves. If only Shorty had listened to him and had taken refuge in the quarries they could have gotten clean away.

Finally, when asked why he had surrendered unlike the rest, he threw up his cuffed hands and with a slight laugh of resignation replied: "The wagon was all filled with dead men, and my ammunition was about gone. I don't believe in killing myself. When Dowd tried to do it the first time I argued with him."

The Burlington special from Lincoln steamed into Gretna at three o'clock, triggering a bizarre spectacle that left many locals incredulous and produced headlines of condemnation throughout the country. Morley was spirited from the depot onto the train. There, from the rear platform, he was displayed to the assembly at gunpoint. Prompted by Hyers, he told the outraged citizens that he was sorry the young farmer had died, adding: "I think it was a shot from the posse that killed him." This revelation was greeted by a collective groan from the angry hundreds who listened in mortified silence to his every word.

The part about Blunt's shooting was not what Hyers had wanted to hear, and after Morley finished, something inside the sheriff snapped. In a lame attempt to put the best face on what happened next, a reporter for the *Lincoln Daily Star* wrote of the building tension from four sleepless days and nights of manhunting, until, by Monday, the sheriff, who had been working "like the proverbial Trojan," was almost too sick to stand. The bodies of both convicts were dragged onto the train platform and, in turn, held up by Hyers, so that everyone could see: "This is Gray, the man I killed. How do you like him?" he shouted. Then Dowd was grabbed by the hair "like a dead dog," blood streaming from the gaping wound in the side of his head and forming clots on what remained visible of his ashen face: "This is Dowd, how do you like him?"

The next issue of the *Gretna Breeze* branded this danse macabre a "holy show" and questioned the sheriff's sanity: "It is a wonder to us that Morley wasn't given a couple of guns to help out if the unarmed citizens of Gretna had started to shoot." Hyers's statement to the contrary, the men of Sarpy County could have killed all the convicts long before the lawmen from outside showed up if it had not been for the fear of hurting Blunt. "[Those] officers can't brag much of their own bravery," though Hyers "seemed to be the whole show." Still, there was no denying the fact that "readers of Jesse James and other blood and thunder literature could not conceive that a battle like this could ever be fought in western Sarpy County. It rivaled fiction."

Calling Hyers a "Desperate Desmond," the *Springfield Monitor* censured him for "pulling his guns on people all day, and otherwise making himself obnoxious with his own importance. Somebody should have knocked him in the head. Officers of his stripe make anarchy justifiable."

During the return trip to Lincoln the train stopped at some of the same towns along the escape route taken by the fugitives, drawing large numbers of the curious who grew more hospitable to the lawman the closer he got to home. After Hyers spoke again of how he had killed Shorty Gray, Morley was marched to the rear platform at each stop to repeat his coerced statement of contrition, whose exact words went unrecorded. In hopes of adding gravity to the historical moment, and of firming up his claim to the reward, about which Briggs, Chase, Trouton, and a few dozen others would have something to say, Hyers posed for photographs with the prisoner before escorting him back to his seat. As a partial gesture to decency, he kept the limp bodies inside, propping them up in the windows and letting their heads hang out of the car to the repeated cheers of gaping onlookers. John Cahill, the county jailer from Omaha, was on the train and later spoke of how the sheriff had wanted him to help hold the corpses out the window: "I told him I was along to help take care of the bodies and not to make a sideshow out of them."

At four-forty, while the special was making one of two stops at Havelock, the former stamping ground of Sheriff Hyers, the No. 12 Burlington arrived from Lincoln, headed in the opposite direction. The drawn and grief-stricken face of an aged woman suddenly appeared in a passenger-car window. A reporter for the *Lincoln Daily Star* recognized the widowed mother of Warden Delahunty, taking her son's body back to their hometown of Peoria, Illinois, for burial after the morning's funeral. Whether she saw the corpses of the men who had murdered Jim, he did not say, but it was one of those rare and barely credible moments laden with irony.

During the getaway, Gray had made a point of pumping an extra bullet into the body of the defenseless warden, which everyone took as the ultimate expression of his hatred for authority. Although doubtless true, something important seems to have been overlooked by those trying to comprehend his actions, and it involved Deputy Warden Wagner as well. Appearing in the double column of typed names that made up the witness list against Gray at his trial for burglarizing the Citizens Bank at Giltner was that of Charles W. Wagner. Appended to the same list in a bold hand was the name of Wagner's superior, James Delahunty.

Shorty Gray, it seems, had settled an old score, and the posse had returned the favor, in kind, only days later. For a final few minutes the bodies of the two antagonists lay almost side by side, the one absolved in the eyes of the church, the other defiantly unrepentant, and damned: *Liber scriptus proferétur, In quo totum continétur, Unde mundus judicétur.* ("Lo! the book exactly worded / Wherein all hath been recorded / Thence shall judgment be awarded.")

A crowd estimated at two thousand, and growing, awaited the train's arrival in downtown Lincoln. Police kept as much of the throng behind the surrounding fence as possible, but many, including women and children, swarmed the station platform and spilled onto the tracks. Fearing violence or injury, Burlington officials arranged to have the special continue right on through to the penitentiary, where it would be met by members of the state militia.

The engine entered the yards at a crawl, enabling Burlington Chief of Detectives Malone, two other railroad officials, and a reporter to swing aboard before picking up steam for the quick run through the city. When the crowd realized what was happening, many broke and ran ahead to the O Street viaduct in a hopeless attempt to catch a glimpse of Morley, and the bodies, through the windows of the coach. Others clamored aboard the next prison-bound streetcar, which reached Lancaster just as the special pulled in. But, as the disappointed onlookers soon discovered, the authorities were well prepared; heavily armed militiamen had already occupied all the approaches to the stone ramparts and were not letting anyone pass through their ranks.

It was going on five o'clock, and the March twilight was beginning to descend, when the hissing engine creaked to a stop a hundred yards from the main entrance. Straining convicts looking down on the scene from their cell windows on the west side could just make out the figures of several men, whose movements, softened by distance and the fading light, took on the aspect of a tableau vivant against the far skyline. With his cap pulled over his eyes and looking straight ahead, a handcuffed Morley fell in between two squads of Company F, while the sheriff held on to one arm. The stiffening bodies of Gray and Dowd were lifted from the coach floor and placed on bedsprings doubling as makeshift stretchers, each borne by five trusties who then lined up behind the prisoner and his guardsmen. When all was ready, the spectral column set out for the cement walk at the front of the looming structure, marching through ankle-deep water and slush for most of the way.

Without glancing to either side, Morley passed through the same gates that he and his accomplices had promised themselves never to reenter. Now they were all back. He was led straight through the prison and into the chapel. It was turnkey Pahl who opened the big steel door that Morley, Gray, and Dowd had dashed through Thursday afternoon after forcing the turnkey to submit at gunpoint. As the party was waiting for an official to fetch the keys to the door leading into the yard, Dr. Spradling, the prison physician, approached Morley and asked if he was wounded. Morley shook his head no.

Hyers asked him if he was all right, and Morley, speaking for the first time since he had gotten off the train, replied softly: "Just a bit weak in the nerves."

Moments later, they crossed the yard and entered the wing containing the hospital and solitary confinement, where Acting Warden "Rube" Hyers was awaiting their arrival. The father of the sheriff escorted Morley to the main door leading into the hole, which he opened himself. A few steps more and the prisoner was safely inside a steel-and-concrete cell. He was followed in by the sheriff, who unlocked the cuffs as his father held up the prisoner's hands, making it easier to locate the keyhole in the dim light.

Before leaving, the sheriff claimed Morley's heavy canvas jacket and exchanged a clean uniform for the rest of his bloody and mud-stained clothing. As Hyers was about to step through the door, the convict unexpectedly offered his hand to the departing lawman. The sheriff took it in what a reporter who witnessed the gesture described as a "moment of sympathy." Then Morley was left alone in the pitch dark to relive his final days of freedom with the ghosts of his lost companions.

As Sheriff Hyers left the hospital area he was met by the convicts bearing the pallid corpses, which they delivered to Coroner Matthews and Dr. Spradling. Gray was placed on the operating table first and his clothing removed in preparation for the post-mortem and embalming. One of the trusties on duty scowled fiercely at the dead man and exclaimed: "Lay there, you son of a bitch. I wish I had been the man to have got you instead of the officers!"

The bullet from Hyers's rifle, which Morley said had laid his fellow convict low, struck the murderer in the right shoulder about two inches below the joint, severing a number of blood vessels. According to Spradling, it continued on a downward course through Gray's body, either penetrating or passing close enough to the heart to cause almost instantaneous death before lodging in the large bone of the left arm. The resulting hole was big enough to allow the physician to pass his finger through, which meant that the fatal projectile had been fired from a large-caliber gun. This was the only wound found on the body, with the exception of a tiny bruise about six inches below the left knee, where the skin had been slightly cut. Gray, who was rapidly becoming Taylor again in the press, had bled profusely, his stiff clothing saturated with blood and his face and hands covered with gore.

The condition of Dowd's corpse was even more gruesome. The .38-caliber bullet had entered his right temple and exited two inches in back of the left ear. The young man's hair was matted with blood that had flowed over his face and neck, creating a ghoulish effect. Like Gray, he bore no other wounds of any significance.

A careful inventory was taken of the fugitives' clothing and its contents. Gray wore a brown, sheep-lined jacket and was clad in a pair of new blue overalls, beneath which he still wore his blue-gray prison trousers. He also wore a new black-and-white patterned shirt and new underwear. On his feet were a pair of black, gun-metal shoes, brown socks, and overshoes, all courtesy of S. O. Beal's general store in Murdock. A number of .38-caliber bullets were found in his coat pockets, as well as about half a dozen 12-gauge shotgun shells and a new bone-handled jackknife, from Louis Maxwell's hardware store, plus a brown leather drawstring purse stuffed with matches and $1.50 in silver.

Dowd, whom the papers characterized as a "Beau Brummel," possessed an even larger number of articles, including two blue bandanna handkerchiefs and another one of black silk, which he wore about his neck as if dressing for his own funeral. He had an Ingersoll watch and several shoestrings. In one pocket of his new overalls was a comb and a white-handled razor in a black leather case. According to one reporter, "The nature of the man was shown more prominently in one thing than anything else found." The telltale item was a tube of Colgate's toothpaste. Of the eighty-five cents in Dowd's possession, all but a dime was in pennies wrapped neatly in two separate packets. His apparel was much the same as Gray's, save for a pair of patent leather shoes and brown duck trousers fastened with a belt of the same material. Morley's clothes were new as well, including a blue cap and a black sateen shirt like the one worn by Dowd. The men had supplied themselves with tobacco of various kinds. Both Gray and Dowd carried partially consumed plugs of chewing tobacco, and Shorty also had a package of Rice-brand cigarette papers.

Despite the coroner's conscientious attempt to preserve all the evidence, some of it would never reach his hands. Like much else, Morley's claim that he was very nearly out of ammunition at the point when he gave up the fight simply didn't hold water. When frisked after his capture, several shells were taken from his pockets and confiscated by Sheriff Hyers, who was already handing them out to his friends as souvenirs of the chase.

THE DEATH WAGON

So striking was Sam Melick's resemblance to Buffalo Bill Cody that he could have passed for the legendary showman's twin: flowing mane, cascading beard, barrel chest, light-colored Stetson and all. About the only things missing were the trademark buckskins. Nor was the former sheriff of Lancaster County and U.S. marshal, on whom his associates had bestowed the honorary title of "colonel," any slouch when it came to horsemanship and the handling of a gun.

It was Melick's aura of bygone days, in combination with his long experience as a peace officer, that prompted Governor Aldrich to appoint him the new warden of Lancaster penitentiary, in hopes that he would be able to clean up the mess and help stanch the political hemorrhaging. The president of the First National Bank of Gage County gave the beleaguered chief executive some reason for optimism when he wrote: "Please permit me to congratulate the state for securing so competent a man for warden of our prison, as well as to compliment the governor for his ability in securing a five-thousand-dollar man for a two-thousand-dollar position."

Melick, who had been a member of Hyers's haystack posse on the night of the escape, and had served on the coroner's jury that recommended Prince be indicted for murder, had transported some of the most notorious criminals to and from Lincoln, often forgoing the usual handcuffs and chains to keep his charges from the stares of the curious. Among the men he had delivered to Lancaster were Gray and his two accomplices, Forbes and Evans, pending their trial for blowing the bank at Giltner. Melick had even commiserated with Shorty on his "tough luck," to which the thief responded: "Darned tough luck, Mr. Melick." Large crowds had gathered at the stations along the line in hopes of glimpsing the burglars, but Melick ushered them into the Pullman and drew the curtains. The accused repaid his kindness by acting the part of gentleman, which, for Shorty, was something of a stretch.

When the convicts heard of Melick's appointment they were curious to know all about him. High up in gallery C sat an elderly fellow serving a one-to-ten-year sentence for burglary. The colonel had once escorted him all the way from Sacramento, California, to the local county jail, where he was held for several weeks awaiting trial. "Believe me, he was a feeder," the convict recalled, the revelation streaking through the cells like dry lightning and instantly winning the new warden a measure of goodwill. The universal complaint of men who had spent time in custody was that most of their keepers were "stomach robbers," lining their pockets with taxpayers' money by scrimping on the meals they served.

Early Tuesday morning, the day after the chase, Aldrich met with the new warden while their wives walked the prison's corridors accompanied by an armed escort, occasionally pausing to talk with a convict and discussing the nature of Mrs. Melick's duties as the new matron. Both men were in agreement that stricter rules were called for, and Melick had already begun by stationing a guard at the main door. Only those persons carrying a message to officials would be allowed to pass. As it was later reported, "Newspapermen, morbid visitors, and callers upon officials were

**Warden Sam Melick (Used by permission of
The Nebraska State Historical Society)**

held up at the point of a bayonet," and gained entry only if their request was first approved by the warden himself.

Two market baskets of contraband, laden with everything from butcher knives to a full set of homemade burglary tools, provoked further measures. With the governor's assent, Melick put an end to the monthly visitors' day, during which civilians had been allowed to walk about the shops observing the inmates at work. However, as in the past, relatives and friends would have access to the prisoners on Tuesdays and Thursdays, from two to four o'clock in the afternoon. But instead of sitting on opposite sides of a table separated by a metal grille with openings big enough to pass a gun through, the convicts would now be taken to the chapel and seated behind a double wire screen, an armed guard stationed within hearing distance of every word.

By way of compensation, the warden lifted the ban on newspapers containing accounts of the breakout and chase, much to the delight of men desperate for any news from the outside. He would soon abolish almost all restrictions on what they could read as well, believing that even the "yellow journals" had their place, and that the muckrakers were doing a world of good by driving powerful wrongdoers to cover. The policy of writing only a single letter a week was also jettisoned, and from then on inmates would be allowed to receive as many letters as were sent to them.

Of utmost concern to Melick was the poorly trained and underpaid staff. On meeting with the officials and guards, he discovered that three were partially paralyzed, three others were "cripples," several were drunkards, and some were simply too old to be of any service. These men were issued their final checks and dismissed, as was turnkey Claus Pahl, who, at the moment of crisis, had turned the keys over to the desperadoes and then gone into hiding in the cellar.

The firings resulted in a spate of letters to the governor, mostly from strapping young men hoping to become guards. Aldrich answered each one, and asked those who were at least six feet tall and weighed a minimum of 170 pounds to come by his office for a personal interview. Prodded by both the governor and the new warden, the Board of Public Lands and Buildings moved to increase the pay of guards from thirty dollars a month to fifty. As a further incentive the keepers, like the convicts, could look forward to more ample board, for Melick was about to make good his reputation as a heavy feeder. Before his arrival, all prison food had been steamed. After hiring on a new dining room superintendent, who had once been a chef to American officers in the Philippines, he had a large kitchen range installed so that "the boys" could be served fried meat and potatoes. Soon they would be eating supper to the music of the twenty-two-member Melick Concert

Band, equipped with the most up-to-date instruments and decked out in snappy cadet-blue uniforms trimmed with black braid. Never far away and always angling for a handout was Bob, the band's mongrel mascot.

The governor was tight-lipped when he emerged from the morning-long meeting with the warden, not wishing to become the lightning rod for mounting criticism about the way the posse had conducted itself. He expressed his regrets over the tragic fate of the young farmer, but he also asked the public to keep in mind the fact that the lawmen had desperate fugitives to deal with. Later in the day, he wrote a letter of condolence to Blunt's widow, whom the *Gretna Breeze* described as "prostrated." Calling her husband "an innocent victim" and quoting from Scripture, Aldrich concluded: "'The heart knoweth its own bitterness' and the least I can say to you is that I can only commend you to look to Him who is the comforter of the widow and the orphan."

When a reporter asked if he could interview Morley, the governor absolutely refused. Only officials of the penitentiary would have access to the prisoner: "Nothing this convict can say will be of any worth to the public," Aldrich declared; indeed, to give vent to his statements in print "would prove demoralizing." The rule applied to Albert Prince as well, who was in the same tier of cells as Morley. The governor considered it very unlikely that Prince knew the details of the escape and subsequent recapture of his fellow convicts, though he may have guessed that something was up given the "general excitement and disturbed conditions" of the prison.

The rest of the convicts were still locked down, the idleness weighing heavily on the men. They had just been cleared to return to the shops after days of inactivity when heavy runoff from the melting snows flooded the pumps in the water plant, knocking the machinery out of service. Some inmates grew rowdy while

Aldrich and Melick were closeted, but the guards soon quieted them down with the threat of punishment.

All at once the new warden appeared in the cell houses, looking as if he had just stepped out of a dime novel. Accompanied by Chairman Maggi of the State Board of Pardons, Melick passed from cell to cell, shaking hands, cracking jokes, and listening to grievances. Several deplored the gunning down of Warden Delahunty, and wanted his successor to know that they were not in sympathy with the murderers. Melick responded by assuring them that he would treat them on the square and expected the same in return. What they did not know was that the flamboyant warden had personally taken control of the keys to solitary and was thinking of closing the hole for good once its current occupants had been duly tried and sentenced.

———⋄——⋄●⋄——⋄———

Many of Nebraska's citizens wanted to know what punishment Morley could expect to receive, especially if it proved impossible to show that he had fired at least one of the shots that had killed Delahunty or the others. As one lawyer explained it, such proof was not required for a conviction of murder. All three men were guilty of conspiracy to commit murder; therefore, all were equally guilty of the consequences of that conspiracy. Once the legal process was set in motion, the convict would likely hang. Indeed, someone had already ventured the opinion that Morley and Prince would be mounting the gallows steps together.

If Morley was suffering any pangs of conscience he displayed no signs of it. According to an informer on the inside, Morley awoke with a ravenous appetite and disposed of his breakfast in gulps. The only tangible evidence of his ordeal was his frostbite, which had made his feet so sore that he was having difficulty standing, a condition that would persist for several more days. After eating, Morley was visited by the governor and warden, but he talked very little. Later on, prison officials put him through a "sweating," during which he supposedly admitted that Shorty had made good his threat to kill Blunt if the posse followed them. The youth had attempted to leap from the wagon and, in doing so, had knocked the seat loose, causing it to tumble backward into the box. The commotion attracted the attention of the convicts and Gray shot him. But when Warden Melick was asked if this was an accurate rendering of Morley's account, he refused to comment.

As reported in the *Lincoln Daily Star*, Morley was not the only one being interrogated. The Omaha police had arrested Hanford "Curly" Reed, a thirty-two-year-old ex-convict and petty burglar, on the nominal charge of being a suspicious character, and were putting him through what was described as "a severe sweating." The authorities were hopeful of uncovering a plot to smuggle weapons into the prison, and were especially interested in Reed's whereabouts at the time of the escape, for he was known to be an associate of Gray's. Little of what they learned was revealed to the press, but curiosity was piqued when Sheriff Hyers showed up with an arrest warrant for Reed, who had been released from the penitentiary little more than a week before the breakout.

Things got even more interesting after Reed was brought back to Lincoln. One Lillie Owen came forward to claim that the prisoner had bragged to her that he had furnished Shorty Gray with a gun and a quantity of stolen nitroglycerine during Reed's final days as a trusty. Even more stunning was the revelation that he had supplied Albert Prince with the knife used to kill Deputy Warden Davis. The divorced washerwoman further claimed that she knew Gray personally, and that Reed and Prince had spent at least two nights at her Omaha boardinghouse.

It all seemed too good to be true. Deputy County Attorney George E. Hager, who was already prosecuting Prince for the stabbing death of his own father-in-law, was assigned to the case. In questioning the witness, he got Mrs. Owen to admit that she had previously received pay from the Omaha Police Department for her services in catching some bootleggers. She went on to reveal that she had either received pay or was going to receive pay for coming to Lincoln to tell her story, the details of which suggested that she was doing a bit more in her home to make ends meet than taking in laundry and boarders. A red-faced Hager had heard enough and requested that the charges against Reed be dismissed, but not before attempting to salvage his dignity by reasserting his belief that the scoundrel had truly made the incriminating statements, if only as a "wild boast."

At two-thirty on Tuesday afternoon, the mourners of the slain gathered again, this time for the funeral of Charles Wagner. So far, all attempts to locate the daughter and sister of the deputy warden had failed. After the service, the body was driven from the chapel of Castle, Roper & Mathews funeral home to a special vault at nearby Wyuka Cemetery for preservation in the event that any relatives were found. Ironically, officials were having the same difficulty with the corpses of Gray and Dowd, which were laid out on cooling boards on the second floor of the penitentiary hospital. Warden Melick remained optimistic that somebody would come forward to claim them, but if no one did there was plenty of room in the prison cemetery. A man of sentiment as well as of resolve, the warden, having wearied of death, dug up a little rose tree from the prison grounds and replanted it on the still-fresh grave of his old friend, Ed Davis, who would never be without his Sunday flower.

The funeral had just finished when the late edition of the *Lincoln Daily Star* hit the streets. It contained a copy of a letter written by Sheriff Hyers to Carmellette Blunt. The beleaguered lawman had suddenly become the object of blame for the tragedy of the previous day, and he wanted to assure her that: "No one is more grieved over the death of your husband than I. . . . Your father and Mr. Blunt's brother acted nobly." As proof of his goodwill, he had already written to the governor asking him to recommend that the legislature provide compensation to the widow in the amount of $5,000. Still, Hyers had not done what many were urging him to do: relinquish all claims to the reward in favor of Mrs. Blunt. In answer to a reporter's question about what he thought should be done with the money, he stated that Deputy Eikenbary, Sheriff Chase, Police Chief Briggs, and himself "were perhaps the only men who would claim it or who could claim it with any justice." Hyers had obviously read up on the statute, which limited payment to persons making or participating in the capture.

So far as the citizens of Sarpy County were concerned, nothing the sheriff might say or do could alter their belief that he was evil incarnate. In the words of the *Springfield Monitor:* "The fact that an innocent man had been killed apparently aroused no more feeling on the part of the Lancaster County officer than if he had been shooting rabbits." Luckily, Mrs. Blunt's husband had a life-insurance policy in the amount of $3,000, naming her father-in-law as beneficiary.

Public sentiment was also building against John Briggs, the man the *Omaha Bee* had characterized as a "fearless and intrepid officer" during the heat of battle. Within an hour of the chase, the South Omaha police chief had caught a train to Chicago and the Dexter Pavilion to take part in the American Bowling Congress Tournament as captain of the Jetter Gold Tops. All eyes were on the bull of a man who had helped bring down the infamous Shorty Gray. Briggs played his part to the hilt by holding court for the better part of three days, with the press and dozens of others hanging on his every word. He conjectured that it may have been a bullet from his own rifle that had felled the half-mad convict, then surprised everyone by admitting that Roy Blunt may have gotten caught in his sights as well. When Briggs was contacted by his office and learned of Hyers's letter to the governor, he made up his mind to go that damned county sheriff one better. He dashed off a wire promising his share of the reward to Mrs. Blunt, explaining that at no time had his actions been influenced by thoughts of money.

Meanwhile, Sheriff Grant Chase was sticking to his claim that he was entitled to a chunk of the $2,100. In fact, he told several reporters he was almost certain that he was the one who had actually killed Gray, having seen the convict drop just after he unleashed a volley from his rifle. The conduct for which Hyers had been lambasted by the editor of the *Gretna Breeze* somehow seemed befitting of the local lawman: "In all the melee Sheriff Grant Chase was right on the firing line and proved to be an efficient and capable officer. There's a whole lot of difference between him and Hyers."

One element of the mystery as to who had killed Gray was suddenly resolved by an announcement from Coroner Matthews two days after the postmortem. After passing through the convict's body, the fatal bullet had lodged in the upper bone of his left arm, from which it had been recovered. Matthews identified it as one fired from a large-bore rifle, most likely a .44 or .45 Winchester, whose heavy lead slug had burrowed through flesh like a methodical badger, leaving a gaping wound about the size of a quarter. For purposes of comparison, he asked Sheriff Hyers to supply him with the rifle he was carrying the day of the chase along with a sample cartridge. Hyers turned over his 30–40 Winchester, a high-powered weapon favored by Burlington detectives, and one that likely would have driven a bullet right through Gray and anyone else who happened to be in the way. It would have left a much smaller, cleaner wound than the death weapon, something

Matthews was able to prove to his own satisfaction by placing the two bullets side by side. Equally telling was the fact that the slug removed from Gray did not have a metal casing, as had the ones fired by the Lincoln sheriff.

Matthews had held up his announcement as a professional courtesy to R. B. Armstrong, the Sarpy County coroner, with whom he had been in regular contact ever since the shootings. On Tuesday afternoon, accompanied by a six-member jury that included a physician, a newspaper editor, a salesman, and a retired farmer, Armstrong set out from Springfield for the James and Effie Blunt farm to inspect the body of their son. The examination confirmed much of what had been reported all along: The only wound was the result of a single bullet that had entered the body at a point about one and one-half inches below the top of the left hipbone, ranging downward and to the right and emerging from the groin. Neither the body nor the darkly stained clothing contained any evidence of powder marks that would have indicated Roy Blunt was shot at close range by Gray, as Morley had allegedly maintained during his recent interrogation. Furthermore, the wounds at both the entrance and exit points were large and jagged, making for a compelling argument that they had been caused by a soft-nosed bullet fired from the same rifle used to dispatch Gray.

Owing to the terrible condition of the roads, which made the calling of witnesses next to impossible, Armstrong decided to suspend the inquest until Friday, March twenty-ninth, but not before issuing subpoenas to Hyers, Chase, and Briggs, among other eyewitnesses to the fray. Upon returning to Springfield, he phoned Matthews to tell him the results of the postmortem. It was only then that the Lancaster County coroner summoned newspapermen to his office, where he made a simple declaration: "There is no question in [my] mind that Sheriff Hyers did not kill 'Shorty'

Gray nor did a bullet from his Winchester end the life of the young farmer." What was more, neither of the fatal shots appeared to have been fired by Sheriff Chase, who had been using a borrowed .25-caliber rifle, which makes a rather small-sized wound. This left only Chief Briggs and his .45 Winchester, famous for inflicting the kind of gaping wound that had taken the lives of both men.

Long overdue for some good news, Hyers first met with Governor Aldrich and then came before reporters to announce that he was requesting that any reward money due him should be given to the widow. "I am glad," he said, "to hear that the bullet that killed Blunt was much larger than the gun I was using. While I tried to kill Gray, the fact that I was very much afraid of hitting Blunt may have made my aim poor." This was quite a turnaround for a man who only forty-eight hours earlier had triumphantly brandished Gray's corpse like a victorious gladiator. When Briggs read Hyers's comments he made no effort to conceal his disdain: "For unadulterated untruth and the coining of the same," he told a reporter, "I will have to admit that I must take my hat off to Mr. Hyers. He is the limit."

Responding to Matthews's revelation and the unofficial comments of some members of the coroner's jury, residents of Sarpy County hastily called a mass meeting in Springfield that same night. Feelings were running high and sparked an outpouring of emotions, after which more than one hundred farmers and townsmen gave their unanimous approval to a statement prepared by five local leaders condemning the law officers for the needless death of Roy Blunt. At least two of the farmers in attendance repeated their claims that Chief Briggs had sworn at those who begged him not to endanger the youth, his alleged words echoing through the charged meeting hall like the fatal rifle shot: "To hell with them, we know our business." Characterizing the killing as "the most dastardly and cowardly act ever perpetrated in this part of the state" and as "lawlessness committed in the name of the law," the assembly voted to forward the document to Governor Aldrich as a way of underscoring their outrage. The following afternoon, the Blunts and the Andersons were seen consulting with a prominent Springfield attorney, sparking rumors that they were planning to take legal action.

———— ◦●◦ ◦ ————

Long before the hour of the funeral service, mourners began to congregate in the little, white-frame church on a windswept knoll overlooking Plattford Township. They came singly, and by households, over ice-covered roads in wagons, bobsleds, cutters, and buggies from Gretna, Springfield, Louisville, Chalco, and dozens of farms in between. While waiting patiently, they spoke in hushed tones that masked a deep-seated anger over the death of their young neighbor, whom the newspapers were portraying as both a martyr and a hero. The obituary in the *Springfield Monitor* extolled a Roy Blunt "splendidly equipped physically, intellectually, and morally for success in his chosen sphere."

By eleven o'clock every available space in Plattford Church was occupied, the women filling the chairs and the men lining the walls. Some of the late arrivals among the crowd of 250 were forced to stand outside in the biting March cold, making it easy to forget that this was the first day of spring. The white casket, obscured by wreaths and other floral offerings, was carried by sleigh from the parents' home, only a mile distant, and placed in front of the tiny altar so that "all might steal a farewell glance at the face of the dead farmer." Accompanying the body were the father and mother and their six surviving sons. The eighteen-year-old widow, draped in black like her female relatives, rode with her parents and the Reverend A. J. Warne, the Methodist minister from Springfield, who was in charge of Plattford parish.

For his text Warne chose John 11: 23, on the illness and death of Lazarus: "Jesus saith unto her, 'Thy brother shall rise again.'" Yet much like those who had gathered to pay their respects, Warne seemed less concerned with scripture and the obsequies than with the conduct that had led up to this dreadful moment. "Criminals must be captured for the sake of society," he intoned. "Nevertheless in the light of all the evidence, all the facts bearing on this sad case, it seems to us everything desired could have been accomplished if good judgment, patience, and profound regard for the safety of an innocent party had been sufficiently present in the minds of those who have flaunted their sense of duty, courage, and heroism in statements to the press relative to this case. This tragedy," he continued, "has led multitudes to believe that either our laws or our officers need changing. Some are asking does office delegate the right to commit crime, and before some tribunal this question for Nebraska should with authority be answered."

These were hardly words from which the grieving could take solace, and Carmellette sobbed throughout the brief service. When it was over, the flower-laden casket was carried back out to the small sleigh, while the widow was assisted from the church by her father and brother. The mourners untied their teams and, braving a biting north wind, dropped in behind the improvised hearse and began the difficult drive to Springfield Cemetery, six miles away, with Roy's faithful dog trailing his master's coffin.

When the cortege reached Springfield its citizens stood in respectful silence on the streets, or joined the scores of vehicles on the last mile to the sloping burial grounds that overlooked the town. After the Reverend Warne offered a final prayer, the longest funeral procession in local memory began to disperse. For the next few hours Springfield's main street was filled with friends of the Blunts and the Andersons, who, having nothing more pressing to do, lingered to discuss the case and what to expect when the coroner's jury reconvened to complete its inquest, something no one intended to miss.

It was a week to the day since the escape. Back in Lincoln, at the very hour of Blunt's funeral, Dr. Spradling visited Morley to attend to his frostbitten heels. When the physician entered the cell he was made nauseous by the foul air and informed the warden's office of the need to alleviate the stench. Melick ordered that the doors to the cells of both Prince and Morley be opened for a half hour, enabling them to converse for the first time since Morley's return, albeit from inside their respective chambers.

"How are you feelin'?" Prince called out.

"Oh, pretty good," Morley replied, although he admitted to being "a little shaky." He had told Spradling the same thing, stating that his nerves were starting to work on him again, the sight of the dead bodies a recurring fixture of his dreams.

Prince then asked about the escape and listened intently while Morley recounted the details in a loud voice, including both the gunfight and the capture. The time passed quickly; almost before they knew it the guards had stepped forward and locked their cell doors, abruptly ending the conversation.

That afternoon a man described in the *Lincoln Daily Star* as a "promoter" gained entry to the penitentiary, where he revealed his plans to Major Antles of the state militia. The animated stranger wanted to make a moving picture of the escape and sought permission to use the various rooms, corridors, and grounds as sets. Furthermore, he hoped to stage a mock shootout "in imitation of that of last Thursday, so as to obtain lifelike pictures."

Antles, who was known for his sense of humor and love of practical jokes, told the promoter that he lacked to the authority to grant such permission, but assured him that he could get it by speaking to Detective Schmidt of the Lincoln Police Department.

"He will say 'no' at first," Antles counseled the fellow in mock seriousness, "but you insist. Whatever Schmidt may say, you keep on insisting. You'll get the permission."

———◇———◇●◇———◇———

On the Tuesday before the inquest, Governor Aldrich hosted what may have been the most difficult meeting of his political career. The Andersons, their widowed daughter Carmellette, her sister, Blunt's father James, his brother Lloyd, and Professor Moltzer, a Lincoln musician, from whom Miss Anderson was taking music lessons, all gathered in the chief executive's private office to discuss what was likely to happen next. The meeting lasted an hour, and when the parties came out to face reporters Peter Anderson admitted that the relatives were anxious to have the responsibility for the killing of his son-in-law "definitely fixed." He was about to say more when his unmarried daughter took him by the arm and cautioned him not to talk, supposedly at the request of the governor. Aldrich himself would say only that the families had asked him to take part in the inquest, to which he had responded that the law contained no provision for it. "I am not an examining magistrate or a coroner's jury and cannot assume their prerogatives," he said. "However, I will cheerfully lend any assistance I can, within the scope of a legal inquiry, to bring out the truth."

As painful as their visit with the governor had been, the most traumatic part of the day, by far, still lay ahead for the relatives. They were driven out to the penitentiary, where Morley was awaiting their arrival after having agreed to meet face-to-face with the widow and parents. Before walking him to the deputy warden's office in the chapel, Warden Melick asked the convict if he was still willing to go through with it. Morley nodded and, treading gingerly on sore feet, he was escorted to the small room where Wagner had gone for his gun—and paid dearly for it—two weeks earlier. Morley sat down before the families, drew a deep breath, and calmly proceeded to answer all the questions put to him.

To begin with, Morley was of the opinion that Mrs. Blunt's husband had been far more concerned for her safety than for his own, and he seemed unable to comprehend that she had run away to warn the neighbors of the convicts' presence, a revelation that must have stung the widow like a blow on a bruise. Later on, during the pursuit, Blunt gave no signs of fearing the posse, believing that he would be safe as long as he remained in clear view atop the wagon. Otherwise, Morley conjectured, he could have climbed down onto the double tree and seated himself on the tongue.

As to the person who had fired the shot that killed Roy Blunt, the story that Morley told previously—the one that singled out Gray as the culprit (whether true or false)—was not the one that he told his horrified, but rapt, listeners. Although Morley could not be absolutely certain, he fingered the man sitting next to the driver of the carriage that had been nearest the fleeing wagon, and that would have been the big policeman, Chief Briggs. Yet Morley was a walking contradiction with few equals; for all anyone knew, he was simply telling the aggrieved what they wanted to hear now that Briggs had been publicly identified as the shooter. The main thing on Morley's mind was shifting his share of the blame.

On the eve of the inquest, James Blunt issued a statement in which he claimed to have interviewed every eyewitness to the battle, declaring that "no stone would be left unturned to learn the facts of the killing." Any citizen who believed that the families were interested in making money on Roy's death was badly misinformed: "We have no thought of damages, but we want the man. I want to make sure who murdered my boy."

The first theatrical performances in the Springfield Opera House had taken place on the nights of February 19 and 20, 1892. The long-forgotten melodrama, a western entitled *Border Land,* was full of blood and thunder, having to do with cattle rustling, six-shooters, and false identities. The house was filled to capacity both evenings, and the play was pronounced a great success. Still, there were those who thought it a sin to attend the theater unless the show was free, in which case they arrived early in the scramble for the best seats.

No one was about to miss the show scheduled for March 29, 1912, the price of a ticket ranging from journalistic curiosity, to pathos tinged with anger. For this time the drama, which also contained many elements of a western—desperadoes, shootouts, kidnapping, horse thievery, and posses—was for real and held the promise of being the most riveting the locals had ever seen. Almost at the break of day farmers attired in their Sunday best began lining up their teams at the hitching rack in front of the general store, undeterred by country roads hub-deep in soft mud and spring freshets. The hotels and boardinghouses had been booked for days, as were seats on the incoming trains whose late arrival held up the ten o'clock proceedings before which nearly fifty witnesses had been summoned to testify. Newspapers too far away to send reporters were relying on the Postal Cable and Western Union companies, both of which strung wires from outside poles through windows and onto the stage, where expert telegraphers concealed in the wings were prepared to click out the most important testimony.

The long benches of the two-story clapboard building were quickly filled to capacity, requiring the addition of dozens of chairs and stools. Late arrivals flooded the stage, straddled railings, and stood cheek by jowl in the aisles. Parents hoisted their wide-eyed youngsters onto the windowsills, from which they stared down

**Old Hickory (Used by permission of
The Sarpy County Historical Museum)**

quizzically on the animated throng like unfledged birds. When the
structure could hold no more than the five hundred already inside,
officials were forced to close the large double doors, turning away
additional hundreds who left muttering under their breath. The
disappointed gathered outside the hall's main entrance, which was
the scene of a heart-wrenching spectacle. The death wagon, its
giant wheels caked with mud, and its spring seat back in place,
stood next to a walk from which the curious stared into the dark-
stained box and poked fingers through a hole in the end gate, created, it was believed, by the same bullet that had felled Blunt.

For days, rumors had been circulating that there might be
trouble, which the impassioned gathering of citizens a week earlier had done nothing to dispel. Taking no chances, county officials swore in extra deputy town marshals, dividing them between
the opera house and the streets. Chief Briggs arrived with a body-
guard of no less than nineteen burly policemen, described by one
reporter as "a formidable array." Wearing firearms, they stared

down the none-too-friendly locals and seated themselves in the center of the auditorium, ringing the star witness. County Attorney William Jamieson conferred with officials about the advisability of collecting weapons when it became clear that many citizens were also packing guns. But after a lengthy debate it was decided not to do so for fear of antagonizing the already hostile crowd.

The coroner's jury was seated in the so-called "baldheaded row." Directly facing them was a table at which were arrayed the coroner and the county attorney, as well as the lawyers representing the Blunts, the Andersons, Police Chief Briggs, and Sheriffs Hyers and Chase. The bereaved families filed in slowly and took seats nearest the witness chair, the women in black taffeta and heavily veiled, the men in dark suits and bow ties. Seated with them was the Reverend Warne. Together on the stage were a "young army" of newspapermen and two flashlight photographers.

After checking with the stenographer and telegraph operators to make certain that all was in readiness, Coroner Robert Armstrong called the inquest to order half an hour late. The coroner himself was the first to take the stand for questioning by County Attorney Jamieson. After Armstrong illustrated the nature of the fatal wound, Jamieson asked that Blunt's clothing be labeled exhibit one. Armstrong pointed to the absence of powder marks on the trousers and shirttail as proof that the bullet had not been fired at close range by one of the fugitives, whose revolvers included a .38 and a .32 but no .44s, as had been described to reporters by farmer Elmer Hall. At this point both Carmellette Blunt and her father-in-law broke down, burying their faces in their hands. The coroner finished by discussing the nature of the wound, and the fact that it had been caused by either a .45 Winchester, or a weapon similar to it.

The moment all had been waiting for came when Armstrong stepped down and the name of John Briggs was called. A rising

murmur passed like a wave through the crowd as the brawny officer approached the witness chair and sat down, meeting the angry
glare of the audience with a look of defiance. The purported
killer of her husband was seated so close to the wraithlike Carmellette that she could have easily reached out and touched a hand to
his massive shoulder. Her overwrought mother suddenly lost control, exclaiming, "You wretch!" Then Mrs. Anderson bowed her
head and remained silent throughout the intense questioning
while her daughter stared off into space.

Many in attendance had just been alerted to Briggs's remarks
in the morning edition of the *Omaha World Herald* and didn't
much care for the officer's sarcasm: "I have been taught a lesson,"
he growled. "The next time there are any desperate men to be
rounded up the thing to do will be to send out some preachers
and the rest of these wise people who know all about how to effect
a capture without risk or accident, after everything is all over. All

Police Chief John Briggs (Used by permission of
The Sarpy County Historical Museum)

of this prejudice has been stirred up by newspapers and a few parties who were many miles away when the bullets were flying." Still, he was feeling the pressure of the impending legal proceedings and had decided to retreat from his earlier statement that he might have killed both Blunt and Taylor: "I do not believe that I killed Roy Blunt, or that such will be the finding of the inquest. I know the position I took when shooting and the angle a bullet takes. There were plenty of men using soft-nosed bullets besides me for I was asked for ammunition."

Speaking in a husky voice, Briggs recounted the chase in detail, telling of how as many as a dozen rigs on the Gretna-Chalco road had turned out to let him take the lead. He first saw the outlaw trio clearly as they were nearing the second schoolhouse, and he had pushed hard to prevent them from reining in and taking the children hostage. "There were fifteen or sixteen shots fired before I shot once," he declared.

"How many times did you fire altogether?" Jamieson asked.

"About fifteen," replied the witness.

Briggs then told of calling upon the men to surrender at least half a dozen times. "They kept right on going, and all there was to do was to shoot. When the wagon stopped, I got right out and went ahead. I was after them, and nothing could have stopped me except a bullet. I was using two guns, both high-powered rifles of .44 and .45 caliber." He remembered Morley stepping up to him and asking for mercy. "I thought it might be a trick or something and believed the other two were alive in the wagon. Morley told me both were dead. I went up to the wagon, but I told Morley he wouldn't live a second if it was a trick."

Next came the question everyone had been anticipating for the past two weeks. Had Briggs ever shouted, "To hell with Blunt, we are after those men?"

"Where did you get that?" he snapped.

"I asked you if you made such a statement," his interrogator persisted.

"I certainly did not," was the emphatic reply.

The witness went on to explain that Blunt's name had never been mentioned by any of the buggy's three occupants during the flight. Neither had he promised Lloyd Blunt to refrain from shooting until his brother was safe. "I simply told him I'd be careful."

The attorney persisted: "Did you realize that an innocent man was in the wagon and that his life was in danger every time you fired?"

"No more than my own."

"Didn't you think that you might be taking the life of an innocent man?"

"I didn't think anything about it," Briggs calmly responded, shocking the audience with his candor, yet gaining a measure of grudging respect for not giving an inch. "My life was as much in danger as was Blunt's. I was the center of the attack and after I was started I was bound to fight until dead."

Having answered all the questions put to him, the witness was dismissed at eleven forty-five a.m., after spending a little over an hour on the stand.

Sarpy County's own Sheriff Chase was the third person to be called, and he picked up the story at the point where Trouton had taken over the reins from Rose, who had gotten out of the buggy, fearing for his safety. Chase was in the backseat as they were approaching Mowinkle school. "As we drew nearer the men I stood up and called to the convicts. I told them who I was, that I would stand between them and the rest of the posse coming on behind." In a twist to the story not previously told, Chase spoke of the fugitives' treachery. "All three of them stood up in the wagon with their hands up and Briggs said, 'drive on, Trouton, they've quit.' Trouton lashed the horses . . . and as we drew closer to them the

Inquest into the death of Roy Blunt, Springfield Opera House, March 1912. Carmellette Blunt is the woman in the lower right-hand corner. (Used by permission of The Sarpy County Historical Museum)

convicts yelled, 'Come on, you sons of bitches, come on,' and opened fire on us." The lead was so thick that he and Briggs were forced to crouch down in the buggy. Contradicting his previous statement to the press, the sheriff claimed not to have fired his borrowed rifle because the sights had gotten muddy when he had tried to bring down one of Blunt's horses. His enthusiasm was further dampened after being struck in the head by a spent bullet when he stepped out to take aim. Like Briggs, he recalled promising Lloyd Blunt that he would be careful, but he denied the charge that anyone had ever cursed his brother or, for that matter, any other member of the posse.

C. A. Peterson, who farmed along the Gretna-Chalco road south of Mowinkle school, took issue with the law officers' testimony. It was not the convicts but those chasing them in the buggy who had fired the first shot, the one that struck Roy Blunt. He saw a second man fall after several more shots were fired. The farmer was also singled out by the newspapers for his witty asides to questions put to him by the lawyers representing Briggs and Chase; these prompted several outbursts of laughter, bringing the first smile in days to the lips of Blunt's widow.

Every twenty minutes or so the photographers would make "an awful disturbance." The claustrophobic audience would have just settled down after one flash of brilliantly colored light and acrid smoke when—"sputter whooey"—everyone would close their eyes, the witness would falter, and the lawyer doing the questioning would utter a not-too-muffled expletive.

Sparks also flew among the lawyers, and the crowd relished the dramatics. During one such clash between Coroner Armstrong and the Blunts' Springfield attorney, William R. Patrick, the latter proved himself the more adept at repartee, eliciting a "lusty cheer" from the spectators, in which the women took "a prominent part." Mostly, though, the audience remained orderly, intent on catching every word of testimony.

Another twenty witnesses took the stand during the afternoon session, all of whom had participated in the chase. Their testimony varied as to whether it was the convicts or the posse that had fired first and "left the question of gravity in doubt." Several swore that Briggs and those with him had been told that the convicts carried only shotguns and pistols, but when Lloyd Blunt was called to the witness chair late in the day, he told of warning Briggs and Chase that the men were armed with rifles as well. Tall, gaunt, with an angular face and protruding ears, Lloyd helped clear the air when he was asked about the supposed cursing incident. Sheriff Chase, not Chief Briggs, had yelled "to hell with them," Lloyd explained, but he took it as a reference to the convicts, and one that had nothing to do with his brother.

Conspicuously absent from the proceedings was the much reviled Gus Hyers, who was enjoying a measure of vindication now that the deaths were believed to be the handiwork of Briggs. According to the *Lincoln Daily Star*, the sheriff was not called to appear at the inquest, although he had notified Coroner Armstrong that he would be at home and available, if needed. But the fact that he was represented by counsel, and that buggy driver John Trouton had not put in an appearance either, suggests that the next day's edition of the paper contained a more accurate report of what transpired Both men were summoned but neither had honored his subpoena. The matter was put to the jury, which decided to do nothing for the moment, despite all the evidence of their active participation in the chase. There were other ways of dealing with the absentees should it come to that.

When the inquest had begun, it was thought that at least two days would be needed to hear all the evidence. But because only half the witnesses were called, testimony was completed by six-thirty Friday evening, leaving the jury to begin its deliberations. Before the six men filed out, Armstrong read aloud a three-page letter he had just received from Governor Aldrich, whose large photograph overlooked the proceedings from the wall above Carmellette Blunt. Aldrich had never meant for this hastily drafted, and convoluted, document to be made public, having written it in hopes of persuading local officials to conduct the inquest behind closed doors, both in the interest of public safety, and in fairness to the many parties involved. It was a position that Armstrong himself had argued for that very morning, but to no avail. Though the letter's contents were now moot, the coroner regarded it as something of a personal vindication, little anticipating the depth of feeling he was about to arouse.

"I have been informed," Aldrich wrote, like a father scolding a wayward son, "that it is the purpose . . . to hold this inquest in the opera house so that the crowds may be accommodated. Gentlemen, this is a serious and grievous mistake. You start in by [making] . . . this proceeding a form of . . . entertainment. It mars the solemnity and dignity of the occasion. Entertainment or satisfaction of curiosity seekers is not the aim or object in this matter. . . . The yellow newspapers of the country would seize upon it as something to color up in glaring headlines." As to the lawmen whose conduct had come under suspicion: "Remember . . . that these officials were in pursuit of desperate men, mere human devils, as it were, and that in the pursuit and capture of these desperados, the officers took their own lives in their hands and courageously performed their duty, and if what may seem to be an unnecessary taking of life occurred, remember that it was . . . accidental." Above all, "two wrongs never make a right and . . . two extremes never solve a problem. It will avail no one anything to proceed with undue haste, or arrive at a conclusion based upon prejudice, passion, and feeling."

A red flag had been unfurled. The way the residents of Sarpy County saw it, the governor had as good as called them yokels incapable of conducting a dignified inquiry or applying the law in an evenhanded manner. His unapologetic comments on the killings sounded like a legal brief for Briggs and Hyers, the one self-righteous and stubborn, the other so disdainful of his fellow citizens that he hadn't even bothered to show up, sending a slick, big-city lawyer in his place. And what about poor Roy Blunt lying cold in the ground only a mile away, his grieving dog refusing to leave the grave? Not a word about the victim and his little widow, remembered by everyone as high school sweethearts of more innocent days. Cries of outrage echoed through the opera house, half barn and half church, nearly forcing Armstrong from the stage. It was the jury—not the sanctimonious Aldrich or his toady the coroner—who would make the decisions around here, and it was well past the time to get on with the business at hand.

It became a battle of attrition as the clock slowly ticked away the hours. Believing that the jury was hopelessly deadlocked, many reluctantly surrendered their hard-won seats, collected their sleeping children, and headed home through the spring darkness, after having asked those staying behind to telephone the moment there was any news. It was half past midnight when the exhausted jury members filed back in with their verdict. They had deliberated for six hours. The groggy telegraphers, who had long since spread the contents of the governor's private letter across the land in time for it to make next morning's front page, started to attention.

"Roy Blunt," the verdict read, "came to his death on the 18th day of March, 1912, from the effects of a gunshot wound inflicted by a .44 or .45 caliber rifle ball fired from a rifle in the hands of Chief of Police John Briggs of South Omaha. We also find that Sheriff Hyers of Lancaster County and John C. Trouton of South Omaha were accessories and we recommend that they all be held to the district court." For the Sarpy County sheriff, who was one of their own, the judgment was less harsh, and not easy to square with the treatment of Trouton, who had his hands full driving the buggy and never fired a shot: "We further find . . . that Sheriff Grant Chase failed to exercise due authority in restraining the members of the posse from firing into the wagon occupied by the convicts and Roy Blunt, and that he is deserving of great censure in not exercising such authority." Nobody could say for certain what the three would be charged with, but the attorneys present pretty much agreed on manslaughter.

Whether the reading of Governor Aldrich's letter influenced the jury's deliberations was never revealed, but there is good reason to suspect that it had. So upset were the jurors, all but one of whom were between the ages of thirty and forty, that they composed a supplemental document, separate from the verdict, containing a scathing denunciation of the chief executive: "The members of the coroner's jury . . . resent the interference of the governor of Nebraska in sending a letter to the coroner and citizens attending the inquest, indicating their inability and lack of intelligence in handling a matter of this serious character." It was the governor himself who was guilty of the very bias he ascribed to the jury: "His letter was evidently written with a view to influencing the jury, despite his assertion that they should 'let no excitement or prejudice in any way influence the jury in its investigation.' We consider the aspersions contained in the governor's letter as a stain on the record of a peace-loving and law-observing community."

The moment of catharsis was over, and the last of the bone-weary spectators made their way out of the opera house into the chill night. As they passed the looming silhouette of Old Hickory, someone with a philosophical bent was overheard telling a friend that he figured all this for the last posse, what with the coming of the telephone, the automobile, and everything else.

JUDGMENT DAYS

The first of the early birds were just arriving in Springfield for the inquest when convict Tom Davis, a "half-breed Indian," brought an abrupt end to Sam Melick's twelve peaceful days as warden of Lancaster. At six forty-five a.m., the ringing of the dining room gong signaled that breakfast was over. As the men rose to their feet and formed lines, Davis grabbed Negro convict John Strong from behind by the chin and plunged a four-inch knife, hilt-deep, into Strong's throat, whispering something into his ear. The attacker then drew the razor-sharp blade in an arc, severing the victim's windpipe and showering those nearby with the blood from a spurting artery.

The wound had the unintended effect of a crude tracheotomy, enabling Strong to continue breathing while keeping his feet. He leapt onto a row of tables, scattering plates and utensils as he ran toward the main aisle and the door leading back into the cell house. Frank Dunfee, one of the ten or so kitchen guards that Melick had stationed around the room, thought a fight had broken out and allowed Strong to pass through the door. Staggering from shock and a loss of blood, he made it up the first set of stairs and into the cell room where some trusties, who had begun their regular morning cleaning, caught him before he could fall.

When officials retraced his blood-spattered trail later in the morning they were amazed to find that the running dead man had covered a good sixty feet.

Strong was carried to the prison hospital, where Dr. Walsh, the assistant surgeon, administered artificial respiration with the help of Major Antles. Back in the dining room, Davis, who had dropped his hands to his sides after the attack, was seized by one of the guards and disarmed before being removed from the line and held while the rest of the convicts calmly filed out. Fifteen minutes later, with Walsh and Antles at his side, Strong's raspy breathing abruptly ceased, and he was pronounced dead shortly after seven o'clock.

Afterward, Davis was brought up to Antles's office for questioning. Serving a five-year sentence for forgery, he had no history of violence during the two years he had already spent in Lancaster. He told the major that Strong had threatened his life on several occasions, and there was no way of avoiding him given the fact that they occupied adjoining cells and worked in the same shop: "I beat him to it," he calmly stated, words similar to those he had whispered into Strong's ear.

Davis's claim of self-defense was backed up by a series of violent confrontations involving the twenty-six-year-old Strong, who, together with his older half brother, Jim, had been sentenced to life in prison for a murder they had committed in 1906. The two had been working on a gang digging an irrigation ditch in Sioux County when they got into an argument with the boss. One morning they followed him to the company store and began shooting wildly into the crowd of shoppers, failing to hit their nemesis, but killing an innocent bystander named Orth Crocker, and wounding three others in what was considered a "particularly cold-blooded crime."

A search of Strong's cell yielded a knife with a double-edged blade described as "a highly developed specimen of prison manufacture," one equally useful for slashing or stabbing. Even though every cell had been searched less than two weeks earlier by orders of General Phelps, it was theorized that both the weapon used by Davis, and the one hidden by Strong, had been overlooked, since it would have been difficult to make them in so short a time. The administration also produced records showing that Strong had been one of the most frequent visitors to solitary, mostly for half a dozen knife attacks on his fellow inmates. In another instance, he had tried to brain a convict named Naylor with a hammer for snitching on him. It seems that Strong had told Naylor of his plan to stab Guard Crawford Eikenbary, who had since gone to work for Sheriff Hyers at the county jail. Naylor, in turn, alerted prison officials, for which Strong, vowing revenge, was given another long stint in the hole. On learning of the convict's violent end, Eikenbary sided with the assassin: "Strong was one of the worst prisoners we had there in my day. . . . I can take you to the penitentiary and point out to you the faces of a dozen or more convicts which are marked with knife scars received in affrays with other convicts. Strong has been in several of these."

Warden Melick's short-lived hope of abolishing solitary confinement had been whittled down to a chimera. For the third time in just forty-eight days, a third convict involved in a penitentiary killing was marched to one of the six airless cells and committed to almost perpetual darkness. In a story bearing the sensational headline MURDERERS' ROW, the *Lincoln Daily Star* told of how Prince, Morley, and now Davis were sequestered side by side in what amounted to steel-lined coffins, each awaiting judgment by a higher power.

Clad in prison gray, an old slouch hat, and shielded from a raw March wind by a heavy overcoat, Morley climbed stiffly into the backseat of a buggy for the drive to the courthouse. Major Antles took the seat next to him, and once they were settled in a guard handcuffed the men together. Occupying the seat beside the driver was Warden Melick, who gave the signal to proceed. A newsman, present when Albert Prince had been taken downtown for arraignment three weeks earlier, noted that only two guards accompanied Morley while the Negro had an escort of Sheriff Hyers, Deputy Eikenbary, and two penitentiary guards.

Seated in the chair normally occupied by a prospective bridegroom applying for a marriage license, Morley listened while Sheriff Hyers read aloud the double warrant for his arrest and informed him that he was a prisoner of Lancaster County. Then, with handcuffs removed, he was escorted from the clerk of court's office into the courtroom to face Judge Rissler.

Few spectators had gathered for the arraignment, which was kept secret to avoid the circuslike atmosphere that had attended Prince's first two court appearances. Bent slightly forward, his gaunt face unshaven and covered with heavy stubble, Morley listened carefully to the reading of the first indictment, charging him with having aided and abetted Charles Taylor, alias Shorty Gray, in the murder of usher Ernest G. Heilman. The judge's voice began to drop as he waded through the complicated legal phraseology, and Morley's attention strayed. He stared at a copy of the state statutes on the desk before him, read and reread the title on both front and back, contemplated the inkwell and other fixtures within reach, and only brought his wandering gaze back to attention when asked how he wished to plead.

"Not guilty," he promptly replied in a clear voice.

"About the preliminary hearing?" Rissler asked.

"Oh, I'll let that go, if it's all right."

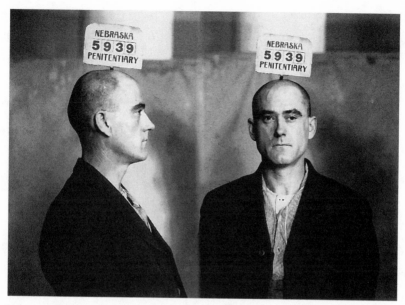

Charles Morley with his second convict number on the eve of his murder trial, 1912 (Used by permission of The Nebraska State Historical Society)

"You'll waive it?"

"Yes."

During the reading of the second indictment, charging him with shooting Warden James Delahunty with a pistol, the prisoner remained more attentive. After he pled not guilty again, County Attorney Strode asked him if he had the means to employ counsel. Morley replied that he did not, and Strode informed him that the matter would be brought to the trial judge's attention. The case was then scheduled for trial in late April or early May, just as soon as Albert Prince had received his day in court. Although Strode was careful never to say so in public, it seemed a foregone conclusion that the two men would be found guilty. Thus the state might as well be spared the trouble of erecting the gallows, taking it down, and putting it back up again.

Morley's composure quickly vanished once the proceedings were over. His hands shook as he answered questions back in the clerk's office while the cuffs were being reattached. One of the reporters whose sleigh had overturned in the storm while they were heading for the Dickman farm told Morley how close they had come to stumbling on the convicts.

"You must have wanted to see us pretty bad," Morley quipped.

"I don't see how you fellows made it over there in the time you did," Hyers remarked.

"I don't either," Morley agreed. "The drifts were waist deep in places."

"If Mrs. Dickman had not been told by Shorty to say you were not there, we would have been over to see you," Melick volunteered. Morley said nothing but smiled his usual slow smile.

Moments later, he was taken out to the buggy for the muddy return to Lancaster. A reporter for the *Lincoln Daily Star* was given permission to ride along and interview the convict, who turned out to be one of the most superstitious men he had ever met. Morley talked about his "hoodoo," or ill luck, and how it had haunted him. He first set foot on Nebraska soil in Omaha, arriving on Friday the thirteenth. Shorty Gray gave him a gun and told him of the plans to escape on March thirteenth, the day before the outbreak. The revolver contained six cartridges to which Gray had added seven more, making thirteen. To avoid any conflict with his hoodoo, Morley had discarded one of the bullets before the shooting began.

The party reached the penitentiary just in time to see the last twenty members of the Nebraska State Militia withdraw after two weeks of service. General Phelps returned to his office at the statehouse, leaving the stowing of equipment and arms to Captain Philip Hall. The next day's *Lincoln Daily Star* reported that "some severe discipline" came to a number of the guardsmen, and that a few who were considered laggards had gotten the opportunity to find out just what it feels like to be shut up in a convict's cell.

The political nightmare that Governor Aldrich had been living for weeks only deepened. Nebraskans flooded his office with mail criticizing him for everything from the firing of Chaplain Johnson and the prison break, to the coddling of inmates and the killing of Roy Blunt. Typical of the letters he received was one written by W. A. Martin, a real-estate broker from Hastings: "It is generally conceded that it is better to let ten guilty men go unpunished than to sacrifice one innocent man, but it seems that this sentiment does not prevail when a reward is offered for the accused. Now, Mr. Governor," an aroused Martin continued, "we the people of Hastings demand that there be a thorough and fair investigation of this matter and that the guilty parties be punished to the full extent of the law. The people here will not gracefully submit to any *whitewash* investigation of this affair. A sweat-box confession from Morley won't go." If Aldrich had any doubts as to the depth of public sentiment concerning the matter, "we can call a mass meeting and pass resolutions that will convince you that this is a correct statement."

Worse yet for a politician eyeing a second term of office, many of Aldrich's staunchest supporters were beginning to waver. Calvin Keller, a Creighton attorney who had introduced Aldrich during his gubernatorial campaign visit to the town, wrote ominously: "There is some sharp criticism of your office in our community. . . . Seven men have been killed . . . and doubtless two more will be hanged later on. It is a dark page in the history of our state. Who, if anyone, is responsible, officially?"

Mixing anger with a degree of self-pity, Aldrich drafted a long reply. "Of course, it is very easy for people of no responsibility to criticize those who are burdened with all kinds of troubles," he began. "The killing of young Blunt was a particularly sad circumstance and in my opinion . . . unnecessary." But the citizens of Nebraska were to blame as well. "They have provided for [prison reform] in a most scanty and meager way and it takes just such a tragedy to arouse public sentiment . . . before the public will do its duty in the care of its wards." Of the "three devils" responsible for it all, Shorty Gray was the worst. But he had been a star member of his Sunday school class "and the teachers implicitly believed in him, and any punishment or severe discipline that had been administered to Gray would have been the cause of a general howl among such reformers." So satisfied was Aldrich with the tenor of his reply that it became the model for his response to others critical of his actions.

From all over the state came telegrams and petitions demanding that every cent of the reward be paid to Carmellette Blunt, even though the governor, as he had told the press ad infinitum, was prohibited by law from doing so. Such were the wishes of the Queen Esther Circle of Blair, the citizens of a now-vanished Cadams, and sixty-five male petitioners of Auburn. Several communities took up collections and sent the proceeds to Aldrich for delivery to the widow. Still, not everyone was feeling quite so charitable. Elmer Hall had contracted the services of Lincoln attorney Orpheus B. Polk and, with his assistance, drafted a two-paragraph letter making "formal claim [to] an equitable portion of the reward . . . offered for the escaped convicts." The fugitives, after all, had stayed at his home overnight, eaten his food, and stolen his shotgun. The following morning, "I furnished to the sheriff of Lancaster County the information [that] led to the apprehension of these men." Nothing was said of Hall's all-night delay in reporting the crime, which may have cost a young man his life. The governor's assistant replied in a scant two sentences and filed the letter with others from telephone operators, railroad employees, unsung members of the posse, and several outright charlatans.

It was only a matter of time before the advent of the muse. One M. D. Sack of Gresham persuaded the editor of the *Spring-*

field Monitor to waive the paper's usual policy of not publishing poetry, especially "the weepy kind." Owing to the widespread public interest in the case, and "not because of its literary merits," the *Monitor* was offering to its readers Sack's "The Death of Roy Blunt," a maudlin concoction of fact and myth in the making.

How they hunt escaping convicts
And in wild and needless strife,
For a bit of coin and plaudits,
Take an innocent young life.

Can you picture those three bandits
As they plunge into that home,
And with guns upon their victims
Send a terror to their bones.

Can you picture that young husband
Forced to leave that trembling bride,
And to start with those three bandits
On that last, that fatal ride.

Can you see him stoop to kiss her,
Can you hear him say good-bye,
Can you picture his young sweetheart
With the tear-drops in her eye . . .

Shall we watch them in their effort
To escape that flying band
In their desperate dash for freedom,
With a foe on every hand.

Over hill and bridge and valley,
On they rush at maddening speed,
Till at last they're overtaken
By the posse on their steeds.

Who with rifles raised and sighted,
For the ending of it all,
Hold your breath—it's just a moment
Until they send that fatal ball.

For they heeded not the warning
Of that brother when he cries,
"For God's sake men don't shoot,
For the boy in danger lies."

Just a crash and all was ended,
And a soul was ushered o'er,
And another life was darkened,
And full many a heart was sore . . .

The beset governor was being pressured just as hard from the other side. Walter K. Williams, pastor of the Home Church in Lincoln, was harboring some peculiarly dark thoughts for a member of the clergy: "Lynching is the awful miscarriage of justice. . . . On the other hand, it seems to me that we are too dilatory in bringing Albert Prince to a lawful trial for the cruel and premeditated murder of Deputy Warden Davis." Morley, too, must pay the ultimate price for his part "in one of the most daring and highhanded triple murders ever committed against the law and authority of the state of Nebraska." The criminal law must not become a net through whose meshes the guilty individual is allowed to escape a sentence of first-degree murder. "If Roy Blunt was killed accidentally the convicts were a thousand times more responsible for his untimely death than were the brave officers who accidentally killed him while in the performance of their duty of taking those desperate men dead or alive."

The pastor's feelings were shared, at least in part, by "133 of the most responsible citizens and businessmen of South Omaha."

Each of them had signed a petition in support of Chief of Police John Briggs, which had been circulated without his knowledge. Headed by business leader A. J. Lepinski, the group called on the governor to make certain that Mr. Briggs was accorded "justice and right" in any future legal proceedings that might involve him. Despite what he had written to attorney Keller about regretting Blunt's death, Aldrich was on record as supporting the actions of the posse, which he again made clear in his reply: "It is quite a relief to get a petition of this kind in view of the number of idiotic petitions we are receiving in here indiscriminately criticizing Chief Briggs without knowing anything about the facts."

From a political point of view, the one advantage of the telegrams and letters was that they could, for the most part, be kept from the prying eyes of the press. What Aldrich could not control, however, were the zealous efforts of bird-dogging reporters. In late March, a newsman for the *Omaha World Herald* wrote an article based on research undertaken in the trial records of Lancaster County. The case in question went all the way back to February of 1898, when Sam Melick testified in district court to having paid $500 to Mayor Graham for appointing him Lincoln's chief of police, the kind of graft usually associated with major cities such as New York and Chicago. On being confronted with this information, a blindsided Aldrich pled ignorance, which may have been true, though it didn't alter the fact that he was left dangling from a limb. "It will do no one any good to bring me stories of that kind," he thundered in his best imitation of self-righteousness. "I know nothing about the facts in the records of fourteen years ago. He [Melick] must stand on his record from this time on, not on anything he may have done in the past."

In trying to push through reforms as quickly as possible, the governor inadvertently subjected himself to additional humiliation. After ordering the purchase of 450 new mattresses for the inmates, he was informed that the manufacturer was withholding delivery for nonpayment. A check with the Board of Accounts confirmed that the state couldn't come up with the money, forcing Aldrich to cancel the order. The best that could be done was to remove the foul-smelling stuffing from the old mattresses, wash the ticking, and refill them with fresh straw.

Despite this and other setbacks, conditions had begun to change for the better. After warning a large packing company about the low quality of meat being shipped to the prison, Warden Melick rejected a large delivery of beef as unfit for human consumption, which, from now on, included convicts. A new icebox and bread chest were ordered for the kitchen, and the butcher blocks—saturated with blood and fat that acted as magnets to rodents—were sawn off in the interests of sanitation. Rotting cupboards were replaced, and also worn-out tableware and badly cracked china. The tables were measured for more sanitary sheet-metal tops on which food of greater variety and quantity was already being served. Of all the improvements undertaken, none was more appreciated by the men than the removal from the bathhouse of the twenty or so rusting tubs that had long been believed to be incubators of disease. For the first time, convicts were able to shower at least once a week, their pleasure heightened by the installation of several hot-water taps. The funding for much else, including the construction of a new cell house for young inmates, and a badly needed kitchen, was dependent on the political will of the next legislature.

Meanwhile, the warden's enlightened policy on mail had hit a temporary snag. Many friends and relatives from other states had underestimated the cost of sending bundles of newspapers to the inmates, and some 160 packages were being held up for postage due. Lancaster's chief clerk found himself reading upward of twelve hundred outgoing letters each month while an estimated five thousand pieces of mail, ranging from postcards to magazines, were arriving during the same period.

Such changes failed to silence reformers who were as much concerned with the moral rot at the penitentiary as its physical deterioration. Speaking before the Social Service Club at its first meeting since the prison break, a deeply vexed Judge Frost decided to make public that to which he had only hinted in his previous attack on the dope trade, and which he had confided to Governor Aldrich. On handing a text of his speech to reporters for publication, the judge asked that readers be warned in advance "of its plain speaking," which they were.

Until his recent isolation from the other convicts by order of the governor, Frank Dinsmore had not only controlled the drug trade at Lancaster, but was also a regular practitioner of "crimes against nature." Luring callow arrivals with the promise of dope, clothing, and better food, "He will take and ravish the person of inmates, mere boys from eighteen years up, ruining them for life." The guards were fully aware of this heinous abuse and would speak of Dinsmore as having "a new kid on the string." Frost himself had interviewed some of the felon's victims, who were reluctant to speak of their defilement at length.

It would have been bad enough if the practice had stopped there, but it hadn't. Dinsmore made the youths available to other inmates for a price, treating them no differently than enslaved women in a brothel. Many of the guards received "tips" in the form of money, alcohol, and drugs for moving the reluctant "prostitutes" from cell to cell, treating the whole thing as a joke. The physically intimidating Dinsmore had been further shielded by his assignment as hospital steward, giving him access to an estimated ninety percent of all drugs taken by the convicts. Having murdered his own wife with arsenic, he was perfectly capable of administering a lethal injection to any man foolish enough to cross him. Indeed, Frost had received unconfirmed reports that a number of men had taken ill while under his care, and a few had actually died. If only Prince and Morley could be persuaded to talk, they were in a position to reveal much about the criminal operations of the convict physician, for they had doubtless obtained most of their dope, or "happy," from Dinsmore.

This was but one of Frost's long list of charges in a speech that required nearly an hour to deliver and took up four long columns of newsprint in the *Nebraska State Journal.* It also acted as a green light for a direct assault by the Reverend Johnson on the reputation of Warden Delahunty; up until now, the reverend had been shadowboxing with the dead man. The preacher chose to publish his lengthy statement in *Appeal to Reason,* the socialist newspaper printed in Gerard, Kansas, whose editor had taken a special interest in the case in part because of Shorty Gray's professed commitment to the teachings of Marx and Debs. Claiming that he had resigned as chaplain, rather than being fired by the governor, as had been reported in the papers, Johnson had no longer been able to deal with the warden's method of handling prisoners: "Delahunty considered a prisoner not a man but a thing without rights or feelings. He believed a prison a place of punishment and I a place of reformation. His methods were brutalizing men and making them desperate. The guards reflected this spirit after convict Prince killed Deputy Warden Davis. I had a premonition of something coming I could not shake off." But no one would pay any attention to his warnings, least of all Governor Aldrich, who had lashed out at him when he broached the matter. "It has taken murder to change things at the prison. All my protests against conditions were received as the vaporizings of a sentimental old man. My suggestions of prison reform were taken as the weakness of a childish preacher. . . . The state doesn't need new buildings half so bad as it does a little humanity at work in the one we have."

Johnson's statement was reprinted almost verbatim in the Lincoln papers, shocking some and outraging others. In a letter to the governor, Sweaney L. Blackmar took Johnson to task for his condemnation of the murdered public servant: "Was there ever a man so erroneously accused and censured as was our friend and late warden, Mr. Delahunty? Chaplain Johnson should be one who would defend his name against criticism. Instead, Mr. Johnson has accused Mr. Delahunty of openly being the cause of the recent tragedy in order to shift the suspicion of blame from his own shoulders." Contrary to what the clergyman had asserted in his statement to the press, it was the "far from modern conditions prevailing at the prison" rather than the "brutal punishment" spoken of by the warden's critic that had triggered the outbreak.

Blackmar closed by telling the governor that he expected no reply. Thus, he must have been somewhat surprised when he received a letter dated just a day after his was sent. Blackmar's sympathetic words had acted like a balm on an open wound, for which Aldrich was deeply grateful. Jim Delahunty had been his friend, too, and he had "never passed up an opportunity, privately or publicly, to express his confidence in him as a man and an official," one more postscript to a complex and morally ambiguous tale.

———— ⸎ ⸎⬤⸎ ⸎ ————

Albert Prince had often told the few with whom he had contact in solitary that he was going to be sentenced and hung for the stabbing death of Deputy Warden Davis, his insanity plea notwithstanding. Seemingly accepting of his fate, he had taken up the study of spiritualism in hopes of learning what becomes of the soul in the "Hereafter." His orders for books from the penitentiary library included treatises on philosophy, astrology, religion, and the occult. An encyclopedia article on the transmigration of souls captured his interest for a while, but in the end he was forced to admit that his entry into the realm of the supernatural had availed him little, if anything: "He knows no more now than he had in the beginning," a reporter wrote.

Jury selection began on April 23, 1912, and it took nearly two days to come up with a panel of twelve middle-aged farmers and businessmen acceptable to both sides. Every seat in the courtroom was filled on the first morning of testimony. The crowd surged over the railing, and the hallway outside was "black with specta-tors," excitedly craning their necks for a glimpse of the prisoner. Off in a small anteroom were seven convicts under heavy guard, waiting for their turns on the witness stand.

Newsmen covering the trial watched the defendant's every move for any signs of the dementia and paranoia blamed by Prince's at-torney for his lethal outburst. At times he seemed to be enjoying his notoriety. Reaching into the pocket of his freshly laundered prison uniform, he would extract a plug of tobacco, break off a piece with all the deliberation of an actor in the limelight, then hesitate for a few moments before putting it into his mouth, a smile inching across his face as he slowly began to chew. At other times he seemed nervous and preoccupied, rubbing his fingers back and forth across the head of a thumbtack, as if he were pol-ishing it. This behavior sometimes escalated into a "violent" drum-ming of his fingers, which one newsman likened to pounding a typewriter or banging out a ragtime tune on a piano, giving de-fense attorney Albert E. Howard some little hope that the jury just might see things his client's way.

Yet at the same time he was attempting to prove that Prince was suffering from diminished mental capacity and irrational sus-picions, Howard seemed to be undermining his own case when he described the convict to the press as "a man of remarkable intelli-gence. He is a socialist—perhaps insane on that point. One thing is sure—he is much brighter than he is credited with being and a man of extraordinary courage. If he hangs, he will go to the gallows absolutely indifferent to his fate."

Some eager spectators immediately got more than they had bargained for when County Attorney Edmund Strode called Mont Robb, a penitentiary trustee, as the day's first witness. Davis's blood-encrusted garments, described as "a gruesome sight," were paraded before the jury, causing women in the crowd to swoon and others to avert their eyes. After identifying the suit and shirt, Robb was excused without further questions.

He was followed to the stand by Dr. Spradling, who proceeded to describe, in clinical detail, the multiple wounds inflicted on the deputy warden. The physician also testified that he had visited Prince in solitary after the stabbing and had asked him what he had against the victim. Prince replied that Davis prevented the convicts from taking hash and hot water to their cells and would not allow him to carry his own fork to and from the dining room. Based on this conversation and Prince's calm demeanor, Spradling concluded that the defendant showed no evidence of being under the influence of drugs—a conclusion bolstered by Prince's admission to having committed the crime, and his willingness to accept whatever punishment the court deemed appropriate.

Spradling's testimony was backed up by that of Dr. Williams, superintendent of the State Hospital for the Insane, and his assistant, Dr. L. B. Pillsbury. The two men had given Prince the same examination as those committed to the institution for treatment. He displayed no signs of paranoia, which Williams described as a degenerative disease. Those so afflicted almost never remember their violent acts, let alone the specific details. Prince, on the other hand, was perfectly lucid and discussed his attack on Davis as he would have any other event in his life. In sum, the man "could not be insane on one question and be perfectly sane on all others."

A stir passed through the courtroom when the name of Frank Dinsmore was called. The controversial murderer, whose own life had been spared by executive clemency, entered the chamber in imposing fashion, striding up to the witness stand while barely glancing at the crowd and ignoring the emotionless face of the defendant altogether. Employing the impeccable English and modesty that were his trademarks, Dinsmore told of receiving Davis at the prison hospital, where he had been steward until a few weeks ago. A winded Prince had come rushing through the door of the operating room, begging to be allowed to finish the job. With one hand on Davis's forehead, Dinsmore had used the other to keep Prince at bay until help arrived.

Three Negro convicts, Lloyd Oliver, James Perry, and Robert Parker, were next summoned by the state. They had all been seated close to the defendant in the chapel when the stabbing occurred and went on to describe it in detail. Each saw the fatal blows struck and each saw the knife pass from Prince to Deputy Warden Wagner, then on to Warden Delahunty. On cross-examination, Howard sought to establish the desire for revenge against Prince as the basis for the men's testimony, to which they angrily objected. They had never asked to testify and produced subpoenas to show that County Attorney Strode had forced them to bear witness against their fellow convict.

Following a full day of testimony, the prosecution rested and the defense called its first witness, former chaplain P. C. Johnson. Howard first wanted to know if he was aware that guards at the prison were addicted to opium and liquor. The state promptly objected, and Howard was admonished by Judge Albert F. Cornish to limit his questions to the issue of insanity.

Johnson then spoke of how he had observed a gradual change in the defendant's personality, marked by sullenness and a lack of attention to what was going on around him. He had been sufficiently concerned to approach prison officials about it, but his warnings had been ignored.

Then Howard asked the witness what may have been the most important question of the trial: "In your opinion, did Prince know enough to be able to distinguish between right and wrong?"

Rather than the unequivocal "no" the defense was expecting to hear, the clergyman began mincing words, fully aware that he was walking a moral tightrope. "Right and wrong as I conceive it is one thing, as Prince may have conceived it another. I think he was able to distinguish between right and wrong as he conceived it." When a flabbergasted Howard asked Johnson to clarify what he had just said, the witness simply repeated himself.

Strode could barely contain his glee as he rose to begin his cross-examination. "Do you think," he asked, "that [Prince] could distinguish between right and wrong?"

"Yes," Johnson tersely replied.

"Would you say that he ought not to be punished?"

"Oh no!" Johnson exclaimed, "I think he should most certainly be punished," the damning statement sending a murmur through the crowd.

Howard tried to claim even more ground by getting the witness to admit that he had assisted the counsel for Prince in the preparation of evidence. Johnson denied that he had done so, but said he had talked with them about the case a few times.

There was nothing evasive about the testimony of another key witness, former warden Tom Smith, whose moral compass points were fixed. "I would have drowned Prince if he had not given up," Smith asserted when asked about the use of the water cure. "It was a question of Prince running the prison or me."

"In that statement," an editorializing reporter wrote, "alarmists and reformers were given a sudden insight upon the other side of the seamy story of prison management, the side of the man who has lived for years on a powder barrel, knowing the suppression of every stray spark was necessary to prevent an explosion, such an explosion as wrecked the peace and safety of this part of Nebraska six weeks ago."

Smith spoke of how Prince had raked an iron bar across his cell door until the sparks flew. At that point the then-warden had ordered the guards to turn on the hose, after which the prisoner was driven from behind the door with a broom handle in the ribs. The conflict of wills had lasted some thirty-seven minutes, easily a prison record. But contrary to the testimony of others, who had witnessed the dousing, Smith attributed Prince's ability to hold out so long to the fact that the hose was rotten and leaked in several places, reducing the force of the stream. Coakley, one of the guards who had manned the hose, followed Smith to the stand: "Since that day," he testified, "Albert Prince has never seemed to be the same man," and was unable, in the opinion of the witness, to tell right from wrong.

With his life literally in the balance, Prince chose to testify in his own defense. Sitting nonchalantly with an arm slung over the back of the witness chair, his hands swinging freely, and one knee crossed, he calmly narrated the story of life in the penitentiary, filled with incident after incident of torture in the hole, petty nagging in the shops and at the dining tables, the careless handling of the men's health and bodies. Convicts suffering from consumption and dropsy were kept at their tasks when they were exhausted by disease. When one such individual was leaving the penitentiary after receiving a medical pardon, he remarked to Delahunty: "Warden, you have caused my death."

The courtroom went absolutely still, the rapt jurors leaning forward in their seats, as Prince demonstrated the three positions used in stringing a man up. The return of Davis as deputy warden had made things worse. The quality of the food, always poor, declined to the point where most men refused to eat it, raiding their meager prison accounts for the money to purchase supplies from town, which they cooked in their cramped cells on makeshift stoves. One by one, privileges were cut off and discipline grew stricter. Things finally got so bad that every time a guard addressed him he cringed and felt the desire rise within him to put the man away. When Prince spoke of the deputy warden the pitch of his voice changed and his speech quickened, reverting to a monotone the moment he switched subjects.

Before leaving the stand, Prince, at his attorney's request, bared his heavily tattooed arm, revealing a trail of needle marks from an opium habit that Howard charged was tolerated, if not directly encouraged, by the state, feeding his client's mental debauchery. Most of his dope had been purchased from drunken and abusive guards. He had never gotten any directly from Dinsmore, although every prisoner was well aware that he was a major source of supply. By the time the defendant rose from the witness chair and returned to his seat at the counsel's table, there was no denying the fact that he had made a powerful impression on the jury.

Despite his outward calm and professed indifference to life's meaning, Prince had begun to falter under the mounting strain, both physical and mental. At night he could be overheard by Morley and Davis praying to God that his fate may not be the gallows, "a weakening viewed with contempt by the other desperados."

The four days of testimony were capped by final arguments that took each side more than an hour to deliver, the defense steeping its presentation in biblical quotes and allusions, the prosecution decrying the breakdown of civil order and respect for the law. Howard spoke of the compassion of Christ and quoted Robert Burns: "Man's inhumanity to man makes countless thousands mourn." Deputy County Attorney Hager challenged the jury to declare "whether the state of Nebraska is big enough and strong enough to enforce her laws," for not only is the defendant on trial but "the very foundation of our civic institutions."

The courtroom was filled to overflowing well before the jury's scheduled return at nine o'clock Tuesday morning. Among the spectators was Mrs. Chester Aldrich, the wife of the governor, who had also been present the day before, listening intently while Judge Cornish delivered his instructions to the jury. No one breathed as all eyes were drawn to the judge's austere countenance when he reached out to receive the verdict. There was a long pause, after which Cornish handed the paper back to the clerk, asking that he return it to the foreman for dating. A reporter described the almost palpable silence as "intense" while the foreman wrote in "April 30, 1912," and returned the verdict to the clerk. Cornish scanned it a second time and then nodded to the clerk, who pronounced the defendant guilty of murder in the first degree, for which the penalty was the scaffold.

The evening edition of the *Lincoln Daily Star* described Prince as "the most self-contained man condemned to hang at the Nebraska penitentiary for many years." He had smiled and joked with his keepers and acquaintances after the verdict was read, and even invited one spectator to the hanging: "Well, you'd better come down pretty soon to the necktie party at the home," he said. Only later did he learn that it had taken the jury eleven ballots to reach a unanimous verdict. Two men had stubbornly held out for acquittal and then, when they could no longer buck the tide, fought for life in prison. Some of the jurors voiced concern about the effect a verdict of not guilty might have on the upcoming trials of Morley and Davis, and this same issue had reemerged while they were debating which penalty to impose. Before he was led away, Prince told Howard that he could find no fault with the attorney's defense, but he wished to apply for a hearing before the state supreme court. While he had no expectation that the verdict would be overturned, it would give him some extra time to put his affairs in order. Howard promised that he would do so, providing his motion for a new trial was overruled.

On the night of April 14–15, 1912, the great ocean liner *Titanic*, thought to be unsinkable and the fastest vessel afloat, went down in the Atlantic south of Newfoundland after glancing off an iceberg. More than fifteen hundred lives were lost, including many notable persons of the time. Yet news of the tragedy was slow to capture the imagination of Nebraskans, perhaps because it seemed so far away, and part of a social and cultural world little related to their own. Whatever the reason, the sinking was overshadowed by front-page reporting on Prince's trial and the lingering echoes of blood and thunder across the Gretna Hills.

In accordance with the verdict returned by the coroner's jury in the Blunt inquest, Sarpy County Attorney William Jamieson filed charges of manslaughter against Briggs, Hyers, and Trouton the first week of April. County Court Judge Jennings Wheat immediately issued warrants for the arrest of the men, and Sheriff Chase, who was lucky to have been spared the upcoming ordeal, set out to serve the papers. All three men appeared for their arraignment on April twelfth and pleaded not guilty. Judge Wheat scheduled a preliminary hearing for the last day of the month before setting bond at $2,500 each, which was posted by their attorneys.

In yet another novelistic coincidence, the defendants returned to court the very day Prince was being convicted of murder and jury selection began in the Morley trial. Tempers had cooled in the six weeks since the tragedy, and the arraignment proceeded without the verbal fireworks that had marked the coroner's inquest at Springfield. Witnesses for the state were positive that Briggs had fired the first shot, and that it was the convicts who had replied in kind. However, they were unable to state whether the police chief fired the bullet that had killed Blunt.

Briggs, Hyers, Trouton, Chase, Empey, and Carpenter, all of whom were in "the thick of it," testified unanimously that the fugitives had been the ones to open fire. Shot splattered the pursuers' faces and bodies; bullets whizzed past their heads in a perfect torrent, luck alone saving them from being killed or badly wounded. Briggs stuck with his story that he had exercised all possible precaution in not firing at the front end of the wagon, where Blunt was perched. When asked by Jamieson about the infamous "to hell" quote, his deep-seated anger stirred: "The man's a liar who says I made that statement!"

Now that it was every man for himself, Hyers emphasized the fact that the small-caliber rifle he was using could not have inflicted the wounds that killed Blunt and Shorty Gray. And Trouton, who had the best defense of the three, declared how he was so busy with the charging team that he never had the chance to grab a rifle, let alone fire a shot. After two days of testimony and legal wrangling, Judge Wheat summed up the facts: There was sufficient evidence to hold John Briggs and Gus Hyers for trial in district court, their bonds continuing in the amount previously set. In the case of John Trouton, the evidence was insufficient to bind him over for trial and he was discharged.

A week later, Hyers's attorney, E. J. Burkett, appeared before District Court Judge Harvey Travis to file two motions, one requesting that his client be given a separate trial, the other that he be granted a change of venue. Henry C. Murphy, who represented Briggs, joined in the petition, and together with Burkett introduced eighty-six affidavits supporting the contention that a fair and impartial jury could not be empaneled in Sarpy County. In rebuttal, Jamieson filed more than one hundred affidavits from residents of the county who swore the opposite. Travis took the matter under advisement after informing both sides that he would make no ruling until the fall term in September, owing to a full docket. Meanwhile, public attention had refocused on the courthouse in Lincoln, where desperado Charles Morley was on trial for murder.

The process of selecting a jury had been long and tedious. Morley occupied a chair directly behind his counsel, William C. Frampton, a granite-faced Christian Scientist with a jovial nature, who was best known for extending public services to various parts of Lincoln during his two terms on the city council. A reporter noted that there was no sign of the "cool defiance" newsmen had come to associate with Morley's public face, but neither was there any hint of tension or fear. He appeared to be keenly interested in the proceedings, writing down the names of prospective jurors as they were called and paying close attention as they answered questions about the defendant's alleged crimes and whether they could impose a sentence of capital punishment, should it come to that.

The number of observers was surprisingly small, and the fact that they were scattered throughout the courtroom combined to create a strangely deserted air. But with the Prince trial due to end at any moment, it was predicted that the legal chambers presided over by Judge Willard Stewart would soon be drawing the largest crowds yet.

Few, least of all the defendant, had any idea that one of the most interested spectators would be his own mother. The once-widowed Alice was still living in Knoxville, Missouri, with her third husband, Calvin R. Ramsey, a mechanic and carpenter to whom she had been married since 1902. Looking considerably older than her fifty-eight years, the bent and frail woman had arrived in Lincoln the weekend before jury selection began and was driven

out to Lancaster by Frampton for a reunion with the son she had
not seen for two years. She was met by Major Antles and taken to
the chapel, where she was seated on one side of a double screen in
the presence of armed guards. Morley was ushered in a few minutes later and sat down opposite the gray-headed woman who had
been transformed by time and grief into a virtual stranger.

"How are you, Charley?" were her first words.

He said he was all right but was not anxious to talk at first.

"Charley, be brave. We have got to fight, you and I together.
The Lord is with us."

He seemed to relax a little at this and the talk soon centered
on relatives, and on Morley's complaint of his treatment, which is
what had led him to break out of prison. When their time was
over, Mrs. Ramsey asked permission to kiss her son, but she was
told that all physical contact was strictly against prison rules.

"I'll see you again," Morley said as he was being led away. After
he had gone, Alice leaned against the wall and burst into tears.

With the jury finally in place, the beginning of the trial was
unexpectedly delayed. On arriving at the packed courthouse,
Morley's guards had discovered that they had somehow forgotten
the key to his handcuffs. A call was placed to the penitentiary and
an employee was sent to deliver the missing item. While everyone
waited, Morley, who was wearing a black coat in place of his
prison issue, appeared perfectly at ease and joked about "unlucky
thirteen"—a reference to the number of men in the jury box,
which included one alternate. The fact that his heavily veiled
mother was with him in the anteroom did not seem to dampen
his spirts.

The story of the breakout, which had been told time and
again in the newspapers, was laid out by the prosecution once
more. The testimony of the state's witnesses varied little from what
had been printed in the past, much of it already familiar to the ju-

rors; indeed, all too familiar from the viewpoint of the defense. Confident of obtaining a guilty verdict, County Attorney Strode moved quickly, taking only the better part of a day to present his case, with few objections from the other side.

Frampton's greatest challenge—and, seemingly, only hope— was to demonstrate that his client was not a party to the conspiracy with which he had been charged, a tall order, considering the dramatic events of the day in question. Before calling his first witness, the attorney did what defense lawyers almost always do in such cases, which was to move that the court instruct the jury to return a directed verdict of not guilty. After the motion was denied, he took the courtroom by surprise when he called Mrs. Joseph Dickman to the stand.

The woman who had been Morley's hostage only six weeks earlier was asked whether the convict appeared to have been under the influence of a drug when he and the others sought shelter from the storm. Strode shot to his feet to voice an objection, which was sustained by Judge Stewart. Frampton suffered another setback when the judge prohibited him from calling other witnesses to testify on Morley's use of dope.

Precluded from inquiring into his client's mental condition, Frampton adopted a different tactic, arguing that because Morley had no intention of killing anyone he was not guilty of murder. The most he could be convicted of was manslaughter, even though the law said otherwise.

Deputy Sheriff Eikenbary was called to the stand and asked to tell about a conversation he had had with Morley after his capture. The deputy asked the fugitive where the guns came from, and Morley told him that all the weapons and bullets were supplied by Shorty Gray. "I said, 'Morley, why did you do it? You killed the best friend I ever had,'" a reference to usher Heilman.

"Morley replied, 'I didn't do it. I never fired a shot.'"

At that point, one of the posse members stepped up to the prisoner and, calling him a vile name, said, "You did and I'll kill you." That was when Eikenbary drew two guns and held the seething crowd at bay while Morley was put in the corner of a wagon with the deputy standing guard over him.

The case went to the jury on May third, a Friday afternoon, over the objections of the superstitious defendant. To Morley, the number three in combination with a Friday was just as bad as the thirteenth or the twenty-third, all Indian sign dates. "I've not got much chance in the face of that jinx," he lamented.

The twelve jurors debated the evidence until nearly ten-forty, when they were taken to their hotel rooms for the night. At eight a.m. Saturday, they were returned to the courthouse and locked up again to resume their deliberations. By midmorning they gave up and started a game of poker. From behind the heavy, oak doors of the jury room came the sound of loud voices punctuated by occasional laughter. Then, to the bewilderment of the packed courtroom, the voices burst into song. The headline from the evening edition of the *Lincoln Daily Star* attempted to explain what was going on: JURY STILL OUT AND APPARENTLY HOPELESSLY DIVIDED—PLAY CARDS AND SING DURING THE MORNING.

The jurors had been instructed that they could select from among three possible verdicts: murder in the first degree, murder in the second degree, and acquittal. The long deliberations seemed to indicate that the twelve had agreed on the guilt of the accused, but were unable to decide whether the punishment should be life imprisonment, or death.

While Morley awaited a summons from the courtroom, a small drama was being played out in the cell next to his. William Hyde, the stepbrother of Albert Prince, was leaving Lincoln after spending nearly a month in the city. After checking the palms of both men, Major Antles suspended the rules and allowed them a final handshake. In contrast to his older brother, who sought to lighten the moment with an attempt at humor, Hyde was moved to tears, causing Prince to remark, "Well, I'll have to admit that while I can laugh and joke still, 'way down in my heart I realize that something is wrong." Hyde then left to take the train east, informing reporters that he would not see his brother again in the event the death sentence was carried out.

Heavy-eyed and weary after a day of singing and card playing, the jurors went to bed Saturday night while Morley lay awake in his cell, cheerful and cautiously optimistic that his hoodoo had been stalemated. At midnight, Frampton told a lone reporter in the otherwise deserted courtroom that the jury was obviously deadlocked and that his client would likely be retried. Alice Ramsey's hopes were also rising. "He is my baby," she told newsmen between spasms of weeping as she sat in the waiting room of the county jail Saturday afternoon. "He was such a good boy and so sweet and good to his mother. They look like good sensible men. Surely they could see that my boy is not a murderer. It is the government that is at fault," she continued, "and then the poor people that make a misstep because it is made so easy for them to have to suffer such terrible torture. I can't understand why it is all as it is in our civilized country." The jailer's wife and some women Sunday school teachers at the penitentiary tried to comfort her, but with little success. They all agreed that it would be difficult for women to change the way things were going even if they had the power to vote. "A few years ago it might have been done," said one, "but now the women are following the footsteps of the men so closely that a great many of them favor their vices."

Shortly before the noon hour on Sunday, the bailiff was notified by the foreman that the jury had arrived at a verdict. Judge Stewart was informed and made arrangements to receive it about two o'clock. In an effort to speed up the process, Morley was brought in from the penitentiary by Sheriff Hyers in an automobile and arrived at the buzzing courthouse handcuffed to Warden Melick, two violets peeping from the buttonhole of his coat, shoes carefully polished, prison clothing neatly brushed. He showed some signs of nervousness by smoking a cigarette and drumming on the back of a chair. "Well, I wonder what it will be?" he remarked to a familiar bystander.

"Cheer up," the man replied, "I don't think they will order you a black suit."

"Or a rope," said Morley, smiling sardonically.

Talk turned to the escape and the posse chase. Morley said that Shorty blew the lock off the metal door with cotton soaked in nitro, the rest of which they kept until the end of the chase. "Didn't you see a package tied up in a handkerchief hanging on a bush at the side of the road near where the fight ended?" he asked a surprised reporter who had been there. "That was the cotton we put there because we were afraid it might get hit by a bullet and blow us up."

He smiled when one of the men asked him about the speeches he had made from the rear of the train, crediting Sheriff Hyers with killing Gray. "When I got out of the wagon after the battle Sheriff Hyers grabbed me by the shoulder," Morley replied, "and told me to say that he had killed Shorty Gray, because that would help him at the next election." The convict joined in the laughter at the lawman's expense, having put another one over on the press.

Judge Stewart, unhappy that the tranquility of his Sunday afternoon at home had been disturbed, arrived and immediately called the court to order. Foreman Ballard handed the verdict to Clark Baer, the clerk of court, and the room went deathly quiet. Morley's eyes shifted from the jurymen's faces to that of the clerk, who began to read the words on which his fate depended. "We, the jury, find Charles Morley guilty as charged in the information, and recommend that his sentence be fixed at imprisonment for life."

An audible sigh of relief swept over the courtroom, filled almost to capacity in spite of the fact that it was Sunday and the hour of the jury's return was not made public until a short time before the verdict was read. Mrs. Ramsey rose from her chair and threw her arms around her embarrassed son's neck. "Oh, my boy, my boy, my prayers are answered at last!" she exclaimed. "At least I can write to my boy." The tearful woman shook hands with each juryman while the crowd looked on in silence. "I'll remember you all my life," she told them. Morley shook hands with Frampton and, "smiling quizzically," was taken into a room out of public view, where he was again handcuffed to Warden Melick.

A reporter asked him how he felt about spending the rest of his life in the penitentiary. "While there's life there is hope," Morley replied. "I'm still a young man yet and have a long life ahead of me. What can I tell you as to what the future will hold?"

Not everyone was pleased with the verdict, beginning with Deputy County Attorney Hager, who had helped get Prince sentenced to the gallows a week earlier. The prosecutor lashed out in anger: "It was a fluke. The people, through their jury, let their maudlin sentiment get away with them." Such a verdict could easily result in "mob rule," for what was to prevent Morley from attempting to shoot his way out of Lancaster again?

The day after the verdict, a petition was circulated in the downtown Commercial Club, demanding that County Attorney Strode have another go at Morley for the purpose of getting him hanged this time. But it was also noted that while many had willingly signed the document, a large number of others had refused because of a growing sentiment against the death penalty.

"Are they going to try me again?" Morley asked a newsman who had been given permission to interview him after his return to the hole. Then he answered his own question by stating that he didn't think they would attempt it.

Otherwise, things were going well. "I am getting the very best of treatment, and Prince, Davis, and myself enjoy ourselves as best we can." Every evening Prince would play his guitar and the three sang along in what they called a "bawl." As Warden Melick and the reporter were leaving the cell house, Prince called out: "Warden, we're going to have another bawl this evening and enjoy ourselves."

"That's right, Prince, that's right," Melick called back.

Two months to the day after the prison break, Morley was taken from solitary confinement to appear before Judge Stewart for the final time. Showing no emotion, he declared that he had nothing to say when he was given the opportunity to address the court. Then he listened passively while the jurist sentenced him to life in prison. On his return to Lancaster, he was taken back to his cell in solitary to collect his meager belongings, after which two guards marched him over to the west cell house, where the most desperate of the convicts were housed. The door to his new quarters opened and Morley, laughing out loud at the irony, stepped into the tiny cell once occupied by fellow desperadoes Shorty Gray and John Dowd.

After lying unclaimed for two weeks, the bodies of Gray and Dowd were transferred to the medical college of the state university and suspended in pickling vats to await dissection by Dr. C. W. M. Poynter's anatomy class. The brains were removed from the skulls and placed in jars of hardening fluid, perhaps to become part of a larger collection of significant criminal types. According to sensationalistic articles in the *Omaha World Herald* and *Lincoln Daily Star,* they were a study in contrasts. Gray's skull was symmetrical and contained a well-formed brain, denoting the intelligence and cunning of a born criminal leader. Dowd's cranium, on the other hand, widened at the back, becoming exceptionally broad. Inside was a brain of the "degenerate type, there being very little frontal elevation and the frontal lobes being almost lacking," both characteristic of a man slow of thought and short on initiative.

Six months later, the press showed no interest when Dr. Poynter published a ninety-six-page scholarly article, complete with a dozen plates and extensive bibliography, titled "A Study of Cerebral Anthropology, With a Description of Two Brains of Criminals." In his conclusions, the author wrote that the organs displayed no anomalies and variations indicative of the so-called "criminal brain." Quite the contrary: "We must conclude that the two cases here presented . . . are both free from evidence of inferiority and degeneration."

Two days after the end of Morley's trial, the mysterious lady in black resurfaced out of nowhere, spurning makeup and without "a single stitch of coloring in her gown." Calling herself Mrs. Brown, as opposed to Mrs. May Woodworth, and claiming to be Shorty Gray's mother-in-law, the middle-aged woman, who was more than likely his wife or lady friend, told reporters that poor health and anxiety had caused her to leave Lincoln for Chicago prior to the escape. The fact that she had departed only a day before the tragedy was merely a coincidence; nor did she possess any knowledge as to how the men had secured guns and explosives.

But it was not the escape that she wanted to discuss. The blame for what had happened rested squarely on the shoulders of Governor Aldrich. He had been warned about what was going on at Lancaster and told to remove Delahunty as warden. "What the governor should do is to enlarge the prison grounds," she scolded. "Let the convicts see a blade of green grass. Let them sit on it and take off their shoes and walk on the soft earth. Then you won't have any more mutinies." Morley, who was awaiting sentencing, should not be hung. "I don't believe in capital punishment," she asserted.

A few weeks later, about the time Tom Davis was acquitted of slashing the throat of fellow convict John Strong on the grounds of self-defense, a new granite monument went up in Springfield Cemetery, purchased with donations sent in from around the state. The inscription read: ROY F. BLUNT. BORN MAY 14, 1890. OUR HERO. MARRIED DEC. 27, 1911. DIED MAR. 18, 1912. Roy's mongrel dog never came home but stayed by the grave all summer long. Twice each week, Peter Anderson would make the seven-mile drive into town, bearing food and water for the animal. Then one day it was gone, never to be seen again. According to family tradition, the dog had simply wandered off and died alone of unbearable grief.

In September, Judge Travis granted both motions filed by the attorneys for Briggs and Hyers. The two lawmen would receive separate trials and changes of venue from Sarpy to Saunders County District Court, at Wahoo, so named for a medicinal shrub made known to settlers by the native Indians. The judge had also arranged to have Briggs tried first, beginning the second week of December.

Nothing during the three days of testimony made a more lasting impression on the overflow crowd than the appearance of the young widow, attired in black and carrying her three-month-old son, Roy Blunt Jr. Carmellette took the witness stand for the first time, telling of how the convicts barged into her kitchen with shotguns, demanding food, and then of escaping to her parents' home with the help of a neighbor. Bearing silent but eloquent witness was Old Hickory, hauled all the way from Springfield in the same condition as on the day of the chase, from the bloodstains in the wagon box to the stolen caps on the floor that had been worn by Gray and Dowd.

Almost as memorable was the appearance of Morley, who had been brought to Wahoo by train, without handcuffs, after he promised Warden Melick that he wouldn't do anything foolish. Wearing a loose-fitting suit, tie, overcoat, and porkpie hat, he little resembled the famous outlaw who had been the only one to emerge from the ill-fated wagon alive. Morley was put on the stand early in the morning, before the courtroom had completely filled, then whisked out of town on the ten-forty-eight train to Lincoln, after testifying that Briggs was the man who shot Blunt.

If any of this troubled the defendant, he gave no indication of it. Indeed, Briggs seemed to cast a spell over the citizens of Wahoo, who formed an entourage that trailed the burly police chief around town as if he were the pied piper. On Friday, December thirteenth, a day that would have given Morley the shakes, the jury pronounced the brash lawman not guilty of manslaughter after having deliberated all of twenty-two minutes. In a display of gratitude, a jubilant Briggs walked the streets, pumping arms, slapping backs, and joshing with the locals, whom he credited with treating him more like a friend or relative than a stranger from another county.

The following week, Briggs applied to Governor Aldrich for $1,800 of the reward money offered by the state. Bound as he was by the law, Aldrich had no choice but to approve the claim, subjecting himself to still another round of political fire. But when Briggs tried to cash the voucher, he was rebuffed by the deputy state auditor, who told him that there was not enough money in the reward fund. It was up to the next session of the legislature to make the appropriation, which seemed most unlikely given the public's lingering anger over Blunt's demise and the recent birth of his posthumous child.

With the prosecutors' best chance of conviction lost, it was taken for granted that the charges against the second defendant would be dropped. Although it was the Christmas season, Sarpy County Attorney Jamieson was not in a holiday mood. Using every tick of the clock at his disposal, he waited until March 3, 1913, before sending his assistant to Wahoo for the purpose of entering a motion to dismiss the case of the State of Nebraska against Sheriff Gus Hyers. The motion was sustained by the district judge, thus bringing to an end bitter litigation that had dragged on for almost a year.

The time had come for Albert Prince to go to wherever the other side of the trapdoor might take him. The state supreme court had denied his appeal for a new trial and set March 21, 1913, Good Friday, as his execution date. At one-thirty in the afternoon, he climbed the gallows steps without the slightest hesitation, turned, and smiled down on the silent crowd, which numbered no more than fifty by orders of the warden, leaving as many as two hundred grumbling citizens in the prison corridors.

Among those present were several of the lawmen who had participated in the running gun battle the previous March, including Sheriffs Hyers, Quinton, and McShane. Moments before the black execution cap was pulled over Prince's face, his attention was drawn to a ray of sunlight coming through a small opening in the doorway. It widened as it traveled across the room, forming a soft halo around his head and shoulders.

Left behind in his cell was an enigmatic letter addressed to Dolly Hyde, his mother in Cincinnati: "My last wish and desire is that you take heed to warning letters I have written you. Don't be headstrong; don't listen to vanity. Why did the apostles suffer death when they might have avoided it? I have asked you this question and you have not answered."

Ten minutes before he was scheduled to begin his march to the scaffold, Prince had been given the required physical examination by Dr. G. E. Williams, one of the six medical men who would shortly pronounce him dead. When it was over, he turned to Williams and said: "Dinsmore lied on the witness stand against me. You may tell him for me that I forgive him that lie before I died." The doctor promised to relay the message to the former hospital steward.

A click sounded through the hanghouse as the trap was sprung by one of the four executioners, and the condemned man shot through the opening. As the rope suddenly drew taut a slight snap was heard, which the doctors later confirmed was the sound of the spinal column severing.

The thing Prince feared most—that his neck would not be broken by the fall, as had happened to the long-suffering Thomas Johnson—did not come to pass. So terrified was the convict of death by strangulation that he was finally allowed to examine the gallows after repeated pleas to the warden. Walking around the structure the Monday before he was scheduled to die, he kept asking the accompanying physician how the hangman's noose worked: "They tell me that it took one fellow twenty-five minutes to die. That would be awful."

"Don't ever worry," the doctor told him. "It isn't necessary to break your neck." Either way, he would lose consciousness a second or two after the button was pushed.

Thus assured, Prince breathed a deep sigh of relief: "Now I can face it much easier," he replied.

Two days after the execution, and before the family could claim the body, the following headline appeared in the *Lincoln Daily Star:* PRINCE'S DEATH IS DOOM OF GALLOWS. The ongoing battle over Nebraska's use of capital punishment, or what some called "hang-'em-high justice," had suddenly been rekindled in the lobbies and corridors of the statehouse. Opponents denounced it as a form of "legal murder" no longer compatible with the aspirations of a higher civilization, while those in favor of keeping it praised its deterrent value. After weeks of debate and recriminations on both sides, the death penalty was retained, but with one significant difference. From now on the condemned would die by the more "modern and humane" method of "causing to pass through the body of the convicted person a current of electricity of sufficient intensity to cause death." To Prince belonged the distinction of having been the last man hanged in Nebraska.

Representative Jedediah M. Gates, of Sarpy County, had something more pressing on his mind than the state's introduction of the electric chair, although he favored the change. In January of 1913, Gates sponsored a bill asking for a legislative appropriation of $23,000 with which to purchase a farm for the use of Mrs. Roy Blunt during her lifetime, after which the land would revert to the state. The measure passed the lower house on March twentieth, two days after the anniversary of Blunt's death, but ran into trouble in the Senate, whose members voted instead for a cash appropriation of $5,000 to be split equally between mother and son.

After much wrangling, a compromise bill was finally hammered out and became law on April 23, 1913. Of the $7,500 in cash awarded by the state, Roy Blunt Jr. received $3,500 and his mother $4,000. The Andersons were incensed. It was announced that Mrs. Blunt would accept the sum appropriated for Roy Jr., but that the widow would not be collecting her share of the money, pending reconsideration of the matter during the next session of the legislature. Two months later, the family underwent a change of heart, and Peter Anderson showed up at the statehouse to request a voucher for the $4,000 owed his daughter. Nonetheless, he told a reporter that Carmellette would be asking for more money just as soon as the legislature reconvened.

The Blunts were not the only ones to benefit from the actions of the state. Guard Thomas Doody, whose shootout with the convicts had left him with a pronounced limp, impairing his efforts to earn a livelihood, was granted $5,000, thus easing the burden of caring for his aged mother. Another $5,000 went to Mary and Ruth Heilman, the mother and invalid daughter of the slain usher. A final appropriation of $928 was made to Sheriff Gus Hyers as reimbursement for the legal fees the lawman had incurred defending himself against the charge of manslaughter, leaving him one up on Police Chief Briggs, who received no compensation for his legal battles and none of the $1,800 in reward money the law said he had coming to him.

On a wall of the jail in the Lancaster County Courthouse hung a painting called *The Chase*. It was the work of one C. A. Dobson, who spent several months each year in a cell with paints, brushes, and canvas while serving out repeated sentences for public drunkenness. Much of the inspiration for the work was supplied by Deputy Sheriff Eikenbary, who described to the artist in detail what it was like to be a member of Nebraska's greatest posse. Captured in the painting was Sheriff Hyers, shooting at the fugitives from the roadside with his rifle resting against a telephone pole. Like medieval pilgrims drawn to a shrine, the curious came for months afterward to compare the painting with their mental image of the mad charge across the Nebraska landscape.

The public was no less curious about Morley, who had been put to work in the new chair factory and quickly became a model prisoner. He had once enjoyed all the notoriety he could get, but now he seemed to shun it. When visitors were shown through the penitentiary he either turned away or held a newspaper over his face to avoid the stares of the curious.

Governor Aldrich was renominated by the Republicans near the end of his first two-year term but was defeated by Democrat John H. Morehead, with much turning on the volatile issue of prison reform. No sooner did the results of the election become known than the convicts circulated a petition asking the new chief executive to retain Warden Melick. Morehead was not so inclined and replaced the grizzled peacekeeper with the younger William Fenton, who would continue to serve as warden until 1934, twenty-two years into Morley's life term.

On Melick's last day, a minstrel show was given in his honor, at the close of which the inmates presented the outgoing warden with a silver service encased in a massive chest, several of the men having pledged all the money in their prison accounts toward the gift. With the new regime came a new chaplain, one who was well remembered by many of the convicts. Almost seventy-eight, and in declining health, the Reverend P. C. Johnson nevertheless returned to the pulpit in 1913, standing up for Jesus at Sunday services until his death a year later.

"My knees are bumping," were a nervous Morley's first words as he sat down before the Nebraska State Board of Pardons and Paroles on January 8, 1941. Balding, pale-faced, and spare, he denied that he was responsible for any of the deaths that had occurred nearly thirty years earlier. His voice was surprisingly steady for a man with so much on the line, and he even joked at times with the board to ease the tension while constantly twirling a small box of matches between his fingers.

In front of each member of the board was the petitioner's application. In answer to the question, "Give the reasons for commutation, pardon, or parole?" he wrote: "The Charles A. Morley who was sentenced to prison (May 1912) for life has long been dead, and in the shadow of his tomb has arisen a new man with a clearer perspective of life and its purpose." In a letter written to this same board some years earlier, he had quoted Portia in *The Merchant of Venice:* "The quality of mercy is not strain'd."

Among the letters Morley had solicited in his bid for a pardon as far back as 1938 was one written by Mrs. Oscar W. Curry, president of the Delphian Literature Club of Edinburg, Texas. While admitting that she had never set eyes on the man, Mrs. Curry had become "much interested" in his writing during a long correspondence: "He has talent and should, and I believe would, do the world a service in the literary field." Mrs. Elmer Hall, who together with her husband had been held hostage by the convict trio, had a more important reason for writing: "Mr. Hall and I are positive we would not be alive today if Mr. Morley had not intervened. We feel Charles Taylor (alias) Shorty Gray would have shot us." Other letters of support came from Missouri's commissioner of agriculture, and from James Hurst, secretary of the Jackson County Board of Paroles in Kansas City, Missouri, promising Morley gainful employment should he be set free. J. G. Withers of the Missouri State Department of Finance wrote poignantly of Alice

Ramsey's death in 1936, after she had been widowed a third time: "I knew his mother well. She died . . . fully believing that her son would yet be pardoned."

There were those on the other side of the issue with equally long memories. Thomas Delahunty, who had moved to Aberdeen, Washington, after the death of his older brother Jim, wrote to the board expressing his hope that "you Gentlemen will be slow to act on this—and will decide to keep this fellow *right where he is* until he *Rots;* he has no business among decent People." Delahunty concluded by stating that he was speaking not only for himself but also for his three brothers still living at Clay Center, Nebraska.

However harsh Delahunty's words may have sounded to some, the trickster in Morley was still around after half a lifetime behind bars. In his application for a pardon, Morley was asked if he had been previously convicted of a crime. He answered "yes," and, as required, gave Springfield, Missouri, as the place and the year as 1905. Strangely, the applicant was not asked to state the nature of his offense, and Morley wasn't about to volunteer one more sliver of information than he had to. He simply wrote that he had been jailed in Kansas City, Missouri, and left it at that.

Morley had in fact served two terms in the Missouri State Prison at Jefferson City, one for murder and the other for armed robbery. The Board of Pardons and Paroles was apparently unaware of the murder charge, but its members did know that Morley had served fourteen months in Missouri for an express robbery committed in 1905, doubtless the unspecified crime referred to in his application. Had they wished to learn more about his nefarious activities, they had only to research old newspaper accounts or the trial record of the crime that had landed him in Lancaster three decades earlier.

The board made much of the fact that the aging convict had sought to improve himself by enrolling in several extension courses. "You have studied a good deal here, haven't you?" he was asked by board member Walter Johnson.

"Yes," Morley replied, "I have taken a course in the University of Chicago in Rhetoic and Rosa Crucian Philosophy and another in English." While his academic record shows that he did, indeed, enroll in English I, in what was called the Home Study program, he failed to submit even one lesson, and the course was finally closed in September of 1925, one year after he signed up. Any record of his purported study of Rosicrucian philosophy remains as obscure as the secret brotherhood that gave rise to it.

After thirty years, Morley still refused to reveal the source of the weapons employed in the escape, finessing the question by sticking to the old story that it was all Shorty's doing, adding only that Gray had told him that they were supplied by a guard. As he was about to leave the hearing room, he turned at the door and addressed the three-member board: "Gentlemen, I'm looking for the good word, and I won't sleep or rest until I hear it."

That afternoon, the board voted unanimously to grant Morley his unconditional release. The man who had told a reporter that he was no longer ill from drugs and could go outside and "trust myself" soon disappeared, presumably headed for Missouri, "a trifle out of time and tune with things" as he put it.

With no relatives left to take him in and no coal mine for support, Morley lasted a year on the streets, gradually drifting back to Lincoln, his only home. What were described as "drinking problems" eventually landed him in the Lincoln State Hospital for a short stay, in 1942, followed by another year in an alcoholic no-man's-land. When he returned, in 1943, it was for good, save for two "brief vacations": the first time on parole, the second after escaping and returning of his own accord, broke and footsore. He was still feisty and going strong in his early eighties when he gave another of his periodic newspaper interviews on March 14, 1958.

Described as a "very clever writer," he had given up contributing to the hospital newspaper because of what he said was "trouble with 'amateur' editors." Like much else in his life, he had never taken writing seriously enough, and now he was too old and failing in eyesight to do anything about it.

One year later, on the forty-seventh anniversary of the chase, he finally "revealed" some of the missing details. A Lincoln preacher abetted by a fellow citizen, who happened to be an ex-convict, smuggled three pistols, ammunition, and nitroglycerine into the prison. The escape was well planned; the weapons were hidden in the machinery of the broom factory and, once on the outside, the trio was headed for Ireland. "We didn't know it was snowing that hard," Morley recalled. "It definitely was one of the big factors in our capture."

Just how closely Morley had followed the fate of others involved in the saga, he never said, but as an avid reader he must have learned quite a lot from the papers. Sheriff Hyers remained on the job until 1916 and then, in the early 1920s, the loyal Republican was appointed state sheriff by Governor McKelvie. In 1927 the lawman left Lincoln for Los Angeles, where he traded in his cowboy boots, Stetson, and star for a business suit, becoming a real-estate broker until his death at the age of seventy-seven, in 1952.

The money appropriated to the Blunts by the state was used to purchase 160 acres from the Andersons for the benefit of their grandson, Roy Jr., who graduated from Springfield High School and studied engineering at the University of Nebraska before returning to farm the land with his wife, Annabelle. The couple built their home out of lumber salvaged from Plattford Church when it was torn down during the Great Depression. On the afternoon of January 29, 1939, Roy, a husky six-footer, had planned to pick up Annabelle and their two-year-old daughter, Jean, who were away visiting his in-laws outside Papillion. When he didn't stop to collect his grandfather on the way, Peter Anderson went over to the Blunt farm to investigate. Minutes later, he discovered the lifeless body of twenty-six-year-old Roy seated in his car, the garage door closed and the motor running. Springfield's Methodist church was filled from balcony to basement for the funeral, after which the body was driven to the cemetery for burial next to the almost legendary father Roy had never seen.

Carmellette forever remained a widow. According to her granddaughter, Jean, she worked "like a man," plowing, planting, threshing, shocking wheat, all without the benefit of a tractor, electricity, or running water. On a hot July day, in 1944, the team she was driving bolted while she was cutting alfalfa. Carmellette was thrown from the mower onto the sickle, suffering a painful cut on one shoulder and lacerations on both legs. Bruised and bleeding, she was driven to Methodist Hospital, in Omaha, where a large number of stitches were taken and she was kept for several days. The wounds eventually healed, but she became ill in late November and was hospitalized again. The last time Jean, who was then seven, saw her grandmother, she remembered being scolded for not wearing the "proper" stockings. Carmellette's condition worsened and she passed away in her sleep on Christmas Day, 1945, at age forty-nine.

None of the Blunts, who sold their land two years after Roy's death and moved to Hawk Springs, Wyoming, where Lloyd opened a filling station and hardware store, was around to read of Morley's passing from heart failure on August 22, 1959. The body was taken from the state hospital to Butherus, Maser & Love funeral home, where it lay unclaimed. Five days later, the remains were turned over to the state medical school for dissection and further anatomical study, but they yielded no more insight into the criminal mind than had the corpses of Gray and Dowd.

Truth to tell, Morley, like Shorty Gray, was a natural-born rule breaker, a boundary crosser—heedless, mesmerizing, threatening—and, above all, elusive. The two were not in crime for family or faith, country or any misguided sense of duty, but for guns, money, whiskey, and dope. Yet these things were subordinate to a higher calling. Drawn to crime like addicts to gambling, they loved the playing of the game—the plotting, the trickery, the cheating, the fraud, the manipulation of pawns, but, most of all, the pitting of their wits against the resources and talents of officialdom by trading in tomorrow for today. Recklessness combined with a capacity for violence were, for them, a form of liberation, indeed of revolution. Their fantasies elevated them to mythic status, where they became the equals of the James brothers, Cole Younger, Ike Clanton, Billy the Kid. Like their misfit heroes, they could never get the world to turn their way and were ultimately betrayed by the shifting winds of time.

The old Gretna-Chalco road is now 180th Street, and seems, to most of those who drive it, as plain and ordinary as its name. The one-room schools are long gone, as are the Mowinkles, the Pflugs, the Jarmans, and the dozen other families who once farmed its borders. From the spot where the posse triumphed, one can just make out the interstate highway connecting Lincoln and Omaha, the big diesel rigs droning across the far horizon like a child's toys. New housing developments are gobbling up the rolling land as the suburbs expand ever outward in concentric circles, impervious to what once was. There is not the slightest trace of the blood and the terror, or the echo of thundering hooves. All has dissolved into the mud and the snow of ninety winters, the spent cartridges long buried beneath the waving stalks of corn and wheat and milkweed that in summer still crowd both the sides of the old gravel road. One day soon this, too, will be gone, as will the lingering ghosts of the vanquished trio.

Standing alone before a gathering storm, I summon them for the last time. Closing my eyes, I listen for the sound of approaching hoofbeats and careening wagons. Against a background of snow-filled ditches, Morley and Gray and Dowd are fast coming on, Hyers and Briggs and a hundred or two others hot on their heels. Shots ring out amid the cursing of men and the shrieks of wounded horses. A young farmer crumples. A bride is suddenly a widow. Desperadoes fall. Haunting as the autumn raindrops that have begun to pelt the dusty road, the story plays itself out as I turn away, shivering, slip behind the steering wheel, and cross back over into my time.

❧ BIBLIOGRAPHY ❧
AND
ENDNOTES

Books

ASH   Loren Eiseley. *All the Strange Hours: The Excavation of a Life.* New York: Charles Scribner's Sons, 1975.

HN   Walter Wilson. *Hell in Nebraska: A Tale of the Nebraska Penitentiary.* Lincoln: Bankers Publishing Company, 1913.

HSN   A. T. Andreas. *History of the State of Nebraska.* Chicago: West Publishing Company, 1882.

SADM   Dom Gaspar Lefebvre. *Saint Andrew Daily Missal.* St. Paul: E. M. Lohmann, 1951.

TSAH   Eduard S. Linde. *The True Story of the American Hymn.* New York: The Abingdon Press, 1921.

YS   Eugene Lee. *Yeggmen in the Shadows.* London: Arthur H. Stockwell, 1935.

Manuscript Collections

BCC   Burt County Courthouse, Tekamah, Nebraska

CCC   Clay County Courthouse, Liberty, Missouri

DCC   Douglas County Courthouse, Omaha, Nebraska

HCC   Hamilton County Courthouse, Aurora, Nebraska

NSHS   Nebraska State Historical Society, Lincoln, Nebraska

RCC   Ray County Courthouse, Richmond, Missouri

SCSN   Supreme Court of the State of Nebraska, Lincoln, Nebraska

Newspapers
(All newspapers are from Nebraska unless otherwise noted)

ADA	*Aberdeen Daily American,* Aberdeen, South Dakota
AP	*Appeal to Reason,* Gerard, Kansas
AR	*Aurora Republican*
BCH	*Burt County Herald*
CCS	*Clay County Sun*
GB	*Gretna Breeze*
GIDI	*Grand Island Daily Independent*
HCR	*Hamilton County Register*
LDS	*Lincoln Daily Star*
LEN	*Lincoln Evening News*
LS	*Lincoln Star*
LSJ	*Lincoln State Journal*
LWC	*Louisville Weekly Courier*
LWS	*Lyons Weekly Sun*
NSJ	*Nebraska State Journal*
NYT	*New York Times,* New York, New York
ODB	*Omaha Daily Bee*
OWH	*Omaha World Herald*
PJ	*Plattsmouth Journal*
PT	*Papillion Times*
RD	*Richmond Democrat,* Richmond, Missouri
SJNP	*St. Joseph News Press,* St. Joseph, Missouri
SM	*Springfield Monitor*

Periodicals

US	*University Studies*

Website

PK	*www.pinkertons.com*

Chapter 1: "Stand Up for Jesus"

1   "The external appearance": HSN, v. 2, 1049.

2   "Come without knocking": HN, 23.

2   "Did you notice": Ibid., 189.

2   "Well, you see": Ibid.

2   "Take a look": Ibid.

3   "Please thank Frank": Ibid.

3   "We have had plenty": Ibid., 118.

3   "Stand up, stand up": TSAH, 221.

4   "It's all right, boys": LEN, Feb. 12, 1912, 1.

4   "splendid physical power": CCS, Feb. 16, 1912, 1.

5   "I am going to leave you": LEN, Feb. 12, 1912, 2.

5   "I want to finish him": NJS, Feb. 12, 1912, 2.

6   "You finish him, Doc": HN, 200.

6   "Let him die": LEN, Feb. 12, 1912, 1.

6   "the most lenient official": Ibid., 2.

7   "What's the matter with you": OWH, Nov. 2, 1909, 1.

7   "Oh, I don't know": Ibid.

7   "Who are you": Ibid.

7   "None of your damn business": Ibid.

10   "I had heard": Ibid, Nov. 25, 1909, 12.

10   "That Albert Prince be taken": DCC Transcript: *State of Nebraska v. Albert Prince*, Doc. 14, no. 148, Dec. 4, 1909.

11   "sizing up the new man": HN, 36.

11   "I believe that": Ibid., 37.

12   "Arms and legs tattooed": Nebraska Department of Correctional Services, State Penitentiary Descriptive Record of Inmates, NSHS, v. 3, no. 5374, Albert Prince.

15   "Forfeit—30 days each": Nebraska Department of Correctional Services, State Penitentiary Daily Journal, NSHS R686, v. 5, 40.

20   "Get up, I want to see you": LDS, April 27, 1912, 5.

20   "He asked me how I was feeling": Ibid.

20   "I told him to come in": Ibid.

21   "I was only making things harder": Ibid.

21   "Coakley pointed it in my face": Ibid.

21   "After the guard had prodded": Ibid.

22   "Delahunty drifts into the city": Ibid., April 10, 1911, 1.

23   "Don't you think that": HN, 184.

24   "Well, I'll take it off": Ibid.

24   "Don't say anything for me": LDS, May 19, 1911, 1.

25   "the melodious tones": Ibid.

26   "And while you are doing that": HN, 184.

26   "I would have put Smith": Ibid., 185.

27   "What got into you": LDS, Feb. 13, 1912, 1.

27   "You have been digging at me": Ibid.

27   "Why, I haven't spoken to you": Ibid.

Chapter 2: Breakout

29   "Give Satan my best regards": HN, 213.

30   "an atmosphere charged": LDS, Feb. 13, 1912, 1.

30   "I had a little tussle": LEN, Feb. 13, 1912, 1.

31   "Calm, cold and self-possessed": Ibid.

31   "Do you wish": LDS, Feb. 13, 1912, 1.

32   "Did you kill Deputy Davis": Ibid.

32   "I would rather not talk": Ibid.

32   "Edward Davis's death": LEN, Feb. 13, 1912, 1.

33   "I do not want to hear": LDS, March 2, 1912, 1.

36   "that a bad condition": OWH, March 3, 1912, p. 7.

36   "hygienic conditions may be": Aldrich, Chester Hardy,
        NSHS, RG1, SG64, Box 4, f. 26, Aldrich to James De-
        lahunty, March 4, 1912.

37   "He is to have nothing": Ibid.

37   "The man has been subjected": LDS, March 9, 1912, 1.
37   "It is generally understood": Ibid., March 13, 1912, 1.
39   "Throw up your hands": Ibid., May 2, 1912, 4.
39   "Give me that gun": Ibid.
40   "Throw up your hands, you": Ibid., March 15, 1912, 5.
40   "You don't get out": Ibid.
41   "I figured it was time": Ibid.
42   "My God, Shorty": Ibid., May 2, 1912, 4.
42   "There was a strange look": HN, 234.
43   "Are you hurt": NSJ, March 15, 1912, 2.

Chapter 3: The Desperadoes

48   "a part of the convicts": Special Orders, Adjutant General, State of Nebraska, NSHS, RG18, SG2, v. 7, March 17, 1921, 184.
53   "where I remained": State of Nebraska, Board of Pardons and Paroles, NSHS, RG34, f. 5939, Charles A. Morley, Dec. 19, 1932, 3.
53   "advantages other kids didn't have": LS, Dec. 9, 1940, 3.
53   "differed violently with": Ibid.
53   "and some other folks": Ibid.
54   "The defendant was addicted": Divorce Records, CCC, *Alice Marley v. John H. Marley,* v. 18, Sept. 6, 1881, 523.
54   "although duly summoned": Ibid.
54   "James Richard Marley": Ibid.
55   "The shock to his system": RD, Dec. 13, 1888, 1.
57   "A fellow drove the thing": LS. Dec. 9, 1940, 4.
58   "two youthful desperadoes": OWH, Oct. 22, 1910, 1.
58   "They did not pronounce": Ibid.
60   "were induced to": SJNP, Oct. 24, 1910, 1.
61   "a carnival of highway robbery": OWH, Oct. 22, 1910, 1.

61 "Say, mister": NSJ, March 18, 1912, 2.

62 "He's a": Ibid., March 16, 1913, 2.

62 "I haven't led": LS, March 14, 1958, 3.

62 "The place was filthy": Ibid., Dec. 9, 1940, 3.

63 "What's the matter": Ibid.

63 "Sure as hell am": Ibid.

63 "I'll get you a drink": Ibid.

64 "Of what": Ibid.

64 "Why brandy, man": Ibid.

64 "In those days": Ibid.

64 "We usually got it": State of Nebraska, Board of Pardons and Paroles, NSHS, RG34, f. 5039, Charles A. Morley, Dec. 19, 1932, 2.

64 "far from a model": LSJ, Jan. 9, 1941, 4.

64 "threatening violence to": Nebraska Department of Correctional Services Penitentiary Daily Journal, NSHS, R686, v. 5, 159.

64 "loafing behind a corn pile": Ibid., 181.

66 "he refuses to state": Nebraska Department of Correctional Services, State Penitentiary Descriptive Record of Inmates, NSHS, v. 3, no. 4231, and v. 4, no. 5762, Charles Taylor.

68 "were considerate and kind enough": GIDI, April 25, 1911, 1.

68 "It's a cinch": Ibid.

73 "Suddenly, and in a place": AR, Aug. 25, 1911, 1.

73 "If I ever see": Ibid.

73 "And there sits the man": Ibid.

74 "to the vilest epithets": GIDI, Aug. 18, 1911, 1.

74 "not bad looking": HCR, Aug. 11, 1911, 1.

75 "of more than ordinary": Ibid.

75 "is a notable writer": Ibid.

75   "while in prison": Ibid.

75   "captured without money": *State of Nebraska v. Harry Forbes, et al.*, HCC, no. 2600, June 22, 1911.

76   "and there kept": Ibid.

77   "With these men removed": GIDI, Aug. 22, 1911, 1.

78   "No peace officer": NSJ, March 18, 1912, 1.

79   "there was not a trace": LDS, March 16, 1912, 2.

79   "There has not been": Ibid., March 15, 1912, 2.

80   "The man who was": Ibid., March 16, 1912, 2.

84   "I had enough": YS, 41–2.

85   "as less than animals": LSJ, Jan. 9, 1941, 4.

85   "It was narcotics or die": Ibid.

85   "I met John Douwd": State of Nebraska, Board of Pardons and Paroles, NSHS, RG34, f. 5855, Frank McCann, June 9, 1913, 1.

86   "I do not think": Ibid., 4.

88   "the sounds did not seem": PJ, Sept. 28, 1911, 2.

91   "only a country boy": Ibid., Jan. 25, 1912, 2.

92   "Dowd turned pale": NSJ, March 22, 1912, 5.

94   "You have convicted an innocent man": PJ, Dec. 25, 1911, 7.

94   "That is true": Ibid.

94   "liberty and freedom": Ibid., Feb. 5, 1912, 7.

95   "midnight assassin to prowl": Ibid.

95   "Omaha was the home": Ibid.

95   "The land is full": Ibid.

95   "Twenty years seems": LWC, Dec. 30, 1911, 1.

Chapter 4: Vanished

97   "Where Gray learned how": NSJ, March 22, 1912, 5.

98   "Gray's later career": Ibid.

98   "He appeared to be": LDS, March 24, 1912, 4.

98   "That was the last seen": Ibid.

99   "I would swear": Ibid.

99   "The warden said": NSJ, March 18, 1912, 1.

100   "In compliance with": OWH, March 23, 1912, 6.

100   "I have been deprived": Ibid.

100   "a man of much force": NSJ, March 22, 1912, 5.

101   "that would do credit to": Ibid.

101   "What I desire to know": OWH, March 30, 1912, 6.

102   "I hope I'll never die": Ibid.

102   "I used to see him": ADA, March 26, 1912, 1.

102   "He was the best hired hand": NSJ, March 22, 1912, 5.

102   "He never drank": Ibid.

103   "Morley will not come": Ibid., March 18, 1912, 2.

103   "Morley is an opium fiend": LDS, March 17, 1912, 6.

104   "A thorough, systematic investigation": LDS, March 16, 1912, 1.

106   "A groan, not riotous": Ibid, March 12, 1912, 1.

106   "No, my boy": HN, 117–18.

106   "I was not surprised": LDS, March 15, 1912, 2.

107   "has been terribly mistaken": HCR, March 22, 1912, 1.

107   "In the shadow": NSJ, March 15, 1912, 6.

107   "Convicts mutiny": NYT, March 15, 1912, 1.

108   "the boys were quiet": HN, 237.

108   "The poison has been spread": LDS, March 16, 1912, 1.

108   "The present regime": NSJ, March 17, 1912, 3.

109   "while in the same interview": LDS, March 16, 1912, 1.

109   "Men such as the three": NSJ, March 17, 1912, 3.

110   "She held up her hand": Aldrich, Chester Hardy, NSHS, RG1, SG24, Box 4, f. 27, March 20, 1912.

111   "Go to Kansas City": LDS, March 16, 1912, 1.

111   "nervous and worried": NSJ, March 16, 1912, 2.

113   "Are you looking for them": Ibid., March 17, 1912, 2.

114   "I was born in": Ibid.

115   "in no uncertain terms": LDS, March 16, 1912, 1.

116   "pathetic in its sadness": Ibid.

117   "Someday when you are grown": ASH, 174.

118   "Look, there are some men": NSJ, March 17, 1912, 1.

118   "My God": Ibid.

119   "We know you": Ibid.

119   "I can tell you": Ibid.

119   "I think all boys": Ibid., March 20, 1912, 4.

119   "I would not be": Ibid.

120   "Would any trouble": Ibid., March 17, 1912, 2.

120   "Oh no": Ibid.

120   "I wish I could stay": Ibid., March 20, 1912, 4.

120   "He paced the floor": Ibid.

123   "I hate to have": Ibid.

123   "Remember, your son": Ibid.

123   "The first man": LDS, March 17, 1912, 1.

123   "You tell him": Ibid.

124   "We started to go": NSJ, March 18, 1912, 1.

125   "I know nothing": Ibid., March 17, 1912, 2.

125   "You can never know": Ibid.

126   "He seemed to be": Ibid., March 18, 1912, 1.

126   "darkest figure": Ibid.

126   "There isn't a word": Ibid.

127   "I have spent": Ibid., March 17, 1912, 2.

Chapter 5: "This Is Awful"

129   "Three convict assassins": OWH, March 18, 1912, 1.

129   "All search fails": NSJ, March 18, 1912, 1.

129   "Trail of Murderers": LDS March 18, 1912, 1.

130   "It is believed": Ibid., March 17, 1912, 1.
131   "will be in a position": Aldrich, Chester Hardy, NSHS,
       RG1, SG24, Box 4, f. 27. J. A. Gustafson to Aldrich, March
       18, 1912.
133   "that is not the business": NSJ, March 19, 1912, 3.
134   "Have you heard": LDS, March 18, 1912, 1.
134   "Well, we are the three": Ibid.
135   "We don't want to impose": Ibid.
136   "The men would read": Ibid.
136   "Your husband is going": Ibid., March 19, 1912, 4.
136   "I can't do it": Ibid.
136   "Then you'll have to": Ibid.
136   "We can't go anywhere": Ibid.
137   "That's bad luck": Ibid.
137   "seemed to favor": Ibid.
138   "shorter but uglier": Ibid.
138   "I am past playing checkers": Ibid
138   "This is awful": Ibid.
138   "bad case of the blues": Ibid.
142   "Thou shalt sprinkle me": SADM, 1795.
143   "Eternal rest give unto them": Ibid., 1797.
143   "And lead us not into temptation": Ibid, 1803.

Chapter 6: Danse Macabre

146   "Friends of both": GB, Jan. 5, 1912, 4.
149   "I'll shoot two": LDS, March 23, 1912, 4.
150   "Well, I haven't any idea": Ibid.
150   "Father, I am not afraid": Ibid.
152   "To the posse": NSJ, March 19, 1912, 1.
154   "telephone girl laboring": PJ, March 18, 1912, 2.
154   "thousand or more men": OWH, March 19, 1912, 1.

156   "It seemed like": NSJ, March 19, 1912, 2.

160   "To hell with Blunt:" Ibid., March 21, 1912, 5. Also see GB, March 22, 1912, 5.

161   "For God's sake": OWH, March 20, 1912, 2.

161   "Go to Hell": PT, March 21, 1912, 5.

162   "Oh, my God": LDS, March 19, 1912, 1.

163   "when we were listening": NSJ, March 19, 1912, 1.

163   "We might as well": OWH, March 19, 1912, 1.

164   "For God's sake": PT, March 21, 1912, 4.

164   "it was all over": Ibid.

165   "dark looks from": LDS, March 19, 1912, 1.

165   "Shoot the son of a bitch": Ibid., 4.

165   "This man is my prisoner": Ibid.

167   "Yes, he was sorry": Ibid.

167   "Doody came in shooting": Ibid.

168   "The wagon was all filled": Ibid.

168   "I think it was": Ibid.

168   "This is Gray": GB, March 22, 1912, 5.

169   "It is a wonder to us": Ibid.

169   "Those officers can't": Ibid.

169   "readers of Jesse James": Ibid.

169   "pulling his guns": SM, March 21, 1912, 1.

170   "I told him": OWH, March 20, 1912, 2.

171   "Lo! the book": SADM, 1799.

172   "Just a bit weak": LDS, March 19, 1912, 1.

173   "Lay there, you": Ibid.

174   "The nature of the man": Ibid.

Chapter 7: The Death Wagon

177   "Please permit me": quoted in HN, 294–95.

178   "Darned tough luck": Ibid., 296.

178   "Believe me": Ibid., p. 297.

178   "Newspapermen, morbid visitors": LDS, March 19, 1912, 1.

181   "The heart knoweth": Aldrich, Chester Hardy, NSHS, RG1, SG24, Box 4, f. 28. Aldrich to Mrs. Blunt, March 20, 1912.

181   "Nothing this convict can say": LDS, March 19, 1912, 1.

185   "No one is more grieved": Ibid, March 19, 1912, 4.

185   "were perhaps the only men": NSJ, March 19, 1912, 2.

185   "The fact that": SM, March 21, 1912, 5.

186   "In all the melee": GB, March 22, 1912, 1.

187   "There is no question": NSJ, March 21, 1912, 5.

188   "I am glad": Ibid.

188   "For unadulterated untruth": quoted in HN, 343.

188   "To hell with them": OWH, March 21, 1912, 9.

188   "the most dastardly": Ibid.

189   "splendidly equipped": SM, March 28, 1912, 1.

189   "all might steal": OWH, March 22, 1912, 9.

190   "Criminals must be captured": SM, March 28, 1912, 1.

191   "How are you": LDS, March 21, 1912, 4.

191   "Oh, pretty good": Ibid.

191   "in imitation of": Ibid.

192   "He will say 'no' at first": Ibid.

192   "I am not": Ibid., March 26, 1912, 1.

193   "no stone would be": Ibid., March 28, 1912, 4.

193   "We have no thought": Ibid.

197   "You wretch": OWH, March 30, 1912, 6.

197   "I have been taught:" Ibid., March 29, 1912, 5.

198   "I do not believe": Ibid.

198   "There were fifteen": Ibid., March 30, 1912, 6.

198   "How many times": Ibid.

198   "About fifteen": Ibid.

198   "They kept right on going": Ibid.

198   "I thought it might be a trick": Ibid.

198   "To hell with Blunt": LDS, March 29, 1912, 1.

198   "Where did you get that": OWH, March 30, 1912, 6.

199   "I asked you": Ibid.

199   "I certainly did not": Ibid.

199   "I simply told him": Ibid.

199   "Did you realize": Ibid.

199   "No more than my own": Ibid.

199   "Didn't you think": Ibid.

199   "I didn't think anything": Ibid.

199   "My life was": Ibid.

199   "As we drew nearer": Ibid.

199   "All three of them stood": Ibid.

201   "left the question": LDS, March 30, 1912, 1.

201   "to hell with them": OWH, March 30, 1912, 1.

202   "I have been informed": Aldrich, Chester Hardy, NSHS, RG1, SG24, Box 4, f. 30. Aldrich to R. B. Armstrong, March 28, 1912.

204   "Roy Blunt came to": LDS, March 30, 1912, 1.

204   "We further find": Ibid.

205   "The members of": SM, April 4, 1912, 1.

Chapter 8: Judgment Days

208   "I beat him to it": LDS, March 29, 1912, 1.

209   "A highly developed specimen": Ibid.

209   "Strong was one": Ibid., 4.

210   "Not guilty": Ibid., March 24, 1912, 4.

210   "About the preliminary hearing": Ibid.

210   "Oh, I'll let that go": Ibid.

211   "You'll waive it": Ibid.

212   "You must have wanted": Ibid.

212   "I don't see how": Ibid.

212   "I don't either": Ibid.

212   "If Mrs. Dickman": Ibid.

213   "It is generally conceded": Aldrich, Chester Hardy, NSHS, RG1, SG24, Box 4, f. 30, W. A. Martin to Aldrich, March 22, 1912.

213   "There is some sharp criticism": Ibid., f. 27, Calvin Keller to Aldrich, March 19, 1912.

213   "Of course, it is": Ibid., Aldrich to Keller, March 21, 1912.

214   "formal claim to": Ibid., Elmer Hall to Aldrich, March 22, 1912.

215   "How they hunt": SM, April 18, 1912, 1.

216   "Lynching is the awful miscarriage": Aldrich, Chester Hardy, NSHS, RG1, SG24, Box 4, f. 28. Walter K. Williams to Aldrich, March 22, 1912.

216   "in one of the most daring": Ibid.

216   "133 of the most": Ibid., Box 5, f. 31. A. J. Lepinski to Aldrich, April 2, 1912.

217   "It is quite a relief": Ibid., Aldrich to Lepinski, April 3, 1912.

217   "It will do no one any good": OWH, March 25, 1912, 5.

219   "He will take and ravish": NSJ, March 19, 1912, 4.

220   "Delahunty considered": AR, March 30, 1912, 1. Also see HN, 259–60.

221   "Was there ever a man": Aldrich, Chester Hardy, NSHS, RG1, SG24, Box 4, f. 30, Sweaney L. Blackmar to Aldrich, March 28, 1912.

221   "never passed up": Ibid., Aldrich to Blackmar, March 29, 1912.

222   "He knows no more": LDS, April 27, 1912, 5.

222 "a man of remarkable intelligence": Ibid., April 24, 1912, 1.

223 "could not be insane": Ibid., April 29, 1912, 1.

225 "In your opinion:" Ibid., April 25, 1912, 1.

225 "Right and wrong": Ibid.

225 "Do you think": Ibid.

225 "Would you say": Ibid.

225 "Oh no": Ibid.

225 "I would have drowned": Ibid., April 28, 1912, 1.

225 "In that statement": Ibid.

226 "Since that day": Ibid., April 26, 1912, 1.

226 "Warden, you have": Ibid.

227 "a weakening viewed with contempt": Ibid.

227 "Man's inhumanity to man": Ibid., April 30, 1912, 4.

228 "whether the state": Ibid., April 29, 1912, 4.

228 "the most self-contained man": Ibid., April 30, 1912, 1.

228 "Well, you'd better come": Ibid.

230 "The man's a liar": PT, May 2, 1912, 1.

232 "How are you, Charley": LDS, April 26, 1912, 1.

232 "Charley, be brave": Ibid.

232 "I'll see you again": Ibid.

233 "I said": Ibid. May 3, 1912, 1.

233 "Morley replied": Ibid.

234 "You did": Ibid.

234 "I've not got much": Ibid., May 4, 1912, 1.

234 "Jury still out": Ibid., 1.

235 "Well, I'll have to admit": Ibid.

235 "He is my baby": Ibid, May 5, 1912, 1.

235 "He was such a good boy": Ibid.

235 "and then the poor people": Ibid.

235 "A few years ago": Ibid.

236   "Well, I wonder": HN, 336.

236   "Cheer up": Ibid.

236   "Or a rope": Ibid.

236   "Didn't you see": Ibid., 337.

236   "When I got out": Ibid., 338.

236   "We, the jury": Ibid.

237   "Oh, my boy": LDS, May 6, 1912, 1.

237   "I'll remember you": Ibid.

237   "While there's life": Ibid.

237   "It was a fluke": Ibid.

237   "Are they going to": Ibid.

238   "I am getting the very best": Ibid.

238   "Warden, we're going to": Ibid.

238   "That's right, Prince": Ibid.

Epilogue

239   "degenerate type": Ibid., March 28, 1912, 1.

239   "We must conclude": "A Study of Cerebral Anthropology, With a Description of Two Brains of Criminals," US, v. 12, no. 4 (Oct. 1912), 65–66.

240   "a single stitch of coloring": LDS, May 8, 1912, 1.

240   "What the governor should do": Ibid.

243   "My last wish": Ibid., March 21, 1913, 1.

243   "Dinsmore lied": Ibid., 4.

244   "They tell me": Ibid., 5.

244   "Don't ever worry": Ibid.

244   "Now I can face it": Ibid.

244   "Prince's death": Ibid., March 23, 1912, p. 1.

244   "causing to pass through": *Laws, Joint Resolutions, and Memorials Passed by the Legislature of the State of Nebraska at*

the Thirty-Third Session (Lincoln: Woodruff Bank Note Company, 1913), 108.

247 "My knees are bumping": LSJ, Jan. 9, 1941, 4.

247 "Give the reasons": State of Nebraska, Board of Pardons and Paroles, NSHS, RG 34, March, f. 5939, Charles A. Morley, Jan. 8, 1941, 2.

247 "The quality of mercy": Ibid., Charles A. Morley to Board of Pardons and Paroles, Feb. 19, 1938.

247 "He has talent": Ibid., Mrs. Oscar W. Curry to Board of Pardons and Paroles, March 2, 1938.

247 "Mr. Hall and I": Ibid., Mrs. Elmer Hall to Board of Pardons and Paroles, May 18, 1938.

248 "I knew his mother": Ibid., J. G. Withers to Board of Pardons and Paroles, May 20, 1938.

248 "you Gentlemen": Ibid., Thomas Delahunty to Board of Pardons and Paroles, March 21, 1938.

249 "You have studied": Ibid., RG 37, f. 5939, Charles A. Morley, Jan. 8, 1941, 3.

249 "Yes, I have taken": Ibid., 2–3.

249 "Gentlemen, I'm looking": NSJ, Jan. 9, 1941, 4.

249 "a trifle out of time": State of Nebraska, Board of Pardons and Paroles, NSHS, RG34, f. 5939, Charles A. Morley to Board of Pardons and Paroles, Feb. 19, 1938.

250 "We didn't know": LS, March 22, 1959, 3.

❦ ACKNOWLEDGMENTS ❦

T he largest collection of materials bearing on this work, including most newspapers, is located at the Nebraska State Historical Society, in Lincoln, where it was my privilege to work with a highly congenial group of staff archivists, librarians, and other specialists under the direction of Ann Billesbach, the head of Reference Services. I am especially indebted to Paul Eisloeffel, Cynthia Monroe, Steven Ramold, Chad Wall, and Steve Wolz. All were helpful in countless ways, generous with their time, patient, instructive, and always willing to offer sound advice when asked for it. The same can be said for Winfield Barber, administrative assistant to Warden Mike Kenney of the Nebraska State Penitentiary, Lincoln. It was Barber who answered a long list of questions about prison life, who provided certain background materials from the prison archives, and who guided me around the grounds of the place once called "Lancaster," enabling me to gain a better sense of the lay of the land, if not the old limestone penitentiary, which is long gone.

Gary Iske, director of the Sarpy County Historical Museum, Bellevue, Nebraska, provided archival materials related to the posse chase, as well as invaluable photographs. H. Margo Prentiss, curator of the Cass County Historical Society, Plattsmouth, Nebraska, supplied newspaper accounts of the Dowd capture and trial. A visit to the Clay County Archives and Historical Society of Liberty, Missouri, put me on the trail of important court records pertaining to the Morleys. Karen S. Yelden of the Nebraska Bankers Association made available an important history of the institution for which she works.

Much of what I learned of Prince, Gray, Morley, and Dowd was derived from district court records generously provided by the following: Burt County District Court, Tekamah, Nebraska; Cass County District Court, Plattsmouth, Nebraska; Douglas County District Court, Omaha, Nebraska; and Hamilton County District Court, Aurora, Nebraska. Copies of the trial record of Police Chief John Briggs were obtained from the Saunders County Museum, Wahoo, Nebraska. Other legal documents came from the following: Bureau of Vital Statistics: State of Nebraska; Bureau of Vital Statistics: State of Missouri; Clay County Courthouse, Liberty, Missouri; and Ray County Courthouse, Richmond, Missouri. The United States Census: 1900, 1910, and 1920, Ray County, Missouri, was of great assistance in tracking the Morleys.

Tecumseh, Nebraska, attorney Thomas L. Morrissey provided me with important background materials on Chaplain P. C. Johnson. Genealogy librarian Sue Kaufman of the Peoria Public Library, Peoria, Illinois, did the same for Warden James Delahunty. The funeral home of Roper and Sons, Lincoln, Nebraska, made their records on Gray and Dowd available, as did Butherus, Maser & Love Funeral Home for Morley, also of Lincoln. I am indebted to Associate Registrar Andrew S. Hannah of the University of Chicago for providing information on Morley's correspondence school record; to Elizabeth Gilliam Beckett, historic sites supervisor at the Jesse James Farm and Museum, Liberty, Missouri, who helped me confirm that Morley was not born at the James place; to Marilynn Sour, reference librarian at the Alexander Mitchell Public Library, Aberdeen, South Dakota, for local newspaper accounts of Dowd's background and trial; to librarian Julie Carlyle of the St. Joseph Public Library, St. Joseph, Missouri, for information on Morley during his sojourn to the city; to officials at Kemper Military Academy, Boonville, Missouri, for making their enrollment records available to me; to their counterparts at William Jewell College, Liberty, Missouri, who did the same; to Sergeant Larry Russell of the Lancaster County Sheriff's Office, Lincoln, Nebraska; to Ronald Reithmuller, records administrator of the Nebraska Board of Pardons and Paroles; to the Ray County Genealogy Association, Richmond, Missouri; to the University of Nebraska Archives at Love Library, Lincoln, Nebraska; and to the Bennett Martin Public Library, Lincoln.

And though I never learned their names, for bylines were few back in 1912, I wish to pay particular homage to the newspapermen whose various accounts of the events in this book made history come alive. Without them I would have had no story to tell.

A very special thank you to Jean Blunt Laughlin, granddaughter of Roy Blunt, Sr. for sharing her family history and photographs of the period, and to Jack R. Haber, grandson of Sheriff Gus Hyers, who did the same. It has been a privilege to converse with these living links to a fascinating past. I spent a memorable day in the company of Lincolnite Morrie Tuttle going over the same ground covered by the fugitives and their pursuers some ninety years ago. Absent his excellent map-reading skills and keen sense of direction, I doubtless would have gotten lost many times over. The University Research Committee at Indiana State University awarded me a travel grant with which to undertake this work, and I was granted a sabbatical by the university during which most of the writing was done. I can only hope the final result justifies their confidence in me. I could have had no finer editor than Brando Skyhorse of Lyons Press. His keen eye for structure and balance have made this a far better book than I ever dared hope. The remaining faults are mine alone. I also wish to thank agent Rebecca Kurson for her efforts in getting the manuscript into the right hands. Finally, to my uncomplaining wife Rhonda Packer, who has heard and read far more about a posse than she ever wanted to, I dedicate this book, small reward for more than two years of steadfast patience and encouragement.

❧ INDEX ❧